I0810339

IMAGES
of America

LONG ISLAND
HISTORIC HOUSES OF THE SOUTH SHORE

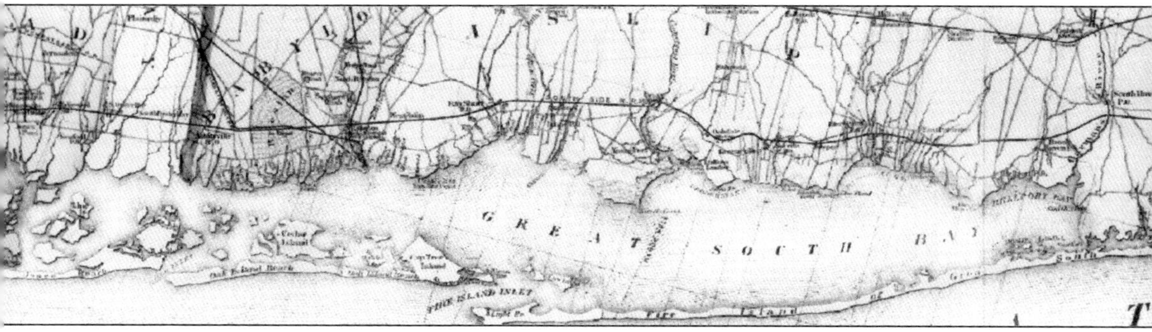

This map shows the South Shore of Long Island, the area covered in this book, from Massapequa to Mastic. (Courtesy *Map of Long Island*, by Beers, Comstock, and Cline, 1873.)

ON THE COVER: This eclectic-style mansion may be the most unusually styled house on all of the South Shore. The mansion was originally built by Edwin Augustus Johnson around 1850. James Neal Plumb eventually owned it and made several architectural alterations, resulting in the unusual architecture of the mansion. (Courtesy East Islip Historical Society.)

IMAGES
of America

LONG ISLAND
HISTORIC HOUSES OF THE SOUTH SHORE

Christopher M. Collora

ARCADIA
PUBLISHING

ISBN 978-0-7385-9803-1

Published by Arcadia Publishing
Charleston, South Carolina

Printed in the United States of America

Library of Congress Control Number: 2012944413

For all general information, please contact Arcadia Publishing:
Telephone 843-853-2070
Fax 843-853-0044
E-mail sales@arcadiapublishing.com
For customer service and orders:
Toll-Free 1-888-313-2665

Visit us on the Internet at www.arcadiapublishing.com

This book is dedicated to my mom for always encouraging me to write.

Contents

Acknowledgments

This book was made possible with the help of the following people who assisted in my research. Thanks to Nancy Melius, president of Historic Long Island Gold Coast Mansions, for encouraging me to report stories on historic mansions. Thanks to author Paul Mateyunas for his encouragement and advice. Thanks to my former journalism professor John Hanc for inspiring me to include the Thomas Jones story and for teaching me to be a better print reporter. Thanks to Chuck and Trish Howlett for their support. Thanks to Ray Lembo, whose expertise on history has been a tremendous help. Also, thanks to Ray's company, Rajen Media (rajenmedia.com), for helping me with several picture scans. Thanks to Mary Cascone, whose outstanding assistance was invaluable.

Additional thanks to the following: East Islip Historical Society president Ray Lembo and Frank Szemko; Suffolk County Historical Society director Kathryn Curran and Ned Smith; Islip Hamlet Historical Society president Victoria Berger; Town of Babylon Office of Historic Services archivist Mary Cascone; Village of Babylon Historic and Preservation Society curator Ruth F. Albin; Bay Shore Historical Society president Barry Dlouhy, Priscilla and Bob Hancock, and Mike Carmody; West Islip Historical Society president Carolyn Agenjo, Katie Hafele, and Bill Jantz; Lindenhurst Old Village Hall Museum director Johanna Sandy; Amityville Historical Society president Pat Cahaney, William Lauder, and Seth Purdy; Historical Society of the Massapequas president Bill Colfer, George Kirchmann, and Lillian Rumfield Bryson; Suffolk County Parks Department, Richard Martin and Eric Crater; Bayport Heritage Association, James Connell; Sayville Historical Society president Constance Currie; Long Island Maritime Museum, Arlene Bakewicz and Barbara Forde; the Post Morrow Foundation; US National Park Service, William Floyd Estate Archives, Fire Island National Seashore, MaryLaura Lamont; Sagtikos Manor Historical Society/George Weeks Memorial Library, Christine Gottsch; Russ and Lynda Moran and Ellen Egelman; Jackie Ruffino; Cathy Gonzalez; Ken Spooner of The Knapps Lived Here (www.spoonercentral.com); the Nathaniel Conklin House Museum, Karen Petz; Sayville Public Library, Alice Lepore; Medford-Patchogue Library, Mark Rothenberg; Suffolk County legislator Wayne Horsley; Beverly C. Tyler of Three Village Historical Society (www.historycloseathand.com/); Patchogue Historical Society, Steve Lucas; Town of Brookhaven historian Barbara M. Russell; Dowling College Library Archives and Special Collections, Diane Holliday; Law Firm of Reilly, Like & Tenety, Irving Like; Bellport-Brookhaven Historical Society, Steve Czarniecki; and Lena Pless.

INTRODUCTION

The South Shore of Long Island is one of the oldest historic regions in the United States. Centuries ago, Native American tribes—Shinnecocks, Massapequas, and Islips—hunted and harvested fish and shellfish for survival. The island's idyllic setting and waterways proved attractive to European settlers as they made their way to the New World in the early 1600s. Religious freedom seekers, who first came to the Massachusetts Bay Colony in 1620 and subsequently began spreading out to new colonies such as Rhode Island and Connecticut, eventually sailed across the Long Island Sound, setting up towns on the far eastern end of the island and its north shore. Far to the west, Dutch settlers began inhabiting Manhattan Island and gradually moved eastward to what are now the New York City borough of Queens and the nearby area of present-day Hempstead.

With the establishment of the new nation in the late 1700s, distinctive patterns of settlement began to take shape as traces of Dutch and New England cultures began to dissipate and a more Americanized version of society emerged. By the late 1800s, although the rural economy remained intact and historic maritime traditions persisted, the modernization and urbanization of American society gradually began impacting the island's development.

At the end of World War II, when I was born and lived in the village of Babylon, one could see the transformation of the island begin to take shape. Many returning veterans, such as my father, who entered the Army during the Great Depression, were ready to live the American Dream. The island was now undergoing a rapid transformation, as the "Crabgrass Frontier" would soon engulf the farms, Colonial-era villages like Babylon and Amityville, and pine forests with the Levittowns of the new suburbia.

Growing up at a very early age in Babylon Village, I began witnessing some subtle changes as new housing developments were springing up just to the east of the village in the hamlet of West Islip and to the north in North Babylon. In fact, in 1950, my father purchased one of the five Cape Cod homes in West Islip. It was the first housing development in that community. Still connected to family in Babylon, where my mother was raised, I continued to spend time in the village, attending the local parochial school there, and at various times, I would walk across the now dilapidated cement bridge that was once part of the famous Hawley Estate—one of the more notable "smaller" mansions on the South Shore, adjacent to the village. As I got older and rode my bike throughout the area, I would ride by the noted Arnold Mansion, where my grandmother, an Irish immigrant, once worked as a domestic and met the famous silent film star Rudolph Valentino.

From Massapequa east to Oakdale, this part of the South Shore became home to many business entrepreneurs, celebrities, and other wealthy personages from the Gilded Age to the Roaring Twenties. Although it did not rival the North Shore's Gold Coast in terms of the size of the buildings, it did have it own lineup of monumental houses and estates. Among them were the William K. Vanderbilt Estate in Oakdale (now home to Dowling College); the Arnold Estate in West Islip, which had its own carriage path from the Great South Bay to the mansion on the north side of Merrick Road; and the Frederick J. Bourne Estate, also in Oakdale (former home of LaSalle Military Academy and now an extended campus of St. John's University).

In addition, prior to postwar suburban development, wealthy investors built smaller, elaborate estates earmarked by clay tile roofs in the tradition of Spanish colonial homes in the Southwest, Tudor Revival with half-timbered facades like the Vanderbilt Mansion, and the more popular Colonial Revival houses where my wife was raised in the village of Babylon. Older homes in the South Shore communities were constructed on canals for quick access to the bay and Atlantic Ocean by private motorized boat and were adorned with beautiful gardens and plush lawns.

Nonetheless, by the 1960s, many of these estate homes disappeared as their land was sold and quickly gobbled up by housing developers. Many of these impressive estate structures were taken down as well and new, smaller homes with the same type and style were erected in their place. Any semblance of what was once a distinctive architectural style to the island's South Shore could only be found in its historic villages (Amityville, Lindenhurst, Babylon, Bay Shore, Islip, and Sayville). The South Shore, like much of its counterparts to the west, north, and east, had been radically transformed with the appearance of housing developments, local school districts for each community, and large shopping malls.

Nonetheless, Christopher Collora, in *Long Island: Historic Houses of the South Shore*, has brought to life an inspiring collection of captivating images of these South Shore estates and community life. His images breathe new life into this bygone age of summer homes, bungalows, and cottages as well as permanent estates, which made the South Shore a wonderful place to visit and, in many cases, to live year-round. This is one way to relive Long Island's past and to enjoy it.

—Dr. Charles F. Howlett
Professor, Molloy College
Coauthor of *A Walk Through History: Community Name Amityville*
and *Amityville's 1894 School House*

One

Life on the South Shore

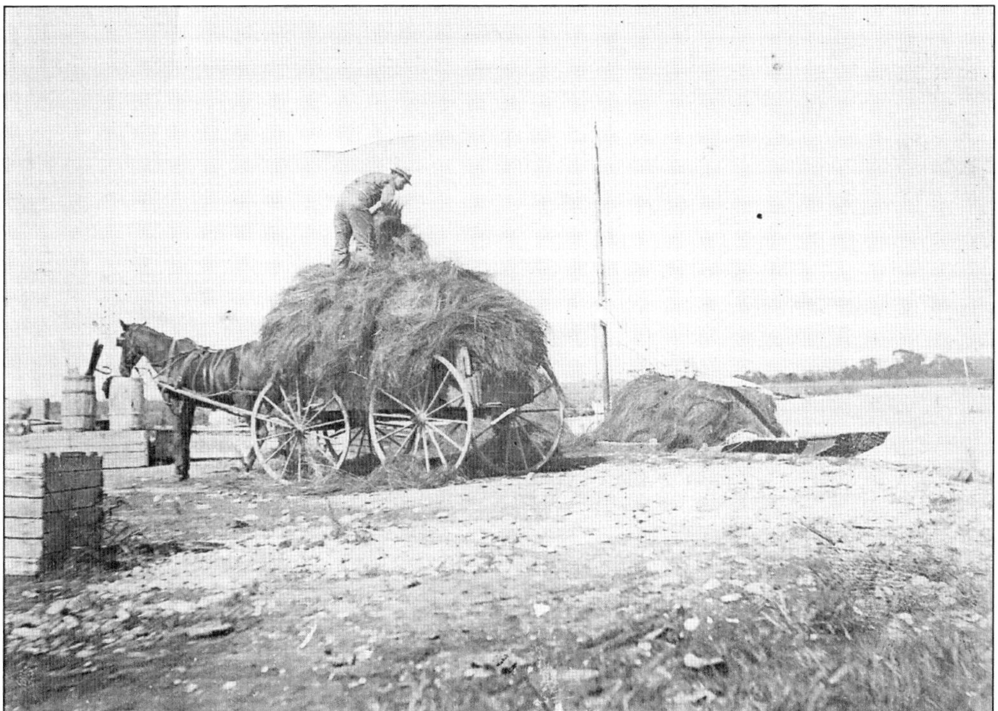

The South Shore of Long Island was not very developed in the early 1600s. Most towns started developing on the North Shore, and the South Shore was considered an extension of the North Shore townships. Marshes and swamplands comprised the South Shore back then. Settlers from the North Shore towns would travel down to the South Shore to collect "salt hay," which was used for feeding livestock and stuffing mattresses. (Courtesy Post Morrow Foundation.)

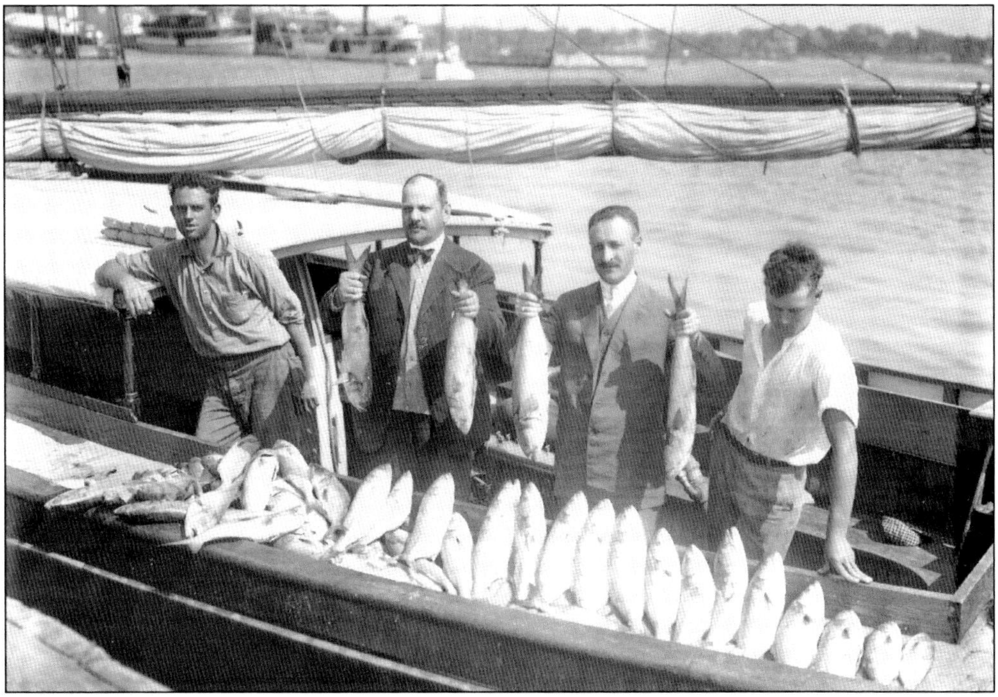

Eventually, the South Shore of Long Island became a draw for recreational pursuits, including hunting, fishing, and water activities along the Great South Bay. Here, two men proudly hold up their catches in Bay Shore in 1927. (Courtesy Bay Shore Historical Society.)

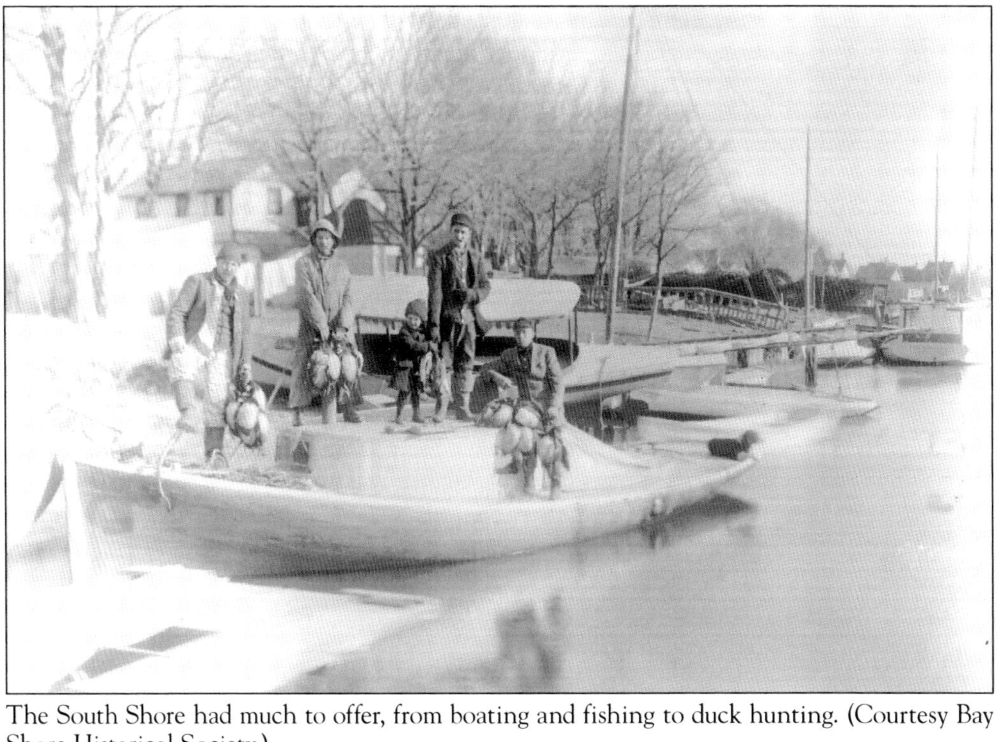

The South Shore had much to offer, from boating and fishing to duck hunting. (Courtesy Bay Shore Historical Society.)

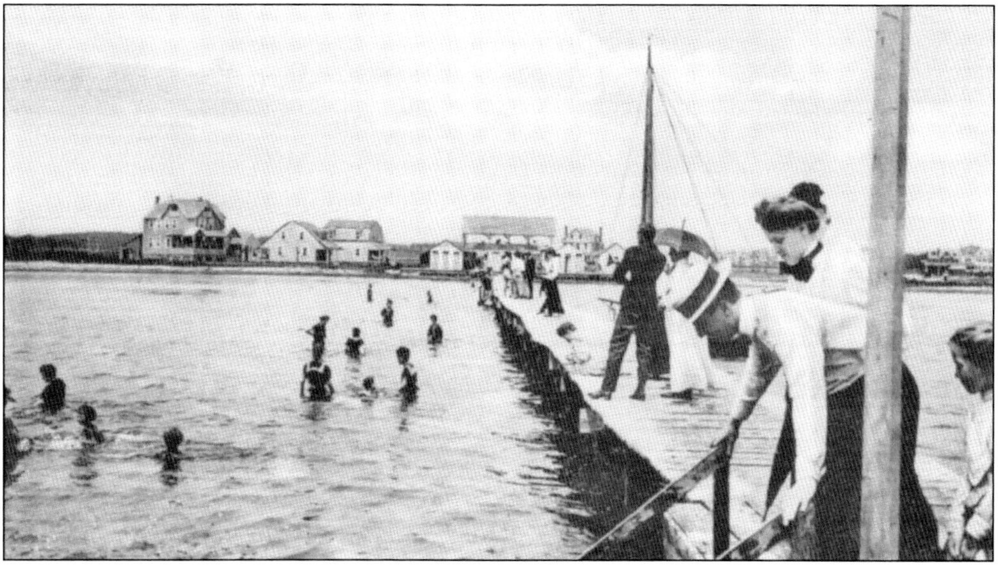

This was a common scene on beaches along the South Shore. This is a Bay Shore beach where people went to the water to cool off during the summer. (Courtesy Bay Shore Historical Society.)

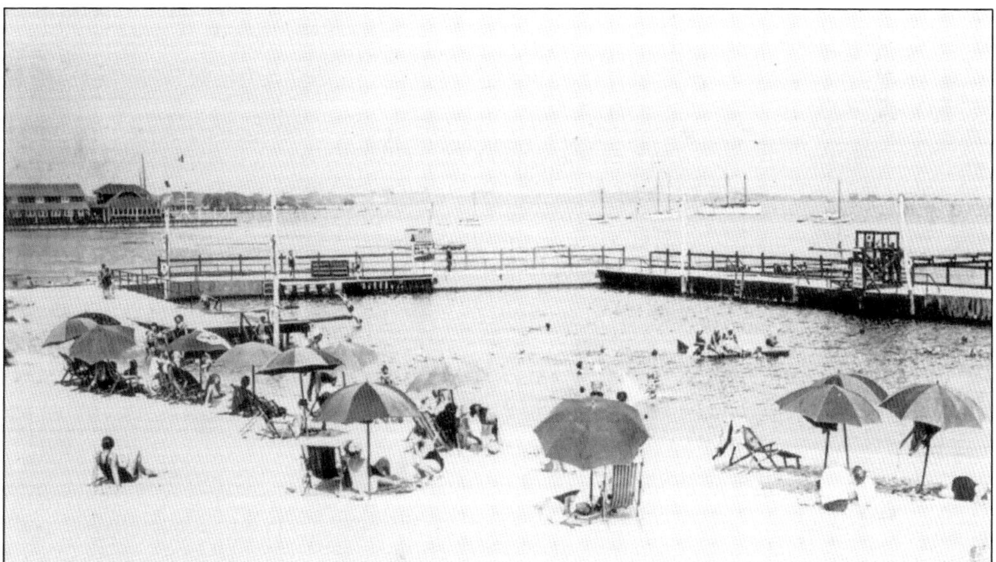

The smooth sandy beaches became a favored tourist spot in the summer as New York City residents traveled to Long Island to escape the heat of the city. (Courtesy Bay Shore Historical Society.)

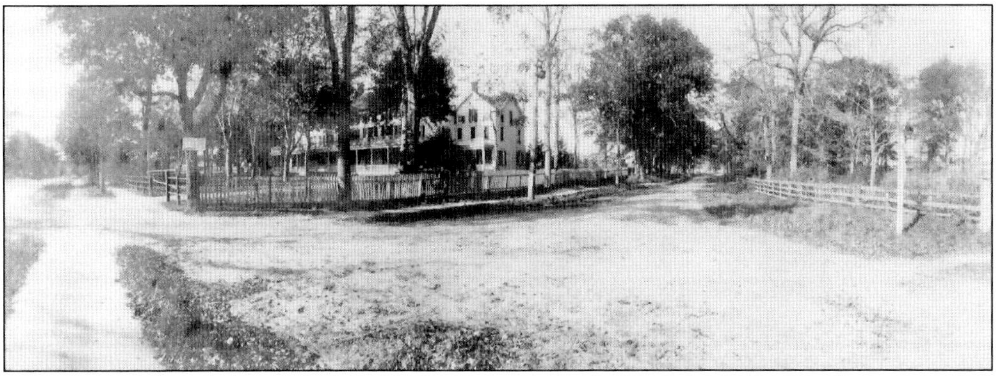

Transportation on Long Island was challenging, as this c. 1900 picture of Montauk Highway and Higbie Lane in West Islip near LaGrange Inn shows. Montauk Highway was still a dirt road. Most early transportation was by stagecoach. In later years, the railroad would provide easier access to the island. (Courtesy West Islip Historical Society.)

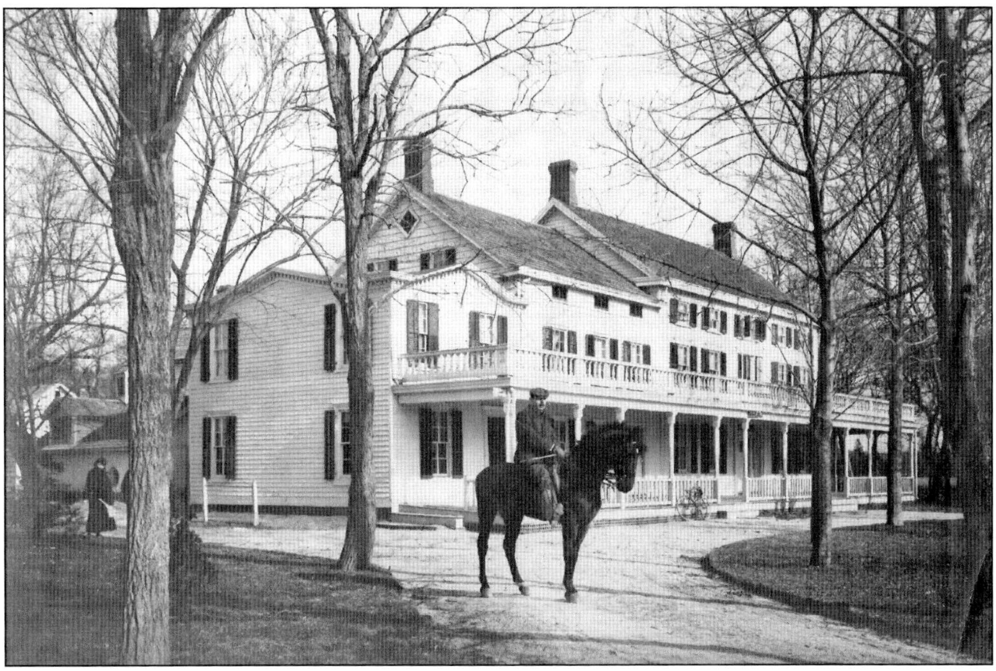

The LaGrange Inn in West Islip was built around 1750 and was, until 2010, open to the public as one of the oldest catering halls and restaurants on Long Island. It was one of the earliest hotels built along stagecoach routes that brought estate owners from the city to their country estates on Long Island. The building still stands but has been closed for several years. (Courtesy West Islip Historical Society.)

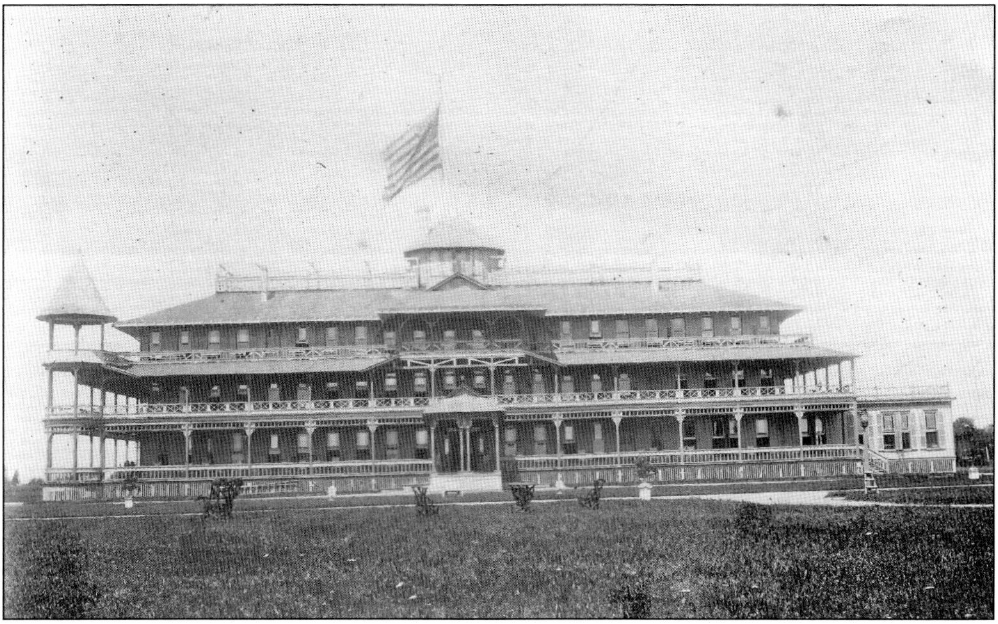

Tourism culminated in the hotel era, when grand hotels like the Massapequa Hotel (built 1888), seen here, were built in nearly every town across the South Shore of Long Island. Tourism was a major industry at the time. (Courtesy Historical Society of the Massapequas.)

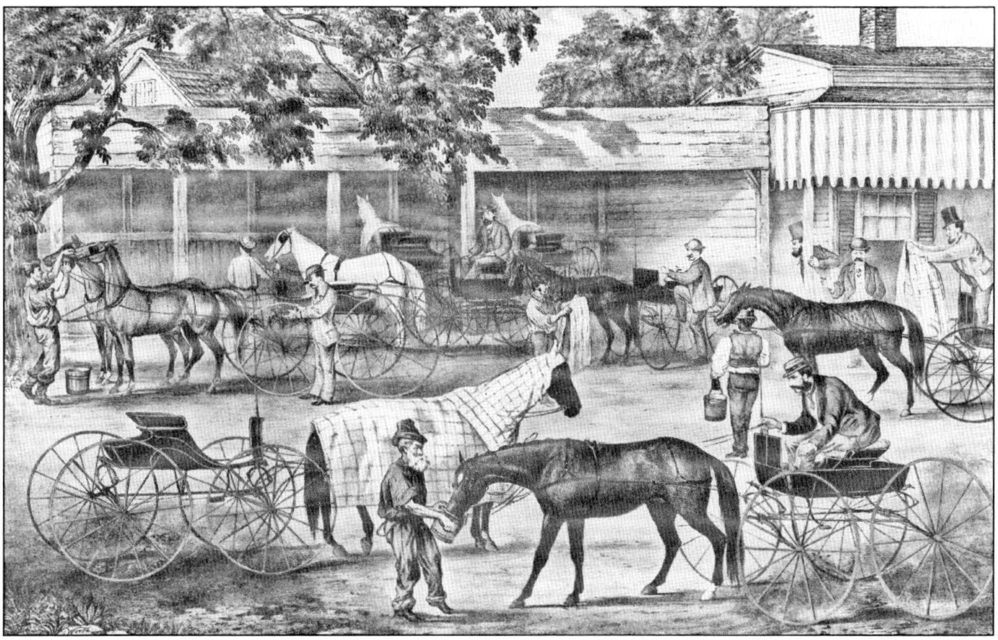

This Currier and Ives print by Thomas Worth depicts Stellenwerf's Lake House, an early rest stop for stagecoaches along South Country Road, today's Montauk Highway. (Courtesy East Islip Historical Society.)

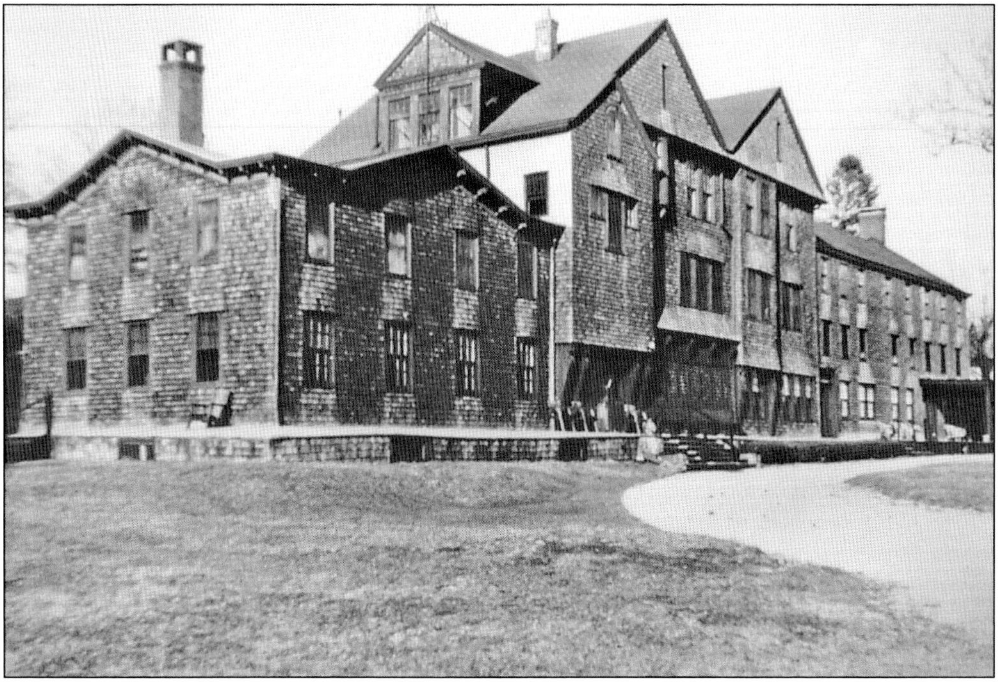

Part of this building was Snedecor's Inn, established around 1820 in Oakdale. The inn offered hunting and fishing, which became a draw to the area for society sportsmen. The sportsmen eventually purchased it for themselves and established the South Side Sportsman's Club in 1866. William K. Vanderbilt Sr., Frederick Bourne, and William Bayard Cutting were members and decided to build their estates nearby. (Courtesy East Islip Historical Society.)

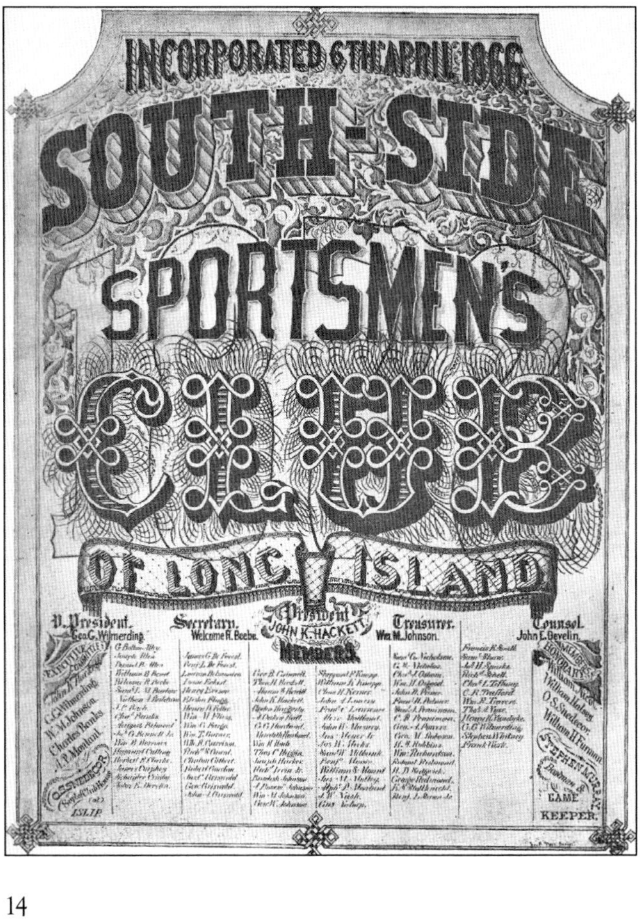

The South Side Sportsman's Club headquarters was in Oakdale in what is today Connetquot River State Park. (Courtesy Suffolk County Parks Department.)

Two

Massapequa and Amityville

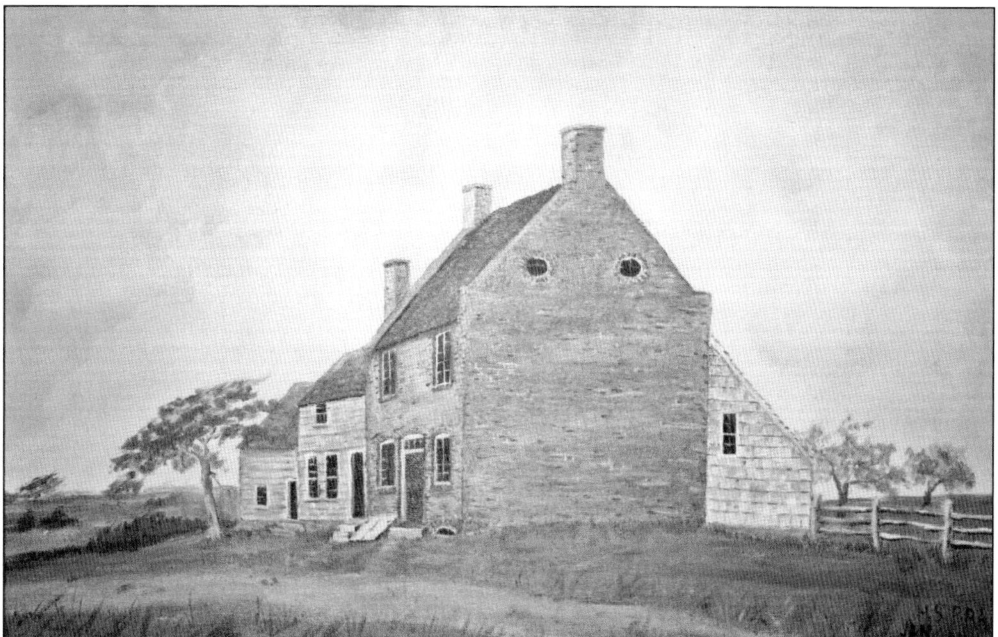

Called the "old brick house," this may be the first brick house on Long Island's South Shore. It was built in 1696 by Maj. Thomas Jones (1665–1713), the first recorded European settler of Massapequa. Thomas Jones was exiled from Ireland after losing in the Battle of the Boyne. He was briefly a privateer (licensed pirate) in the Caribbean before immigrating to Warwick, Rhode Island, and then marrying Freelove Townsend. Jones was presented with the estate in Massapequa as a wedding gift from Thomas Townsend, Freelove's father, who was also Jones's business associate. (Courtesy Historical Society of the Massapequas.)

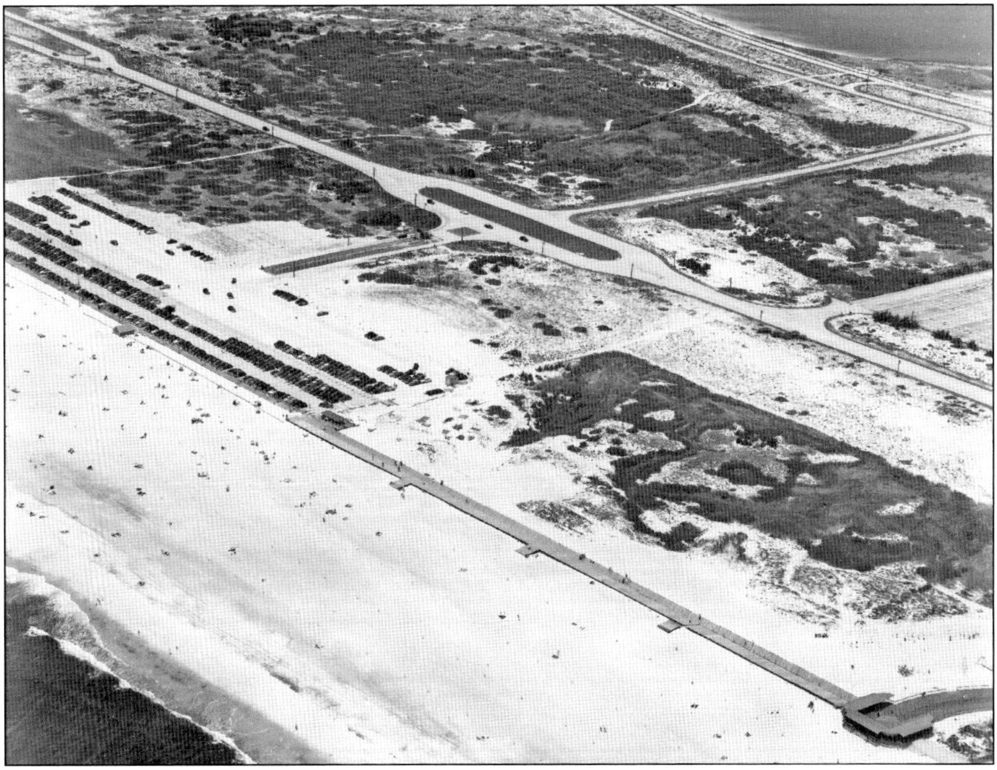

Jones Beach State Park, built by Robert Moses, was named in honor of Thomas Jones, who once owned the land and organized a whaling operation from it. Today, Jones Beach is a major attraction and public park. No known images of Maj. Thomas Jones exist. Legend has it that when Moses was asked who the beach was named after, he said he did not know. (Courtesy Collections of the Town of Babylon, Office of Historic Services.)

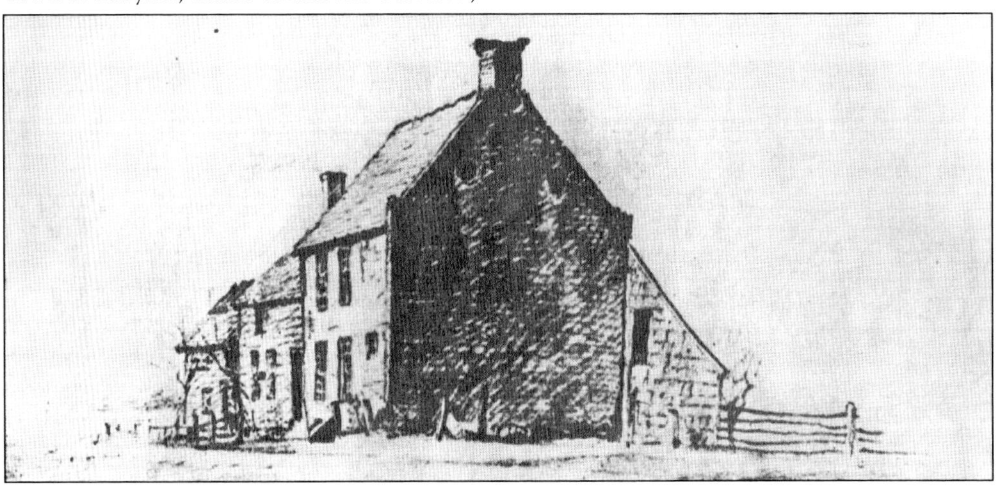

This is a William Sydney Mount drawing of Jones's house. At the time of Jones's death in 1713, a crow flew through his bedroom window and left right after Jones died. Afterwards, the window would never remain closed. Even attempts to seal the window with bricks failed. Some believed the spirit of Thomas Jones still haunted the place. The family moved, and the house was demolished in 1836. (Historical Society of the Massapequas.)

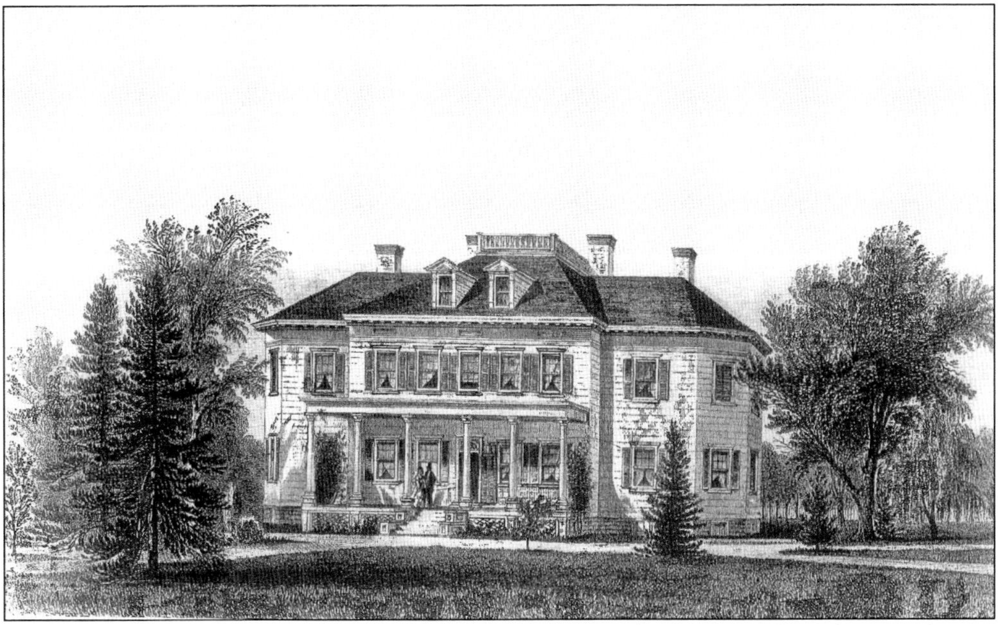

Tryon Hall was the first known mansion on Merrick Road, built in 1770 by Judge David Jones (1699–1775). It was inherited by his son "Little Judge" Thomas Jones (1731–1792). The home was renamed Fort Neck House at the end of the Revolutionary War, commemorating the Indian forts located in the area during the pre-settlement era. The mansion was destroyed by fire in 1940. (Courtesy Historical Society of the Massapequas.)

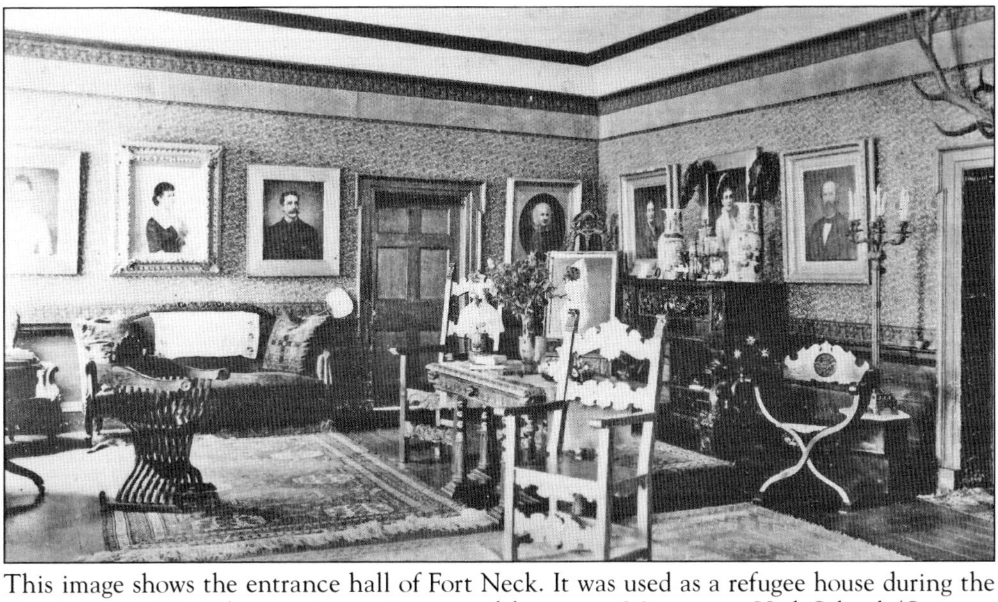

This image shows the entrance hall of Fort Neck. It was used as a refugee house during the Revolutionary War. The mansion sat just west of the current Massapequa High School. (Courtesy Historical Society of the Massapequas.)

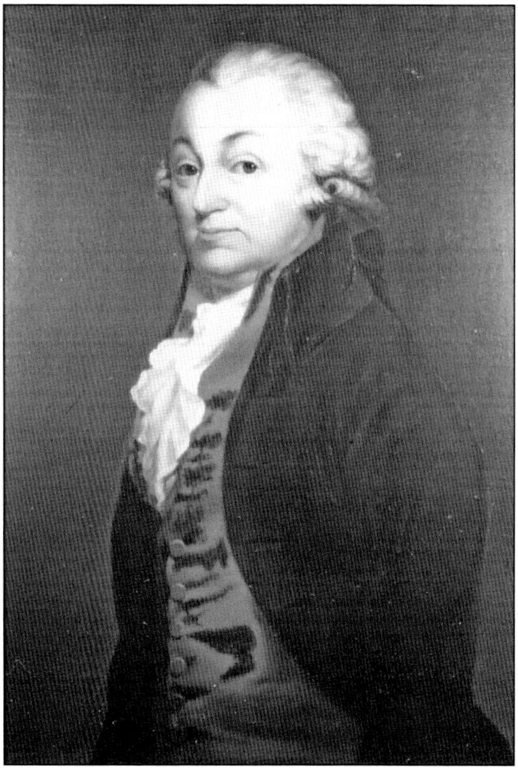

Judge Thomas Jones, grandson of the original Thomas Jones, was a Loyalist during the American Revolution. In 1777, he was captured by the Patriot army and brought to Fairfield, Connecticut, where he was held for several months before being exchanged for Patriot general Gold Selleck Silliman. In June 1781, Jones fled to England, where he died on July 25, 1792. (Courtesy Historical Society of the Massapequas.)

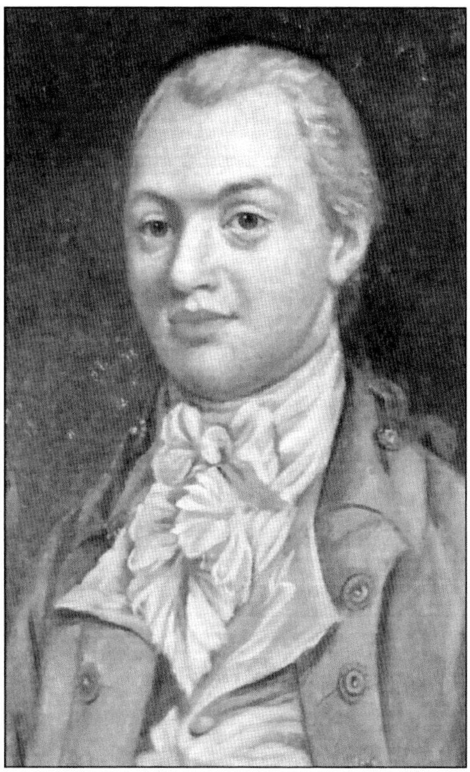

David Richard Floyd-Jones, pictured here, was the first Floyd-Jones. Judge Thomas Jones's sister Arabella Jones (1734–1785) married Richard Floyd (1731–1791), of the famous Floyd family in Mastic, in 1757. David Jones's will said Arabella could inherit the estate if she married a man willing or her children were willing to to take the name Jones. Their son David changed his last name to Floyd-Jones in 1788 to claim his inheritance. (Courtesy Historical Society of the Massapequas.)

Massapequa Manor, built in 1837, was the home of David S. Jones. The mansion was sold to the Caroon family around 1900. It was destroyed by fire in 1952. The family named the mansion Massapequa Manor after the Indian name for the area, meaning "great water land." It is said that because the Jones family used that name, the area came to be known as Massapequa. (Historical Society of the Massapequas.)

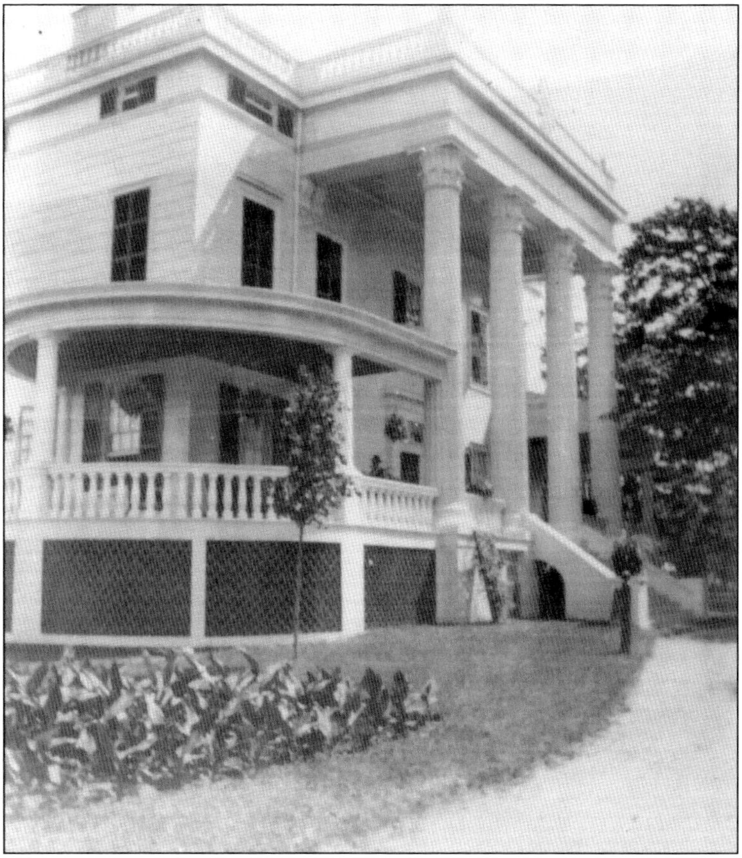

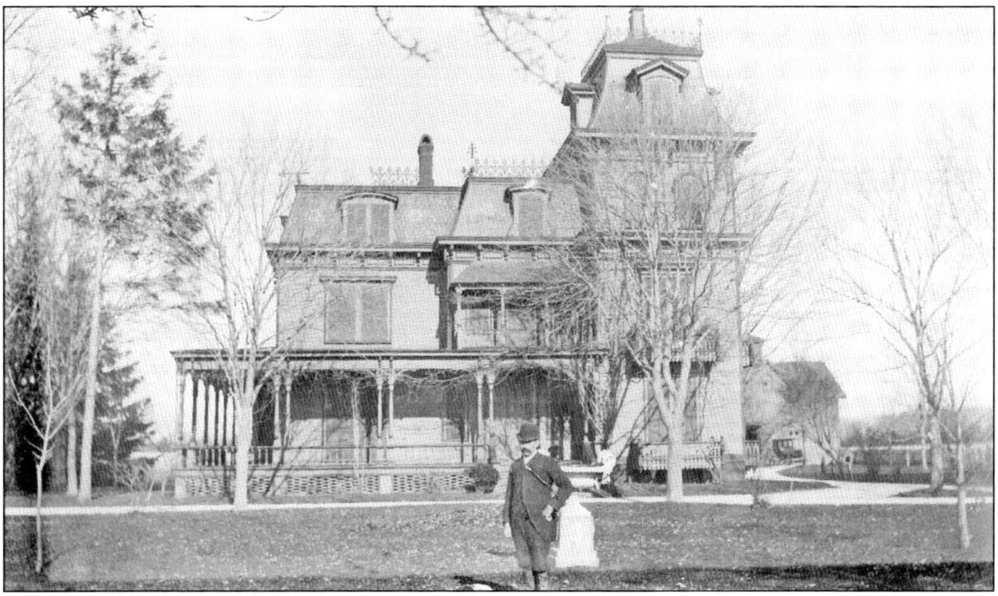

Unqua, also known as Rosedale, was built by Maj. Gen. Henry Onderdonk Floyd-Jones (1792–1862). It sat across from land that later became John Burns Park. It was demolished in the 1950s. A small shopping center currently occupies the land. (Courtesy Historical Society of the Massapequas.)

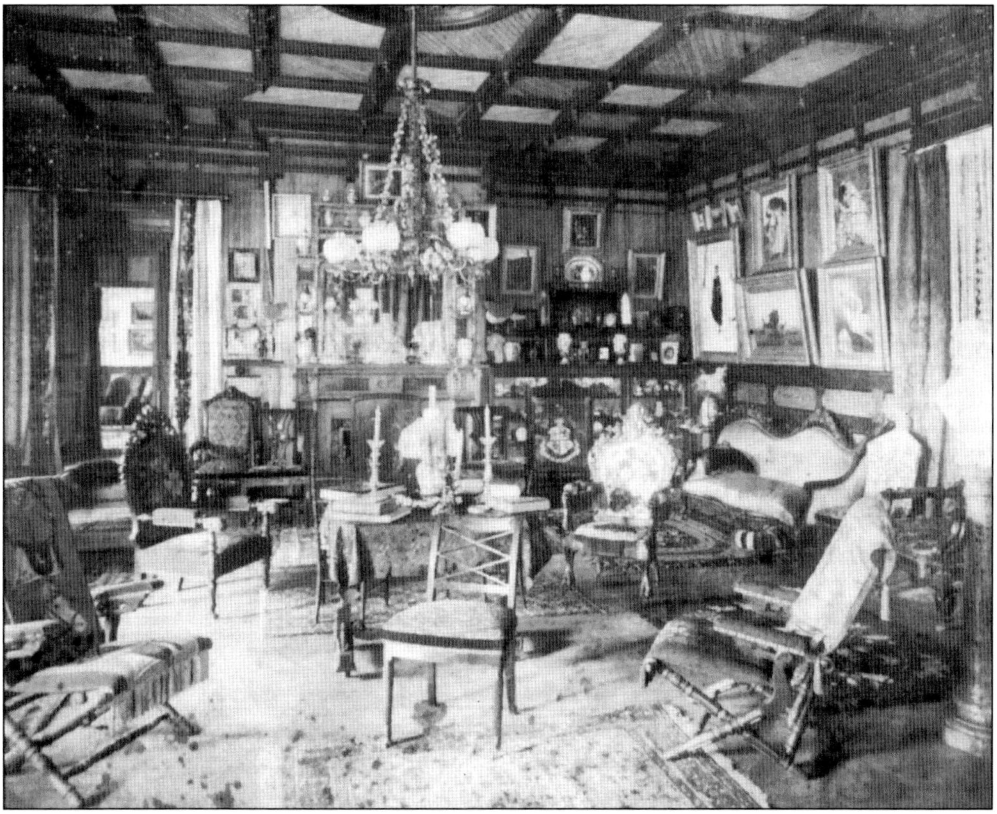

A look inside the impressive Unqua house built by Gen. Henry Onderdonk Floyd-Jones shows the living room of the mansion. (Courtesy Historical Society of the Massapequas.)

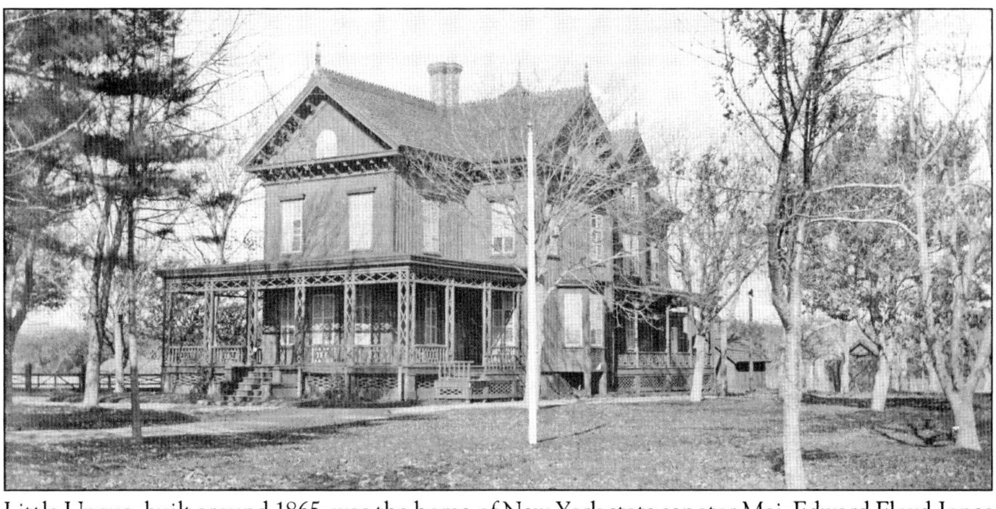

Little Unqua, built around 1865, was the home of New York state senator Maj. Edward Floyd-Jones (1823–1901). It was later inherited by his daughter Louise Ackerly Floyd-Jones Thorn (1867–1961), who married Conde Thorn (1862–1944). The mansion was demolished in 1963. The land became Marjorie Post Town Park in 1965, named in honor of Marjorie Post, the first councilwoman of the Town of Oyster Bay, who helped turn it into a public park. (Courtesy Historical Society of the Massapequas.)

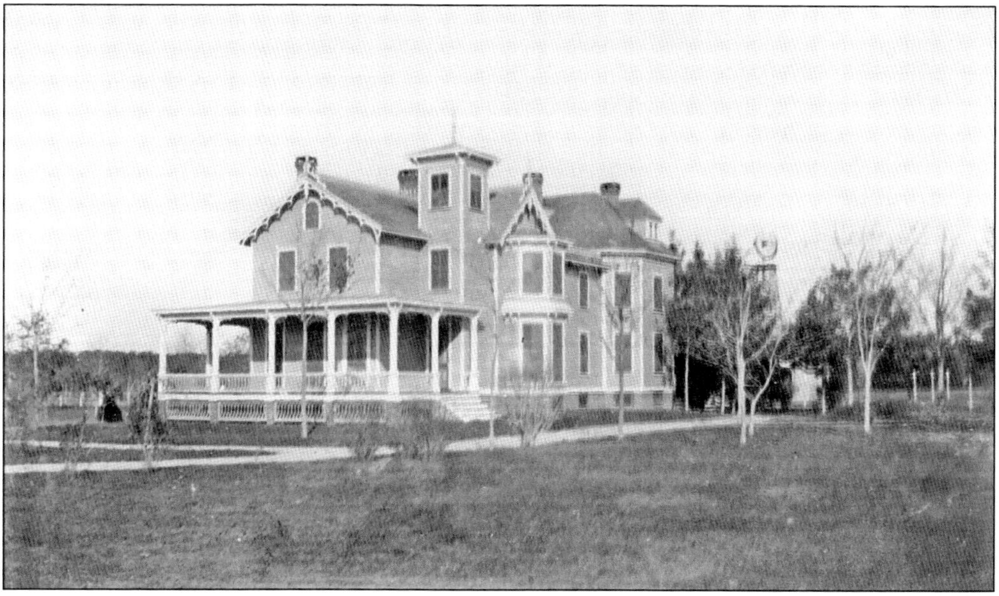

Unqua Lodge/Kaycroft was the home of Walter Restored Twice Jones. Unqua Lodge was remolded in 1913 by Katharine Jones Whipple. The home became known as Kaycroft. The home was demolished in 1950s. (Courtesy Historical Society of the Massapequas.)

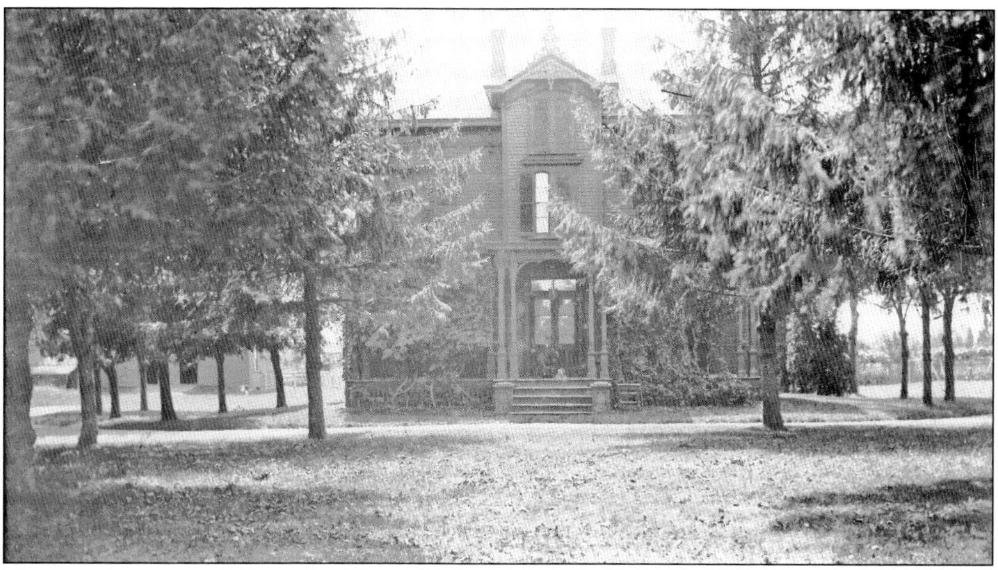

This was the home of Elbert Floyd-Jones (1817–1901), New York state assemblyman. This mansion was built in 1870 and destroyed by fire in 1926 as the result of a Fourth of July fireworks celebration. The Bar Harbour Library now sits on the land. The servants' cottage still exists but was moved in 1986 from its original site. It is now part of the Massapequa Historic Complex on Merrick Road, used to house archives and historic artifacts. (Courtesy Historical Society of the Massapequas.)

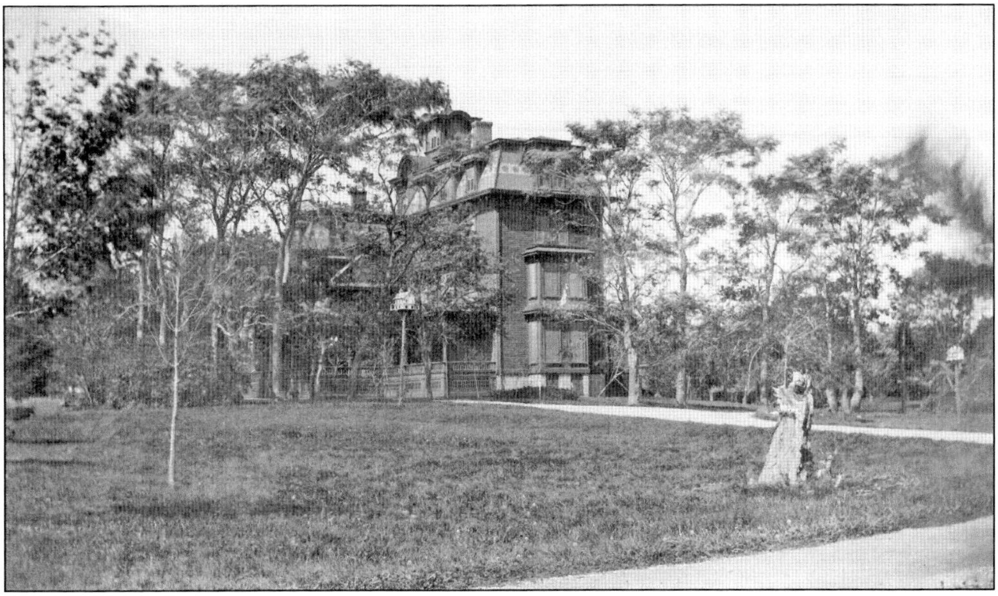

Sedgemoor was built in 1854 by Sara Maria Floyd-Jones (1818–1892), who married Coleman Williams (1805–1891). The mansion was demolished in 1953, and this is now the site of private homes across from St. Rose of Lima Church. (Courtesy Historical Society of the Massapequas.)

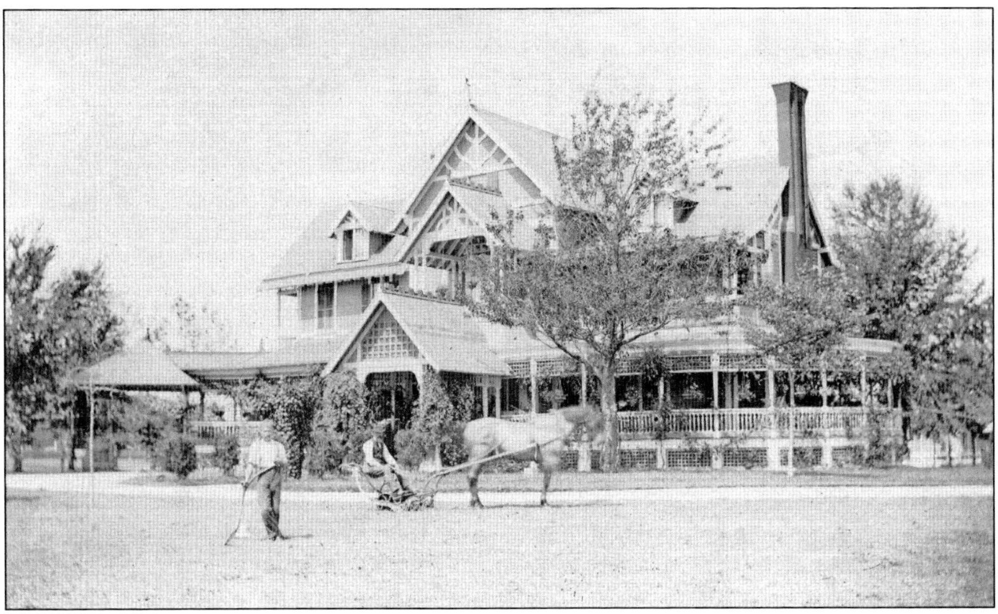

Sewan was built around 1890 by George Stanton Floyd-Jones (1848–1941), president of an insurance company. The mansion fell into disuse in the 1940s. The house was left to the Catholic Church and sold to the school district. It was demolished in 1950s. Massapequa High School now sits on the land. (Courtesy Historical Society of the Massapequas.)

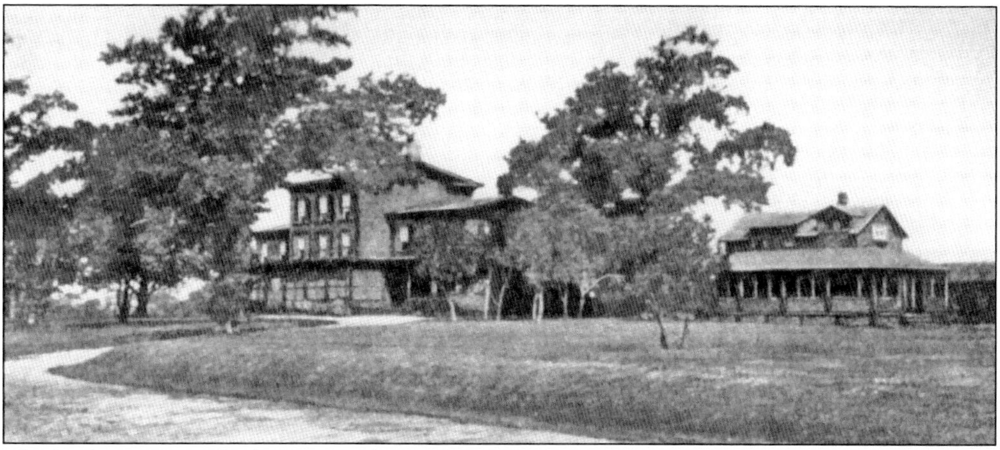

The Red House was built at Merrick Road and Seaford Avenue in 1856 by James Meinell (died 1865). Meinell was a Broadway producer. He built and owned the New Theater in New York City and introduced Laura Keene and her acting troupe. Her troupe is famous for performing the play *My American Cousin* the night Abraham Lincoln was assassinated. This house was demolished 1964. (Courtesy Historical Society of the Massapequas.)

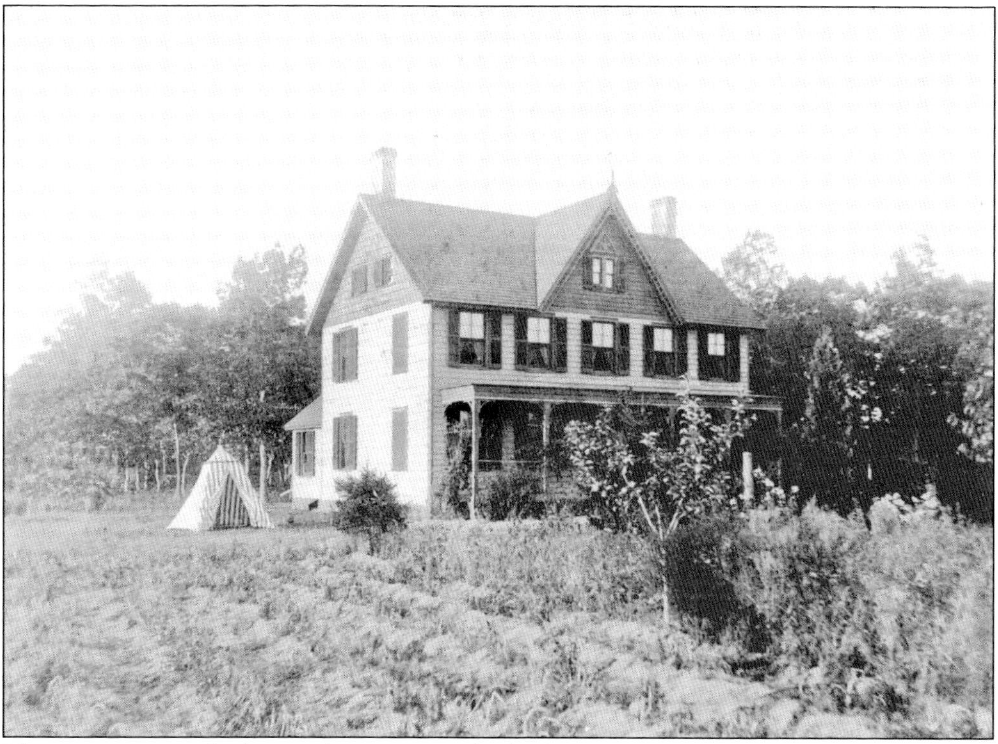

This mansion was built 1880 by Lisette and Charles Schaefer as his private home on Front Street. It later became the first village hall in 1931, when the Village of Massapequa Park was established. Massapequa Park was first known as Stadt Wurtemberg, a community of German settlers. The house was torn down around 1965. (Courtesy Lillian Rumfield Bryson, Historical Society of the Massapequas.)

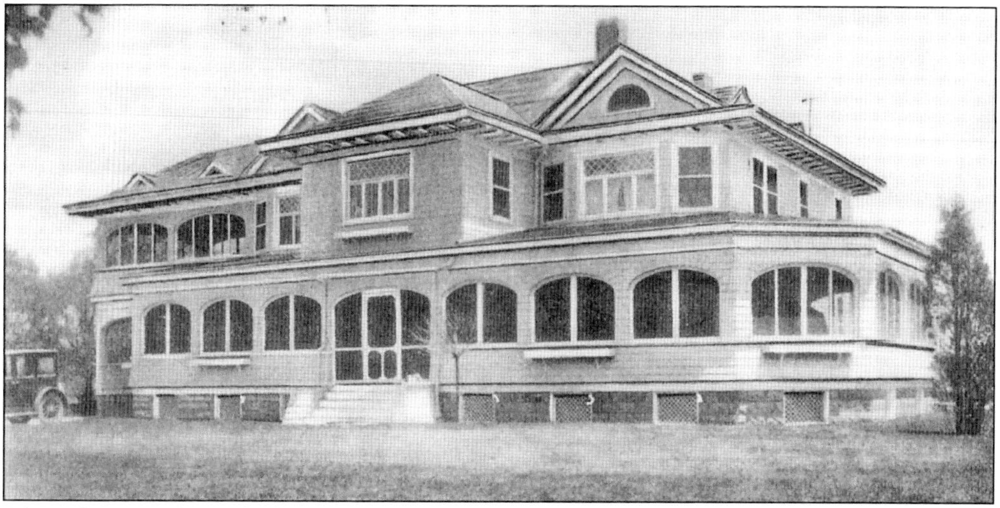

Chin Chin Ranch was the home of actor Fred Stone, who built this mansion on Clocks Boulevard in 1912. Stone was known for throwing celebrity parties. Annie Oakley, Buffalo Bill Cody, and Tom Mix were well-known visitors to Fred Stone's estate. His house contained racetrack stables, a polo field, and several guest cabins. The home is still standing and is in private ownership. (Courtesy Amityville Historical Society.)

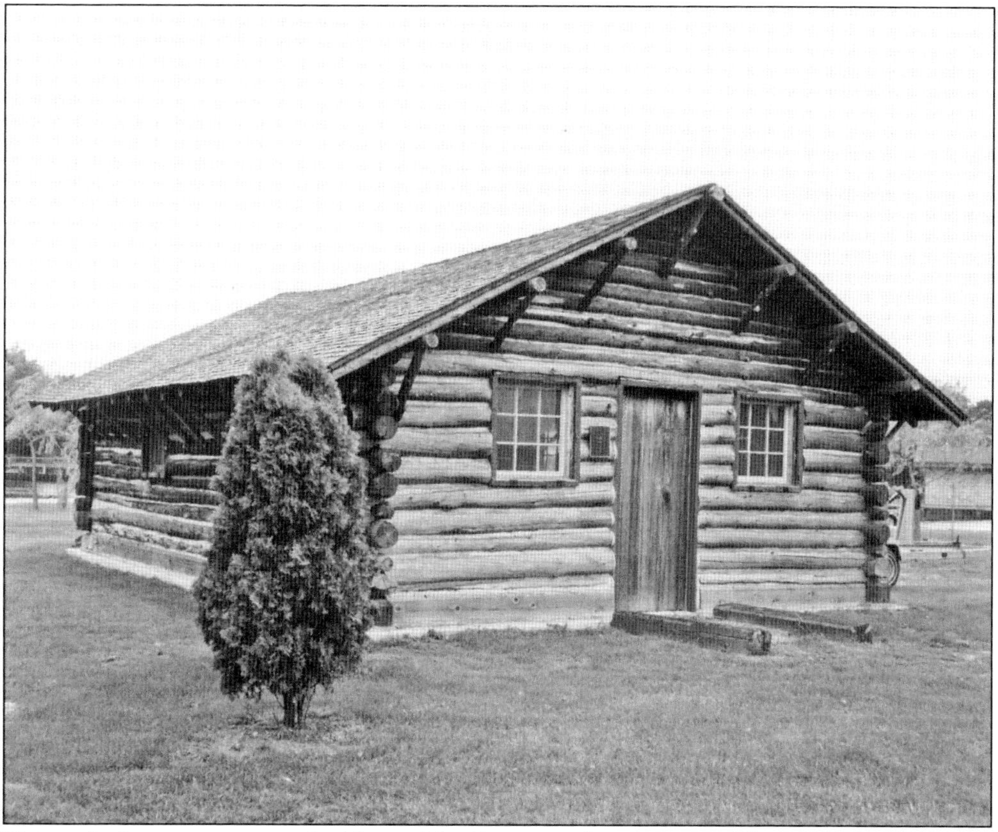

This is the last remaining outbuilding of the Stone ranch; it was moved in 1986 to John Burns Park and is used for storage. (Courtesy Historical Society of the Massapequas.)

Actor Fred Stone (1873–1959) was a famous vaudeville stage and screen actor. He was also the first actor to play the Tin Man in the play *The Wizard of Oz*. (Courtesy Historical Society of the Massapequas.)

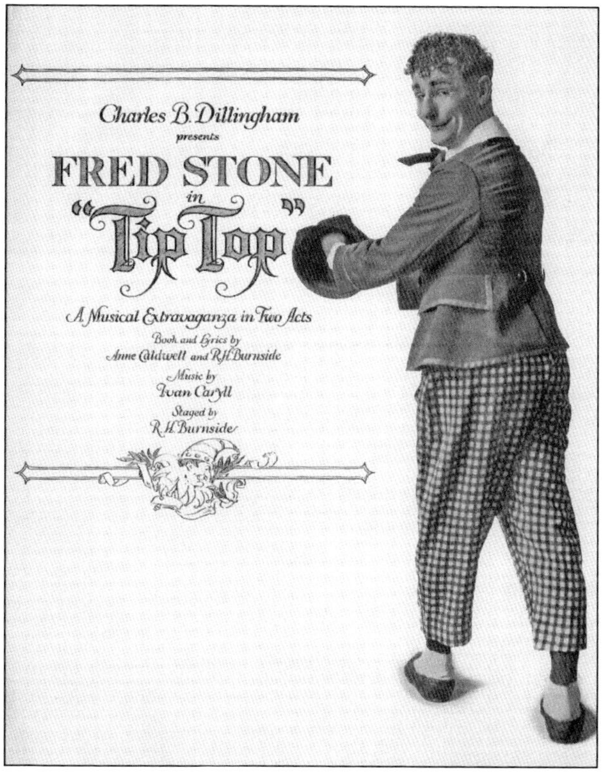

Western-themed stage performer Will Rogers (1879–1935) lived in this c. 1880s house, built across from Fred Stone's estate. Legend has it that Rogers, known as cowboy actor and entertainer, went on to do comedy and political commentary after hurting his right shoulder diving into Fred Stone's Narraskatuck creek. His house still stands and is privately owned. (Courtesy Historical Society of the Massapequas.)

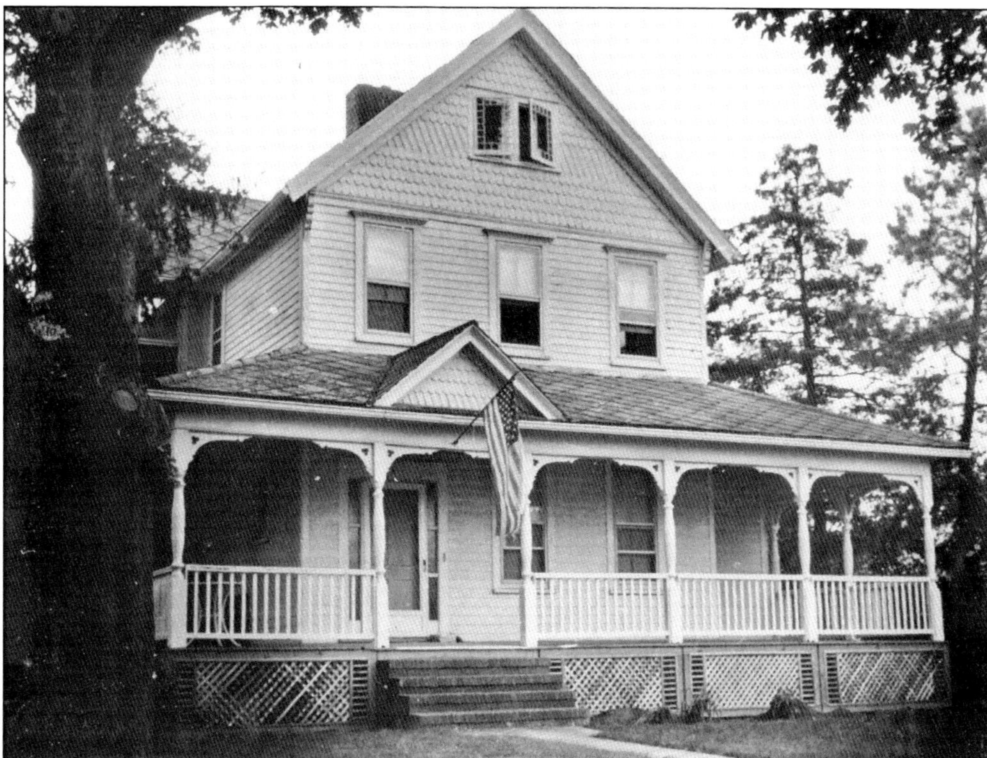

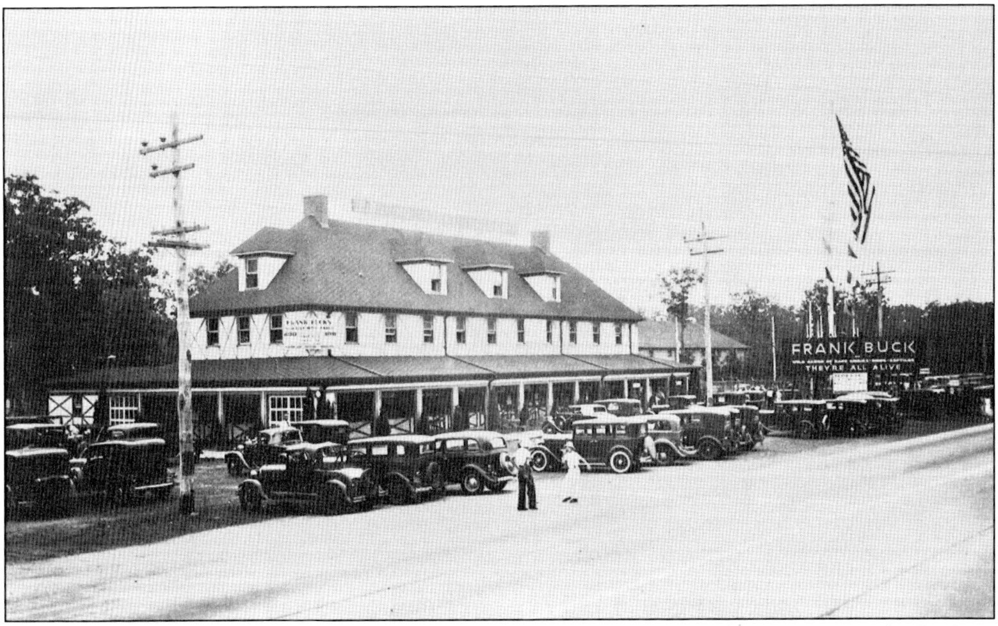

Not all houses on the South Shore were home to people; some were home to animals. Built in 1934, Frank Buck's Jungle Camp was a major attraction for 10 years. The zoo was bought by the Grimaldi family, who transformed it into an amusement park petting zoo. It was closed in 1965. The buildings were demolished except for the Lion House, which still stands in a shopping center. (Courtesy Historical Society of the Massapequas.)

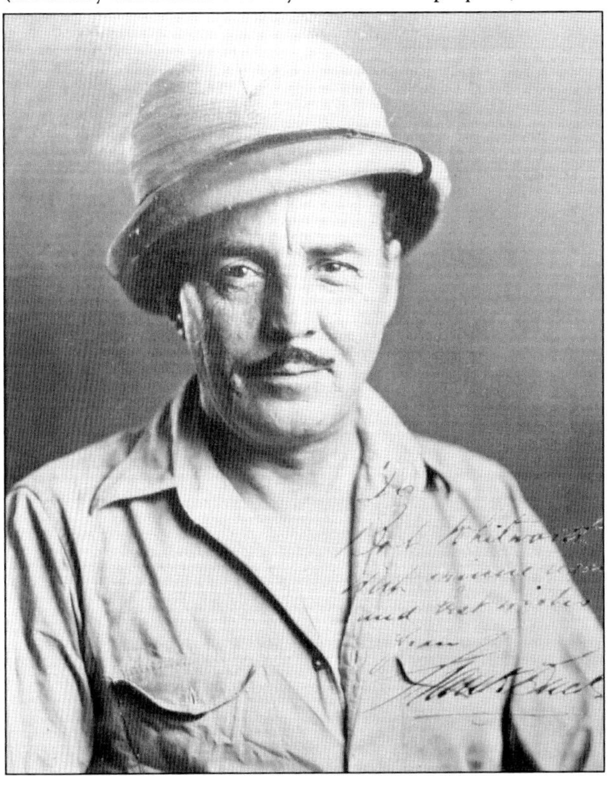

Frank Buck (1884–1950) was a famous animal hunter/exhibitor and filmmaker/actor. His motto was "Bring 'Em Back Alive," meaning that unlike most hunters, Buck never killed the animals he hunted but captured them for transport back to the United States for exhibit. He was also known for his jungle adventure films. (Courtesy Historical Society of the Massapequas.)

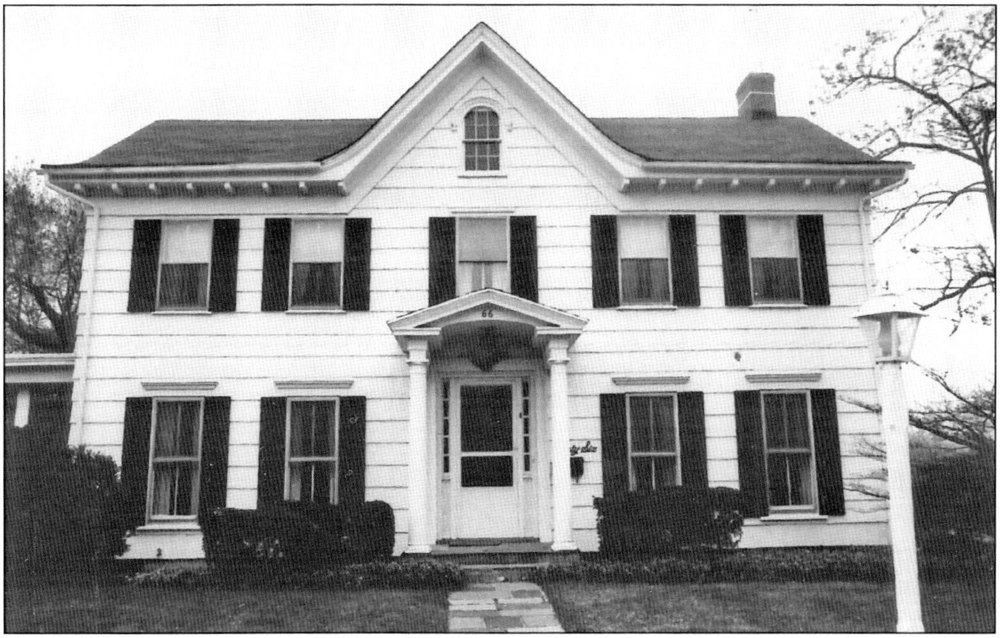

This home was built around the 1840s by Samuel Ireland. The Irelands were among Amityville's earliest settlers. Originally, the town was called Huntington West Neck South. The name "Amityville" may have come from Samuel Ireland's boat, the *Amity*. Another story says the name came from a town meeting where someone said, "What this meeting needs is some amity." The house was later moved to Avon Lake and still stands. (Courtesy Amityville Historical Society.)

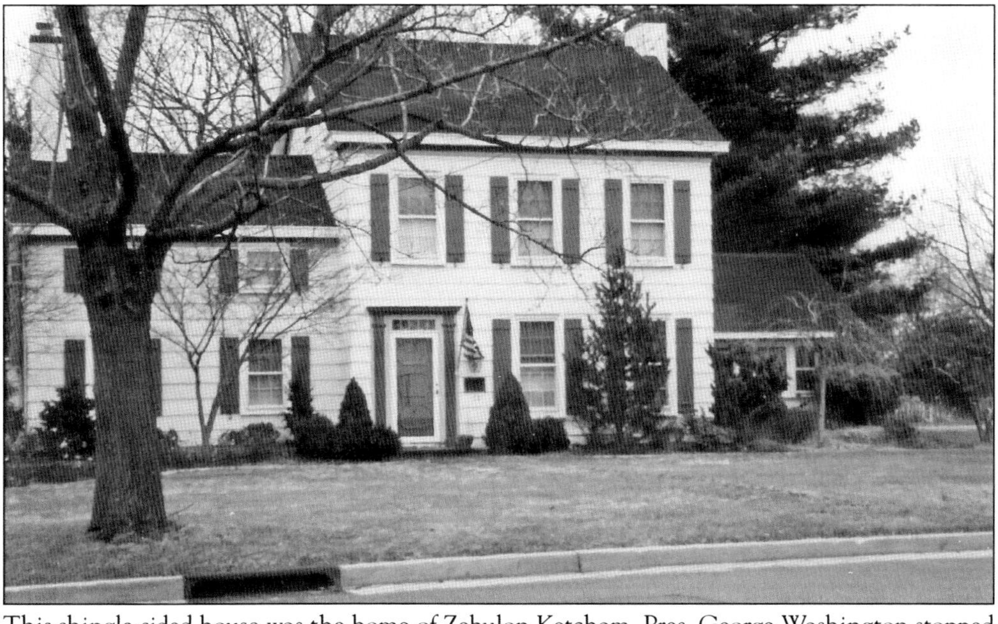

This shingle-sided house was the home of Zebulon Ketcham. Pres. George Washington stopped and ate dinner there on April 21, 1790, during his tour of Long Island. Washington described the house as a "very neat and decent public House." The house was originally located in Copiague but was moved to Amityville in the 1940s. It still stands today on Bayview Avenue as a private residence. (Courtesy Amityville Historical Society.)

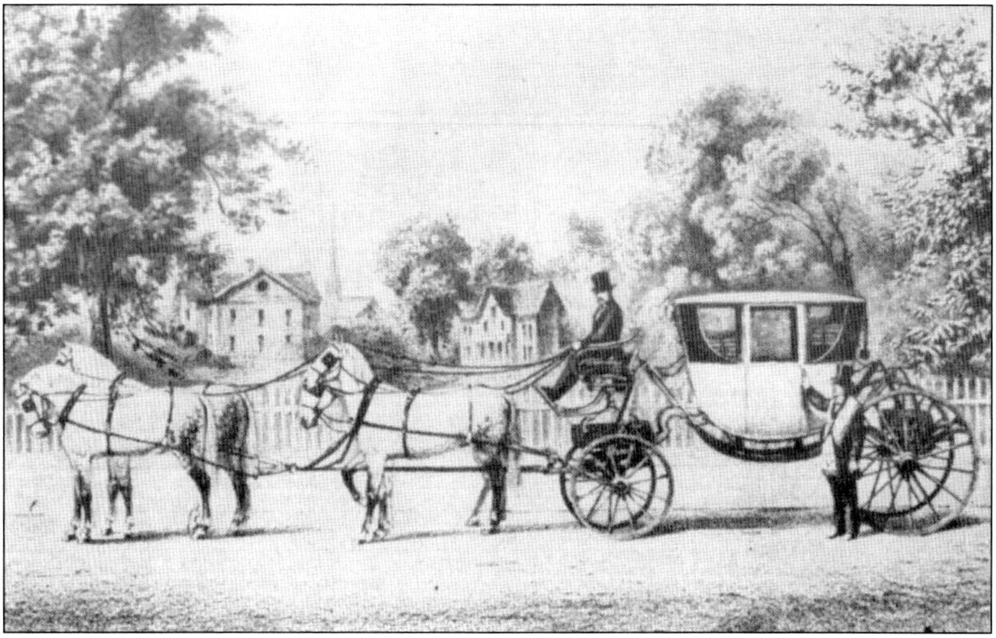

This sketch depicts the carriage Washington used during his tour of Long Island in 1790. He made four stops along the South Shore. (Courtesy Collections of the Town of Babylon, Office of Historic Services.)

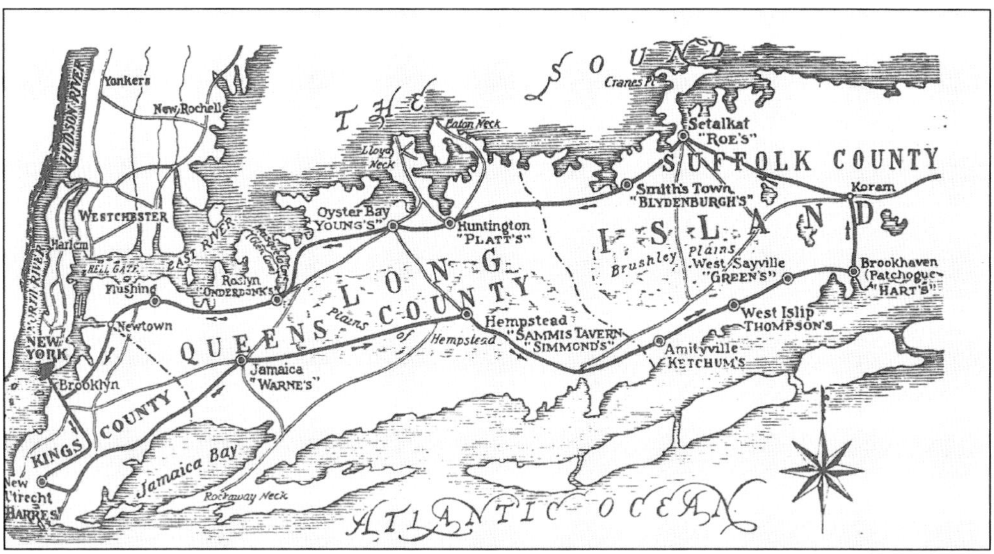

This map shows Washington's route from Ketcham's Inn to Sagtikos Manor and then on to the Green House in West Sayville and Hart's Tavern in Patchogue/Brookhaven before heading to the North Shore. (Courtesy George Weeks Library, West Islip.)

Three

Copiague and Lindenhurst

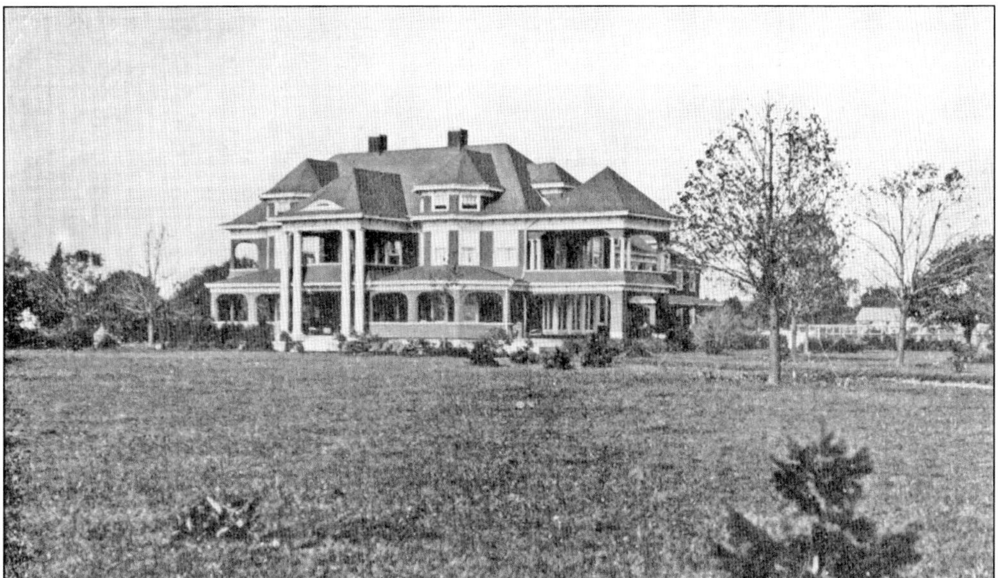

This 40-room mansion, built around 1910, was named Wild Goose Farm. It was the home of William E. Hawkins, president of the American Brass and Copper Company. The farm sat on about 300 acres along the former Strong property on South Country Road (Montauk Highway today). Hawkins reportedly sold the estate in 1926 because of encroaching development and "the din of traffic," which annoyed him. According to newspaper accounts of the time, Hawkins sold the estate to Louis C. Gosdorfer, Inc., for a reported $3 million. (Courtesy Collections of the Town of Babylon, Office of Historic Services.)

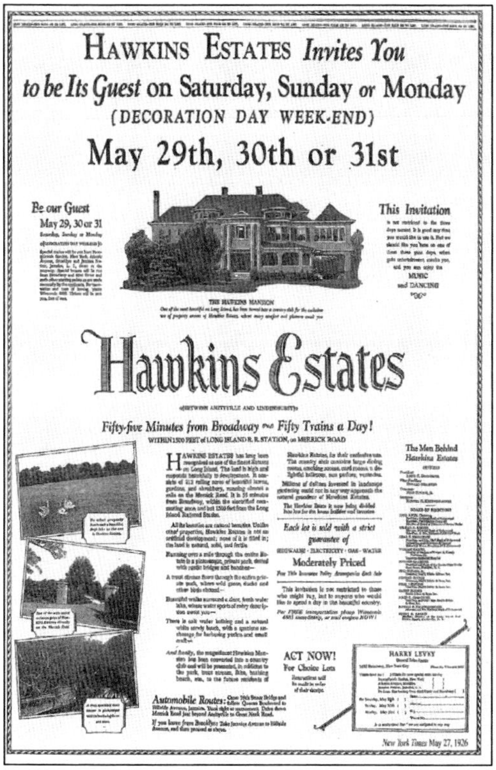

This sale advertisement from 1926 shows Gosdorfer's attempt to use the mansion as a draw to sell his planned estates. (Courtesy Collections of the Town of Babylon, Office of Historic Services.)

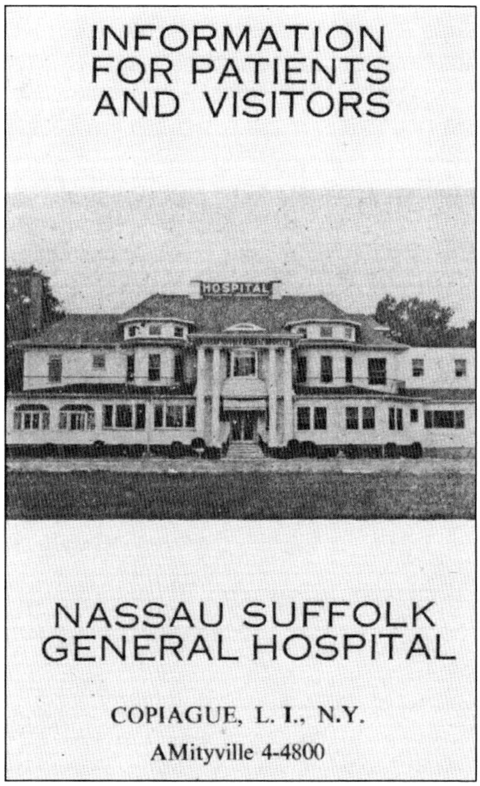

In the late 1930s, the Hawkins Mansion became the Nassau-Suffolk General Hospital; it later changed its name to Lakeside Hospital. It operated until the 1970s. The home was eventually torn down and today is the site of the Lakeside Manor apartment complex. (Courtesy Amityville Historical Society.)

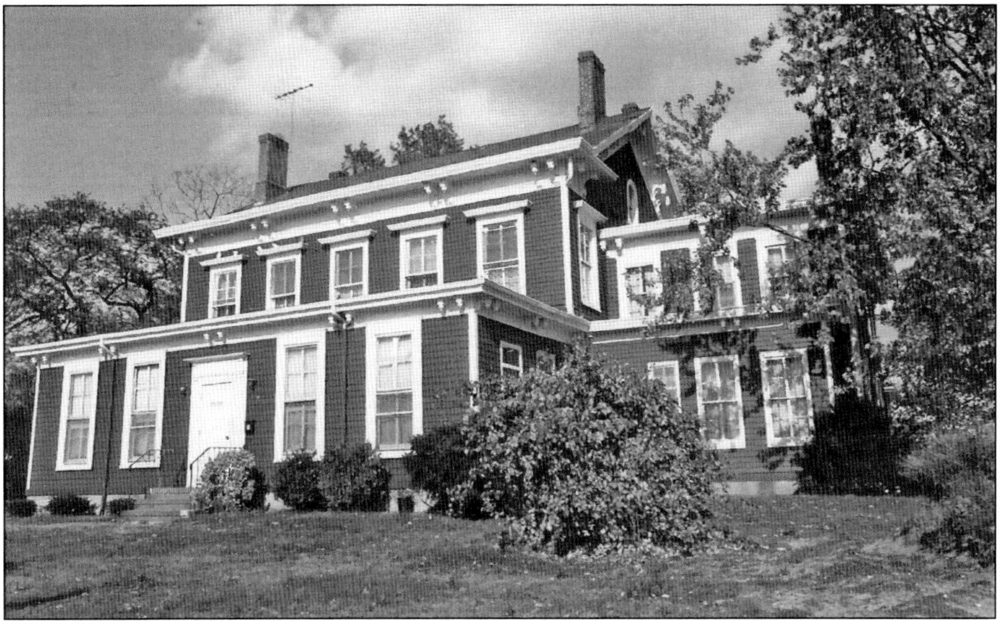

Built in 1860, this was the home of Col. Samuel Strong (1774–1854). Strong originally owned the land that became Lindenhurst. Strong's grandson Elbert sold the land to Thomas Welwood in 1869. Later, the home was used as the Montauk Manor Rest Home until it was demolished in 2004. Currently, it is the site of the Gail Gate Manor West apartment complex. (Courtesy Lindenhurst Old Village Hall Museum.)

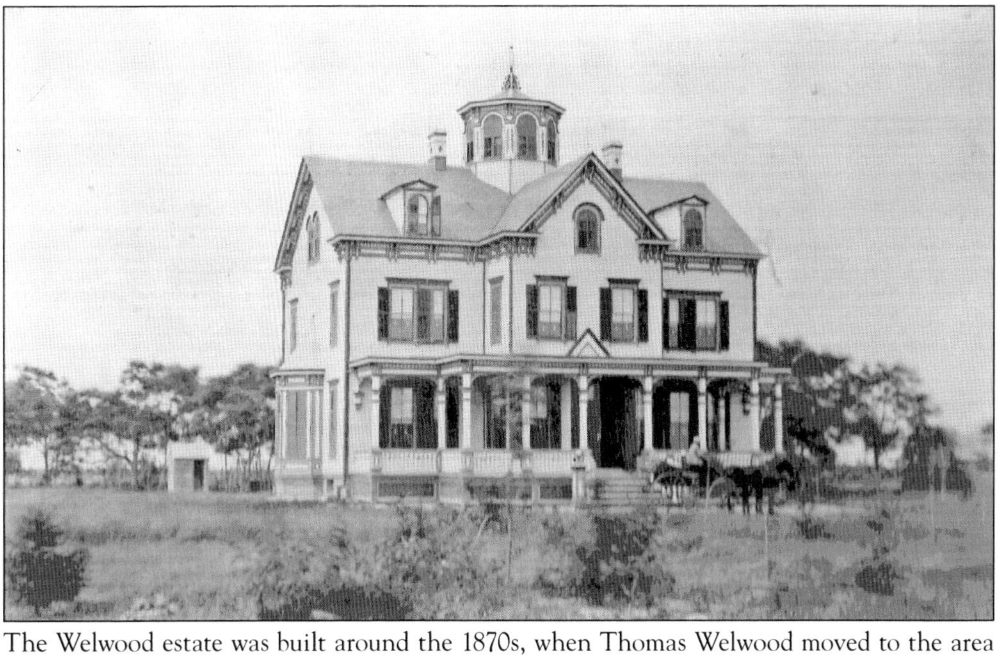

The Welwood estate was built around the 1870s, when Thomas Welwood moved to the area with his wife, Abby. Welwood saw a great real estate opportunity as what was then the South Side Railroad constructed a track to Babylon in 1867. Welwood immediately started buying up property. By 1870, the railroad listed a "Welwood Station." (Courtesy Lindenhurst Old Village Hall Museum.)

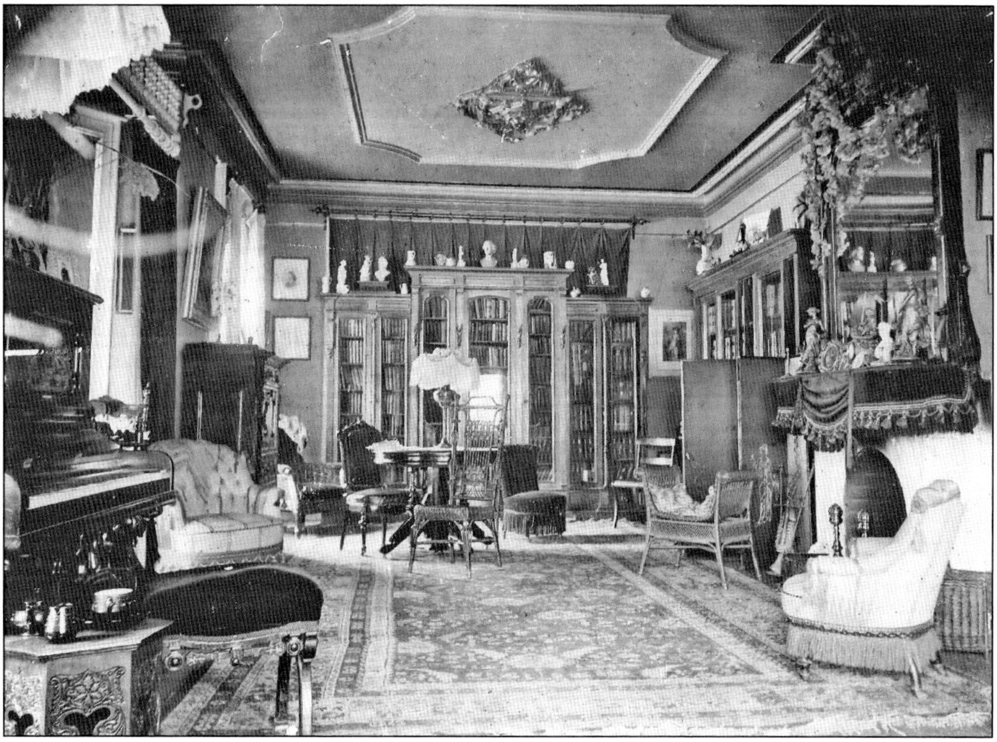

This is a rare photograph of the living room of the Welwood Mansion around the 1870s. The home was demolished around the 1980s. (Courtesy Lindenhurst Old Village Hall Museum.)

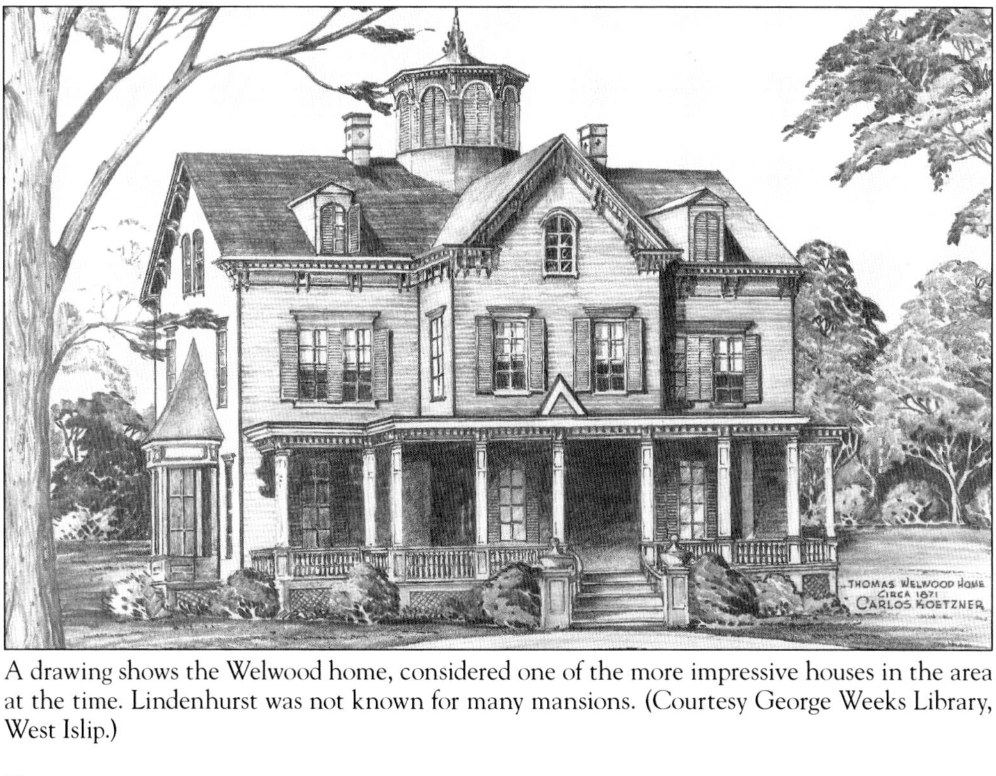

A drawing shows the Welwood home, considered one of the more impressive houses in the area at the time. Lindenhurst was not known for many mansions. (Courtesy George Weeks Library, West Islip.)

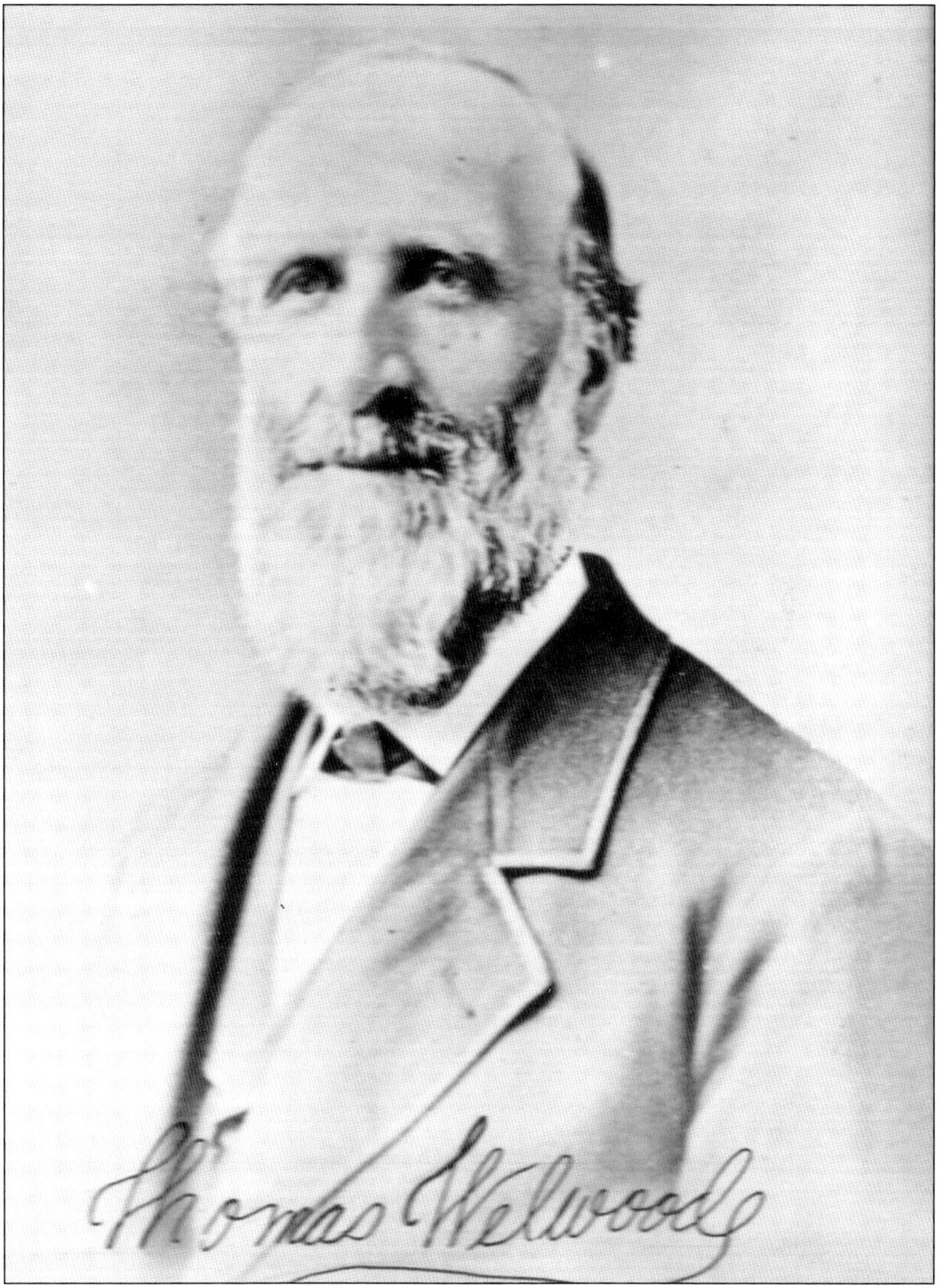

Thomas Welwood and Charles Schleier are recognized as the founding fathers of Lindenhurst. Former Lindenhurst Village historian Evelyn Mentz Ellis wrote in her newspaper column that Thomas Welwood purchased 6,000 acres from Elbert Strong for $30,000 in 1869. Welwood would later partner with Charles Schleier to create a German community then known as the city of Breslau, which is Lindenhurst today. Legend has it that the extra *L* in Welwood's name today came from a misspelled street sign. (Courtesy Lindenhurst Old Village Hall Museum.)

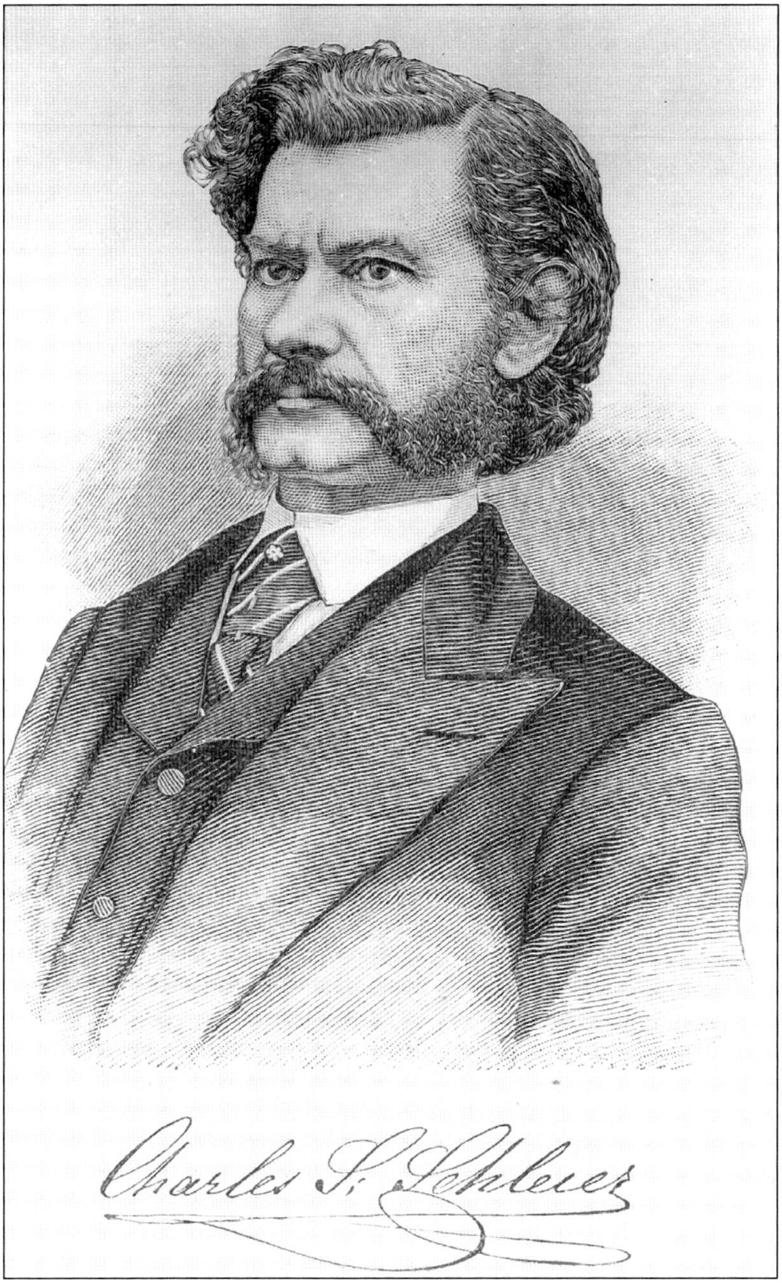

Charles Schleier, originally from Breslau, Germany, came to America in 1850 and settled in Brooklyn. Schleier had a great dream to build a place where German immigrants could live and work. Charles Schleier convinced Thomas Welwood to establish Lindenhurst as a German community on Long Island. The streets had German names. Starting in 1870, it was called the city of Breslau. In 1891, at the request of a large number of residents demanding a name change, the village officially changed its name to Lindenhurst. Legend has it that the name suggestion came from Alexina Cadwallader because she said there were so many linden trees in town. It was incorporated as the Village of Lindenhurst in 1923. (Courtesy Lindenhurst Old Village Hall Museum.)

Four

Babylon and West Islip

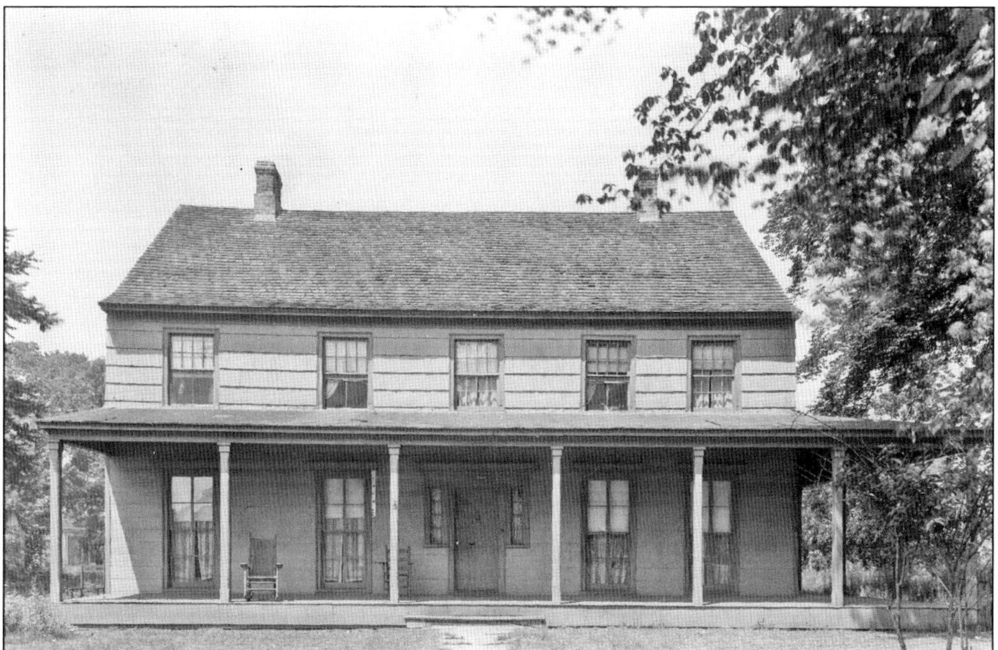

This is one of the oldest houses in Babylon, built in 1803 by Nathaniel Conklin. It still stands today as a house museum on Deer Park Avenue and is open for public tours. (Courtesy Nathanial Conklin House Museum.)

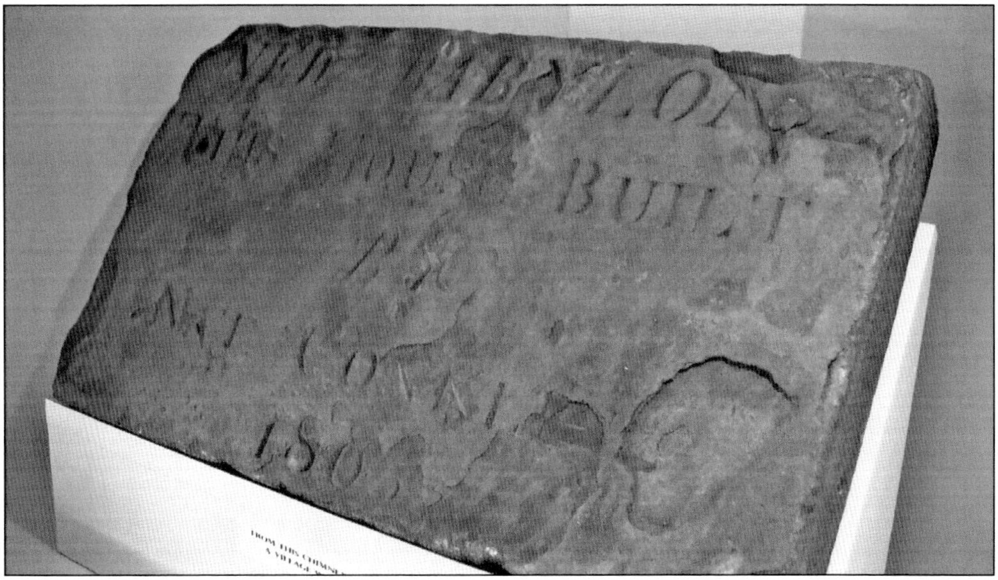

Before 1803, Babylon Village and Town were referred to as South Huntington. Legend has it that Conklin's mother, Phoebe, named the town Babylon in reference to a biblical psalm. Nathaniel responded by saying, "Oh, no Mother, it will be a New Babylon" and inscribed this stone tablet on the chimney of his house. It reads, "New Babylon, this House built by Nathanial Conklin 1803." (Photograph by Christopher Collora.)

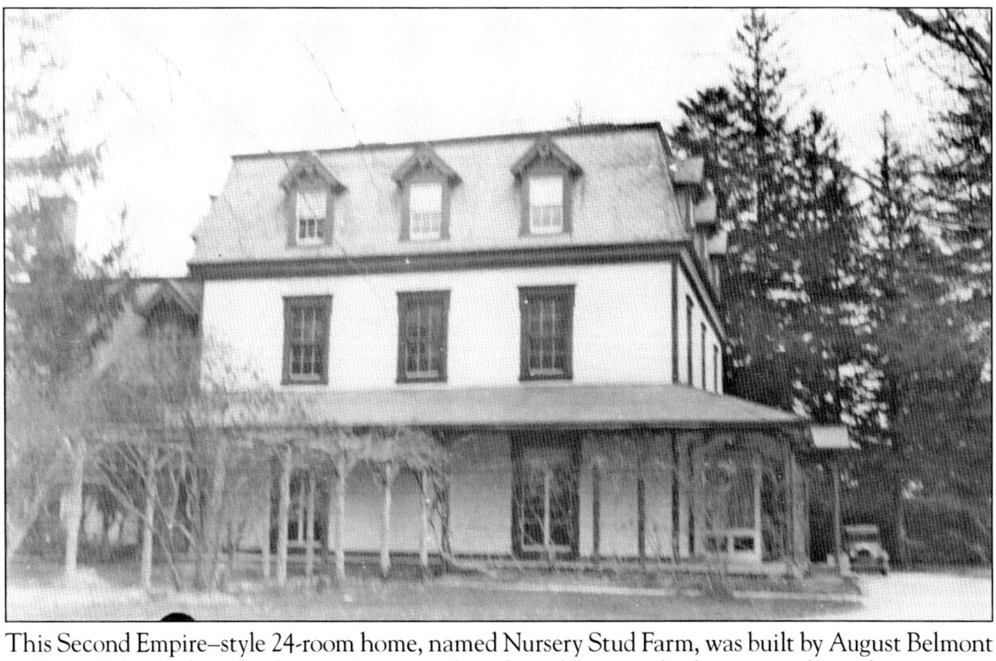

This Second Empire–style 24-room home, named Nursery Stud Farm, was built by August Belmont in 1868. Belmont bought the 1,100 acres to breed racehorses. It had a racetrack on the property. Perry Belmont inherited the estate in 1890. The mansion was destroyed in 1935 by the Long Island State Park Commission, headed by Robert Moses. (Collections of the Town of Babylon, Office of Historic Services.)

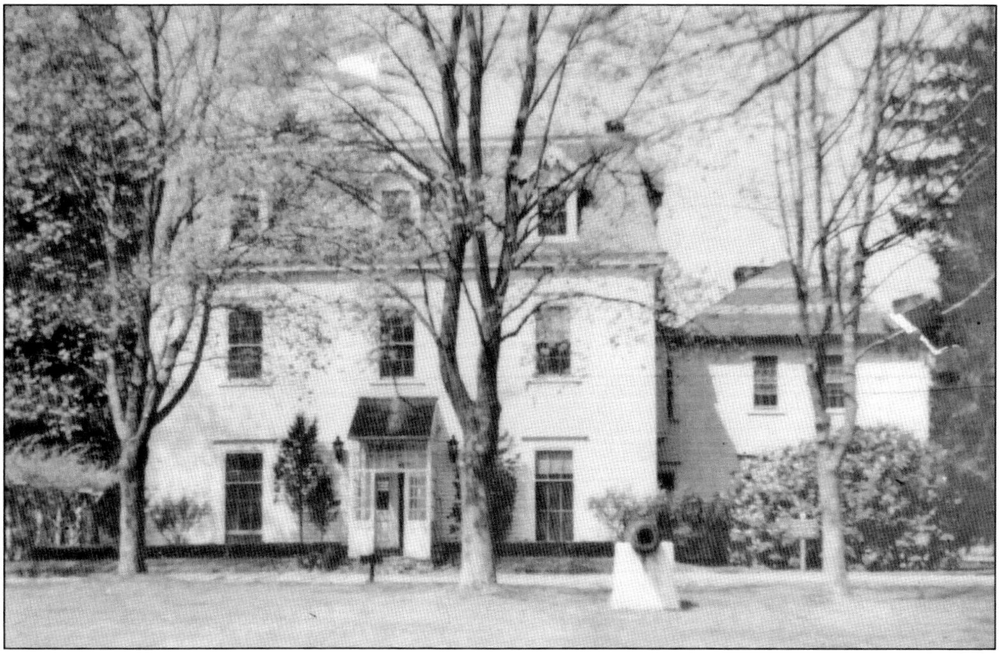

The two cannons that sit in front of the home are from the War of 1812. Legend has it that they were recovered from a British warship sunk at the Battle of Lake Erie by Commodore Oliver Hazard Perry. Today, the Belmont estate is Belmont Lake State Park. It is home to the New York State Park Police headquarters and park administration building. (Courtesy Collections of the Town of Babylon, Office of Historic Services.)

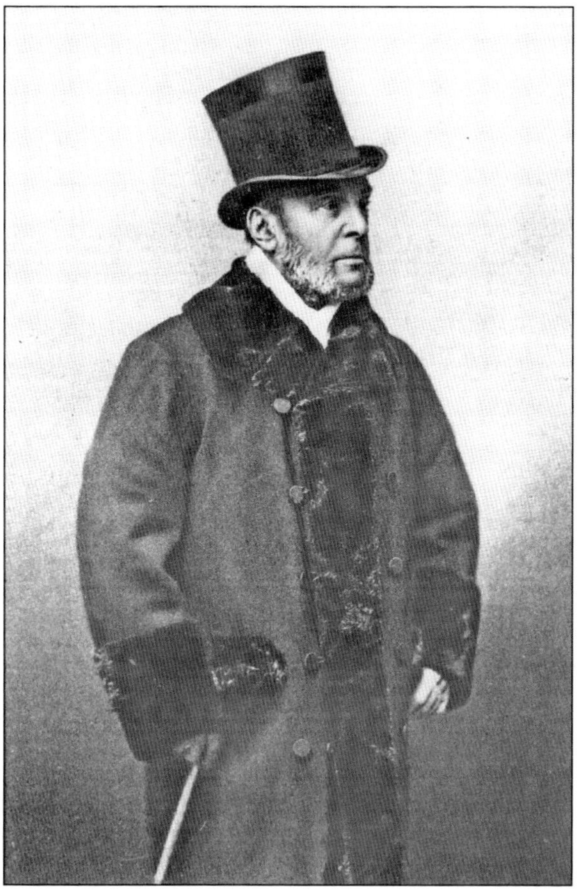

August Belmont Sr. (1816–1890) was an investment banker and politician. He served as a diplomat and was chairman of the National Democratic Committee from 1864 to 1868. (Courtesy Collections of the Town of Babylon, Office of Historic Services.)

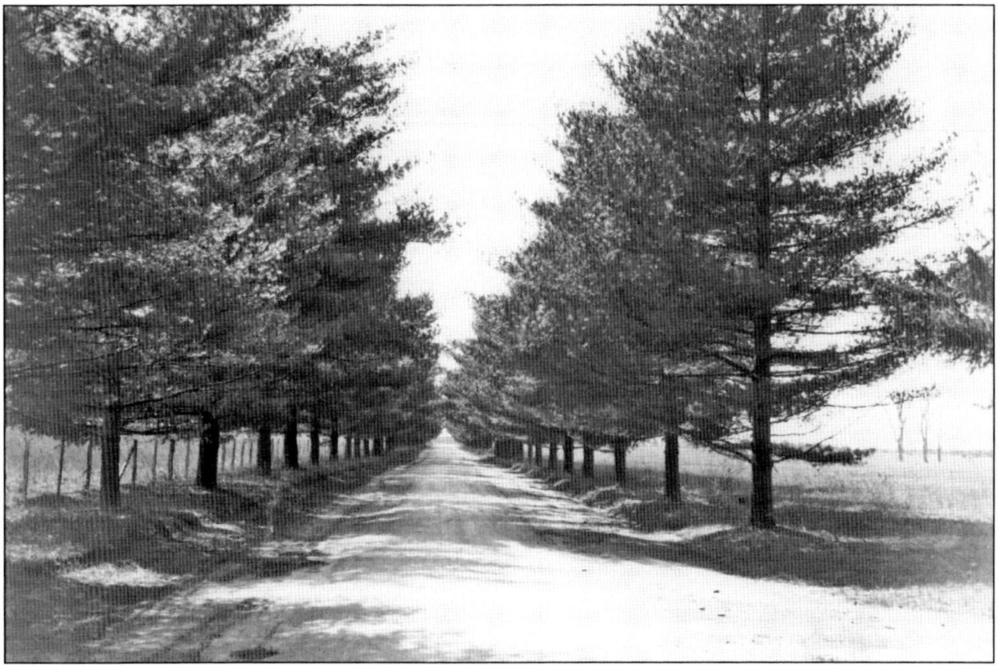

These pine trees lined the driveway to Belmont's estate. The pine trees still stand in the center of Southern State Parkway. (Courtesy Collections of the Town of Babylon, Office of Historic Services.)

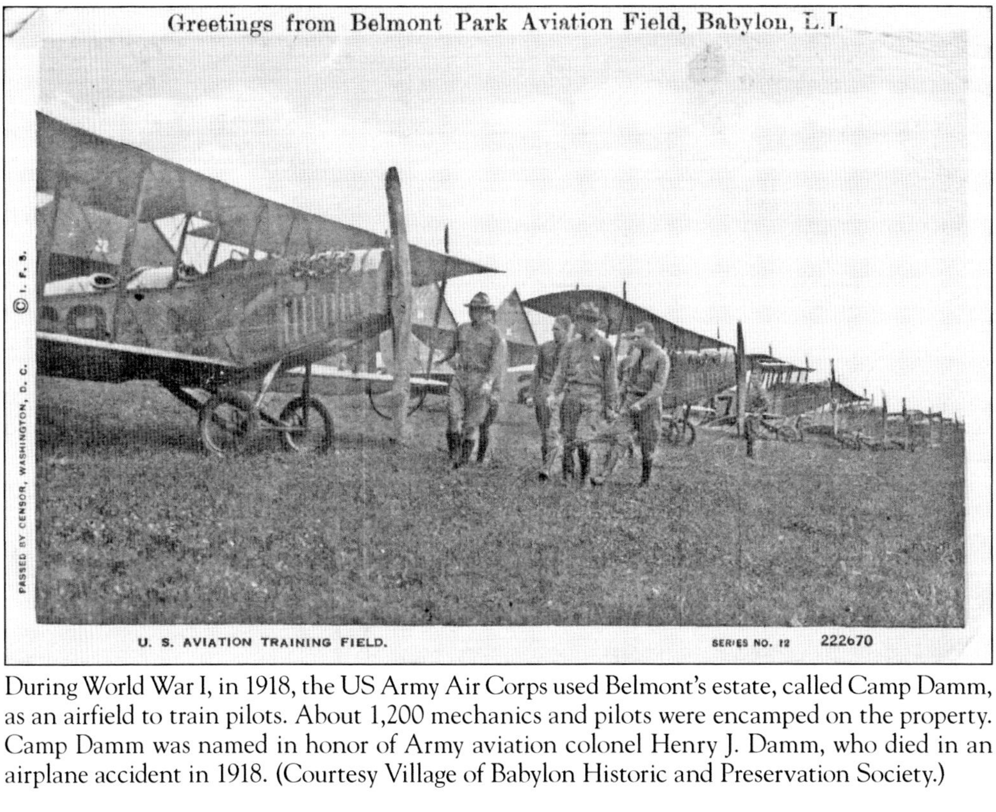

During World War I, in 1918, the US Army Air Corps used Belmont's estate, called Camp Damm, as an airfield to train pilots. About 1,200 mechanics and pilots were encamped on the property. Camp Damm was named in honor of Army aviation colonel Henry J. Damm, who died in an airplane accident in 1918. (Courtesy Village of Babylon Historic and Preservation Society.)

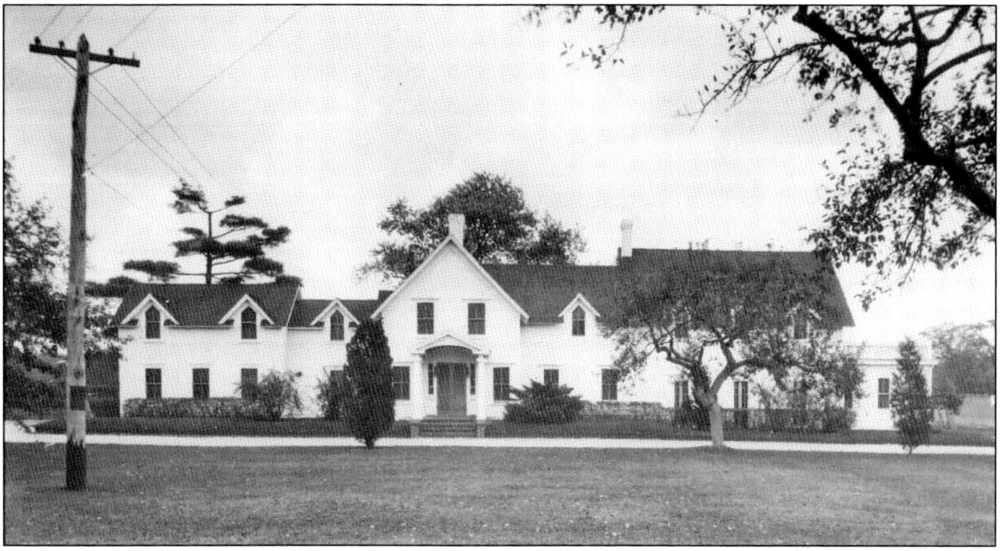

This Colonial Revival–style estate, named Firenze Farm, was the home of Col. Meyer Robert Guggenheim (1885–1959). It was built on Deer Park Avenue around the 1920s. Meyer was one of the sons of Daniel and Florence Guggenheim (Hempstead House, Sands Point) of the Guggenheim family. In 1953–1954, Guggenheim served a brief term as the US ambassador to Portugal. (Courtesy Collections of the Town of Babylon, Office of Historic Services.)

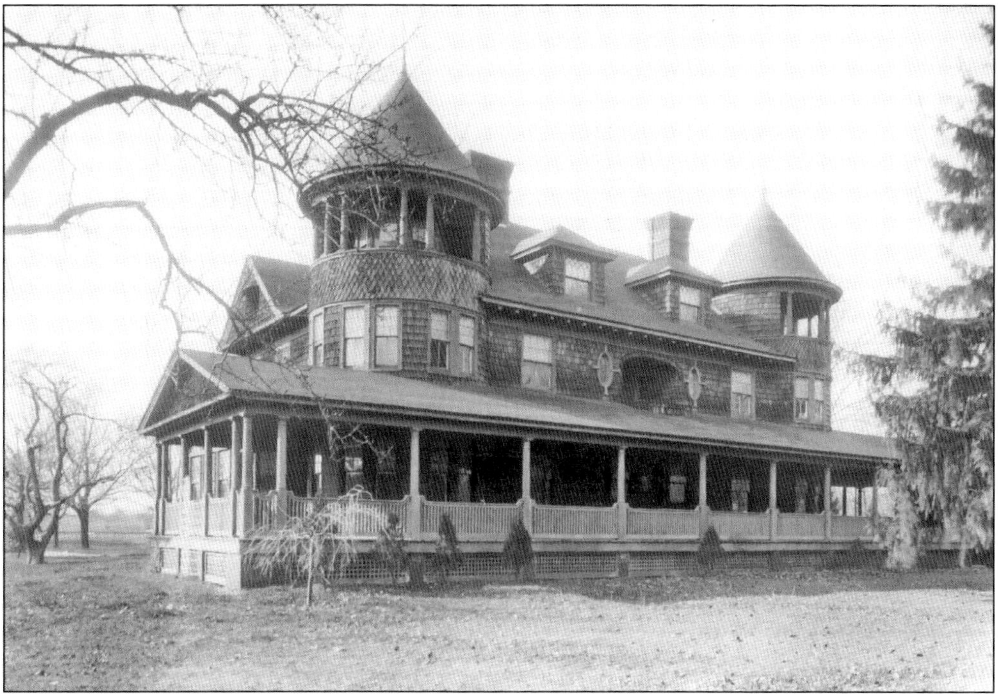

Built in 1895, this Queen Anne–style mansion, named the Towers, was located on the Babylon Crescent and was the home of Judge John Robert Reid (1836–1902). Reid also published the *Suffolk Democrat* and founded and presided over the Babylon Union Free School District Board. Later, the mansion was inherited by his son Willard Reid (1862–1925). (Courtesy Collections of the Town of Babylon, Office of Historic Services.)

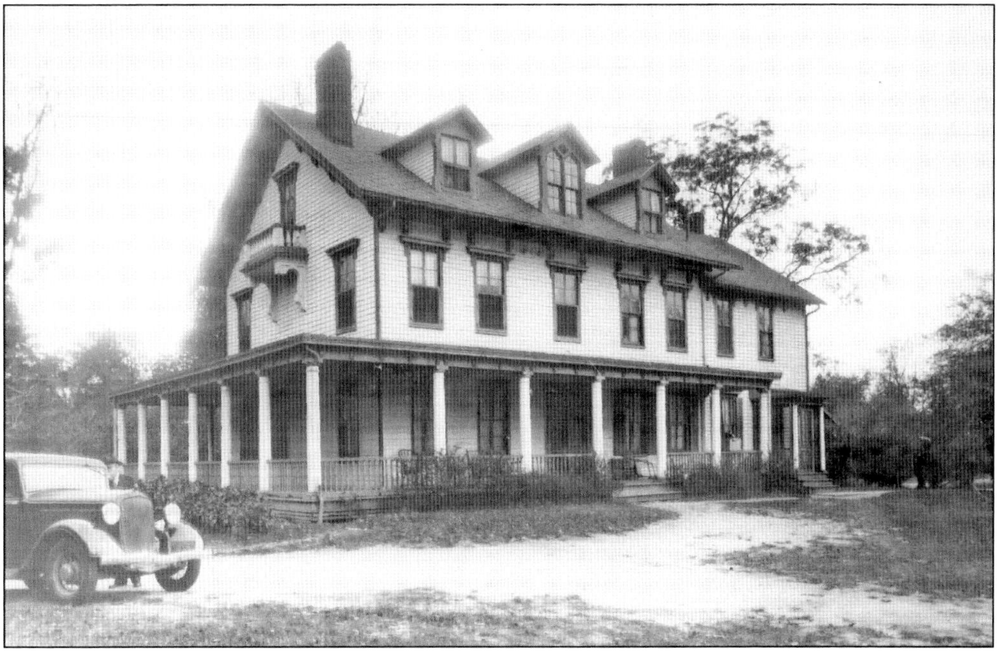

Built in 1864, this 15-acre estate, named Blythebourne, was the summer home of railroad executive Electus B. Litchfield. The house and land was purchased in 1881 by Austin Corbin for $65,000. Part of the land was later used to build the Argyle Hotel. (Courtesy Collections of the Town of Babylon, Office of Historic Services.)

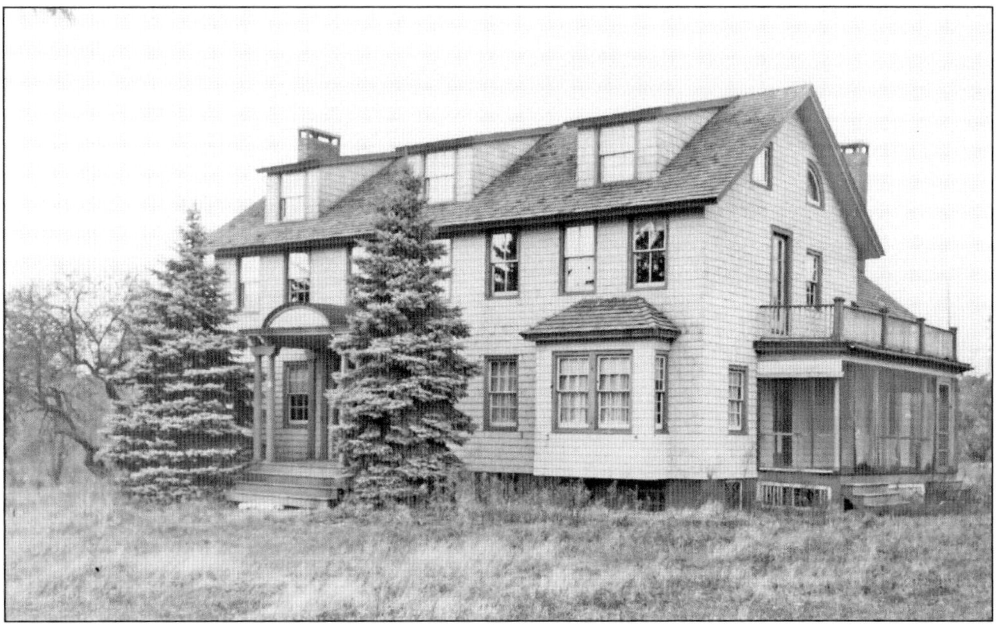

This c. 1875 Tudor-style house, named Forest Farm, was the home of Austin Corbin (1827–1896), president of the Long Island Rail Road. Corbin was rumored to have a private zoo on the property. The property became the dairy farm of A.A. Housman, later owned by Solomon Guggenheim, the copper king. The house no longer stands today. (Courtesy Collections of the Town of Babylon, Office of Historic Services.)

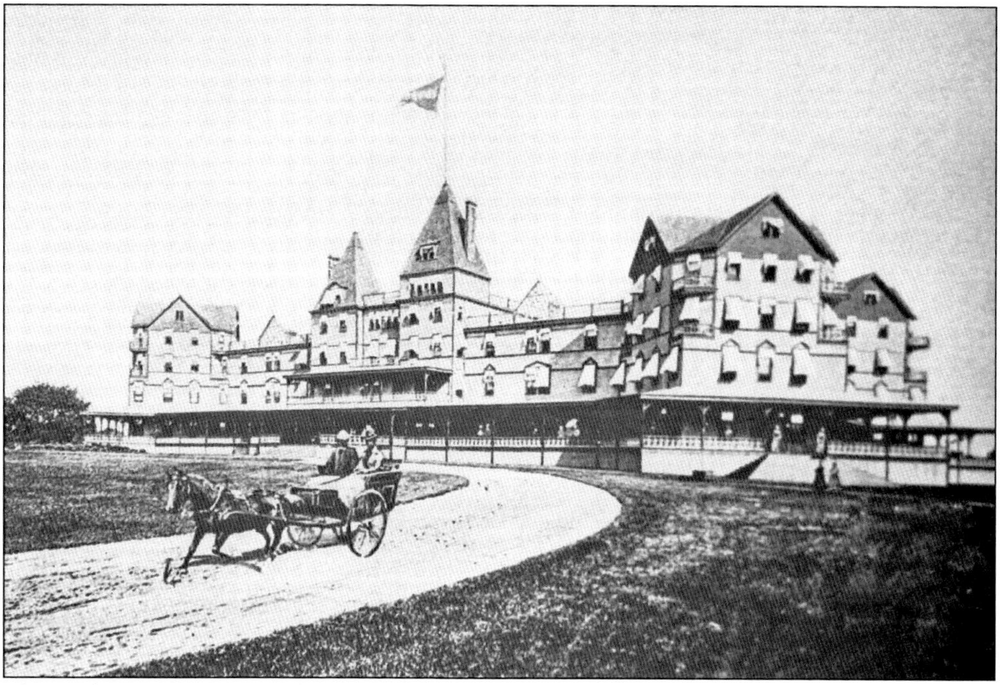

The opulent 350-room Argyle Hotel was built in 1882 on the former E.B. Litchfield estate. The hotel was named after one of the investors, the Duke of Argyll, and included a casino and 14 cottages dotted around the property. Built towards the end of the hotel era, the Argyle was not profitable and was closed in 1897. Austin Corbin eventually sold his hotel interests. (Courtesy Collections of the Town of Babylon, Office of Historic Services.)

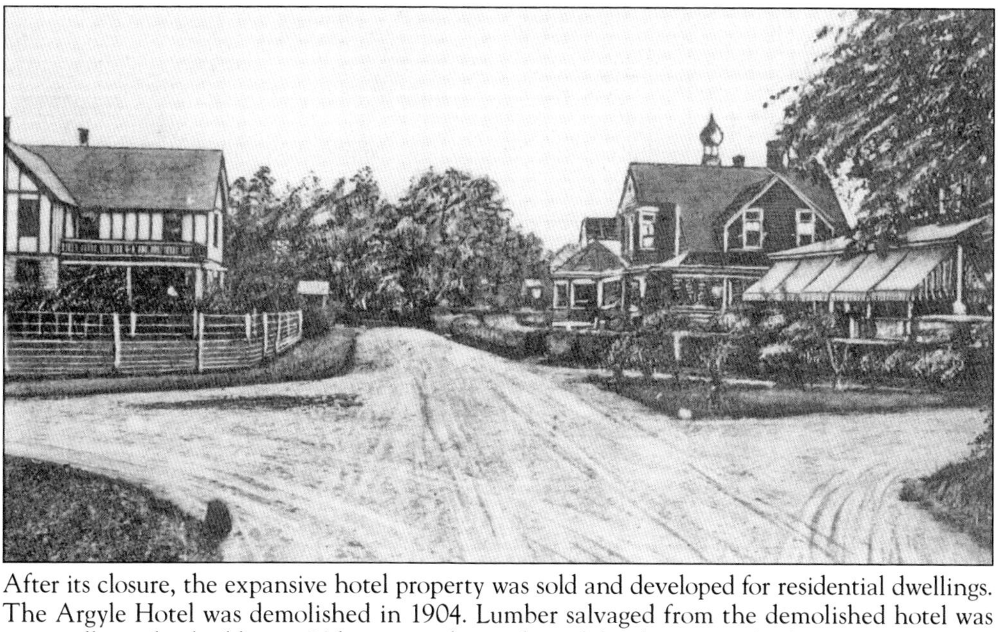

After its closure, the expansive hotel property was sold and developed for residential dwellings. The Argyle Hotel was demolished in 1904. Lumber salvaged from the demolished hotel was reportedly used to build some 20 houses in the residential development, which was named Argyle Park. Many of those home still remain. (Courtesy Collections of the Town of Babylon, Office of Historic Services.)

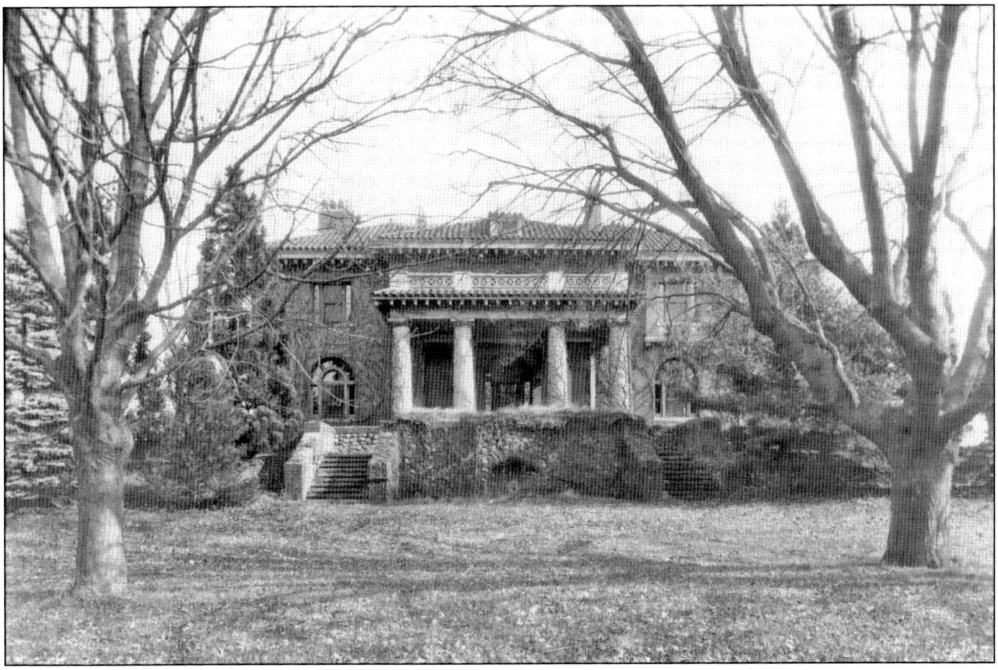

This 40-room Mediterranean villa–style mansion was built around 1909 by J. Stanley Foster II (1877–1925), president of Bowery Bank. The Foster estate sat on 142 acres on the south side of Montauk Highway and extended south to the Great South Bay. The estate was later purchased by the Sampawam Country Club. The house no longer stands today. (Courtesy Collections of the Town of Babylon, Office of Historic Services.)

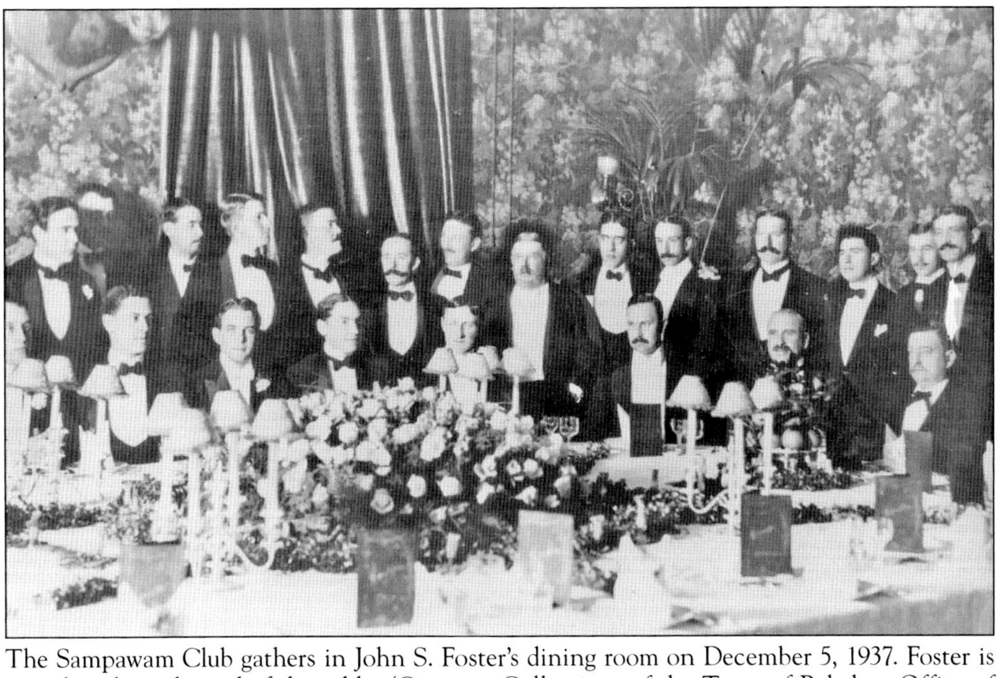

The Sampawam Club gathers in John S. Foster's dining room on December 5, 1937. Foster is seated at the right end of the table. (Courtesy Collections of the Town of Babylon, Office of Historic Services.)

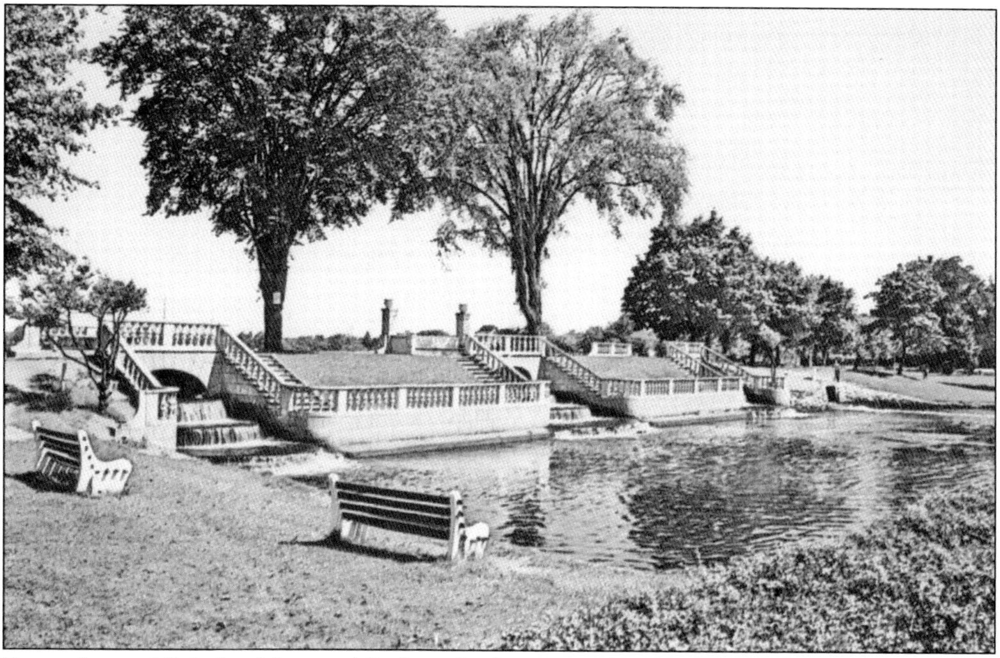

Foster donated Babylon Memorial Park, today known as Argyle Park, to the village in 1924 to honor World War I veterans. Today, the park is a popular recreation spot enjoyed by many residents. (Courtesy Collections of the Town of Babylon, Office of Historic Services.)

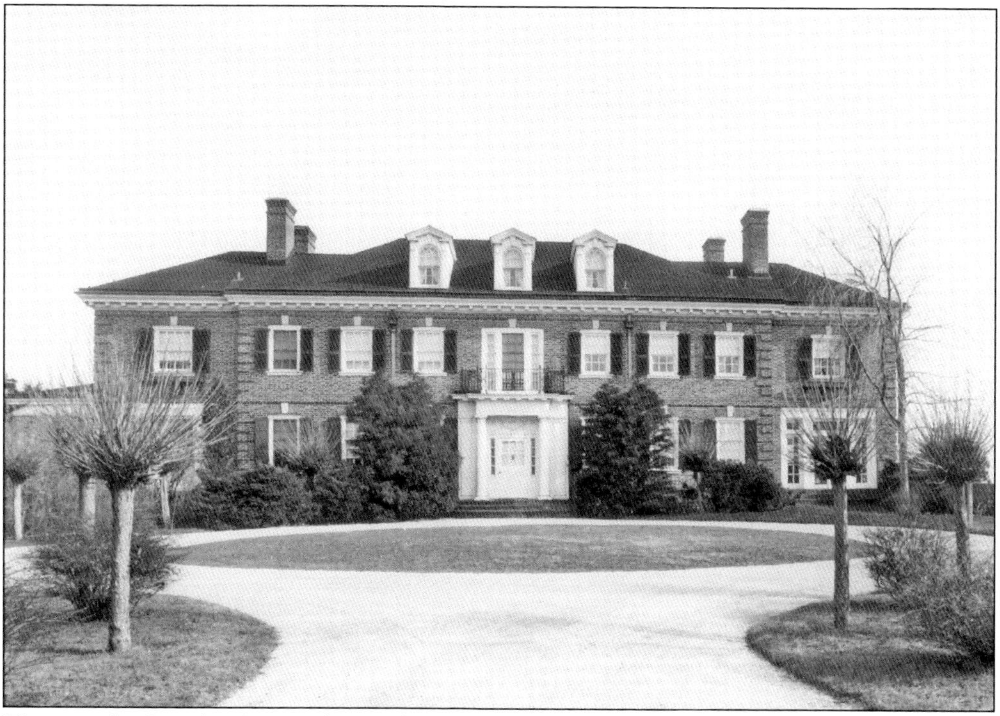

This was the David P. Stewart home, formerly known as the Trenchard Estate, built in 1927 on Little East Neck Road. Today, it is home to the Long Island Yacht Club. (Courtesy Collections of the Town of Babylon, Office of Historic Services.)

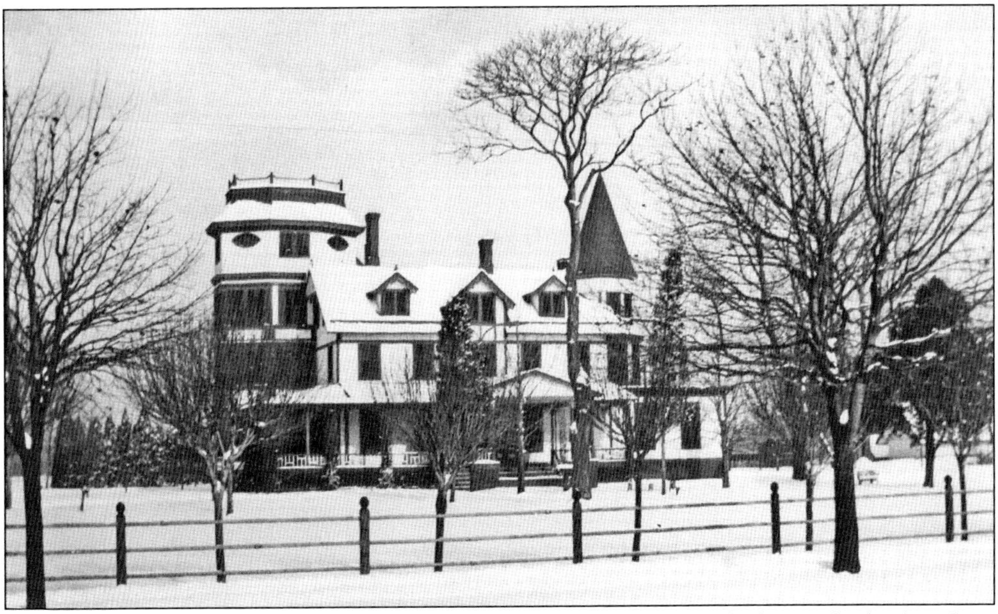

This mansion, named My Fancy, was owned by athlete and writer Malcolm Ford, who bought it around 1892 from the Johnson family. Ford sold to businessman William Guy Gilmore (1847–1921) in 1899. (Courtesy Village of Babylon Historic and Preservation Society.)

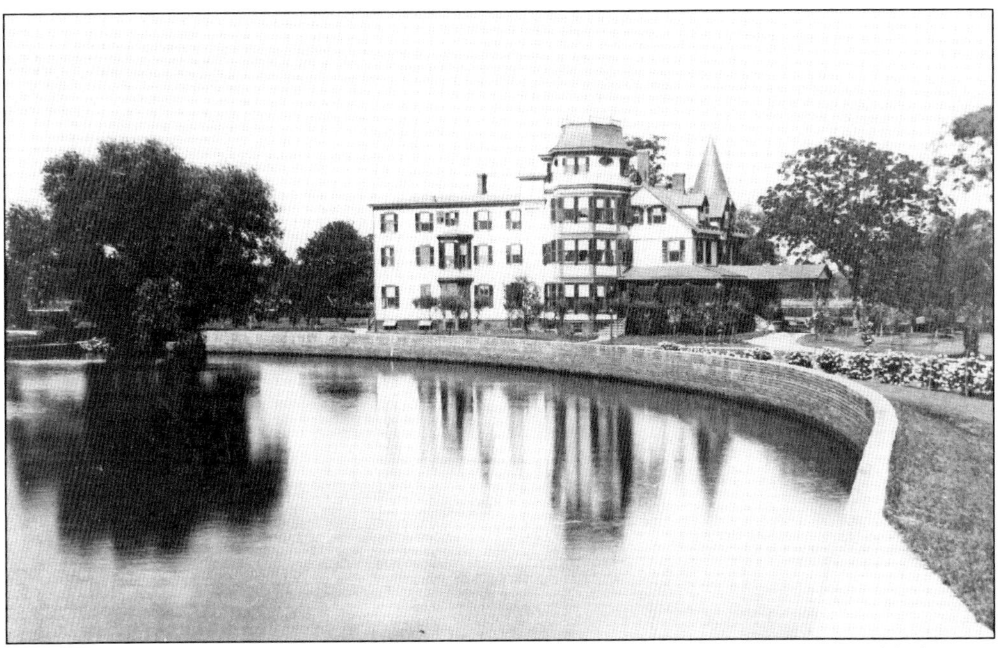

The Gilmore estate sat on over 100 acres in West Babylon. Among the property's highlights was a large freshwater lake famous for trout. Poet Walt Whitman once briefly lived on the land in the 1830s when it was farmland, before the mansion was built. (Courtesy Village of Babylon Historic and Preservation Society.)

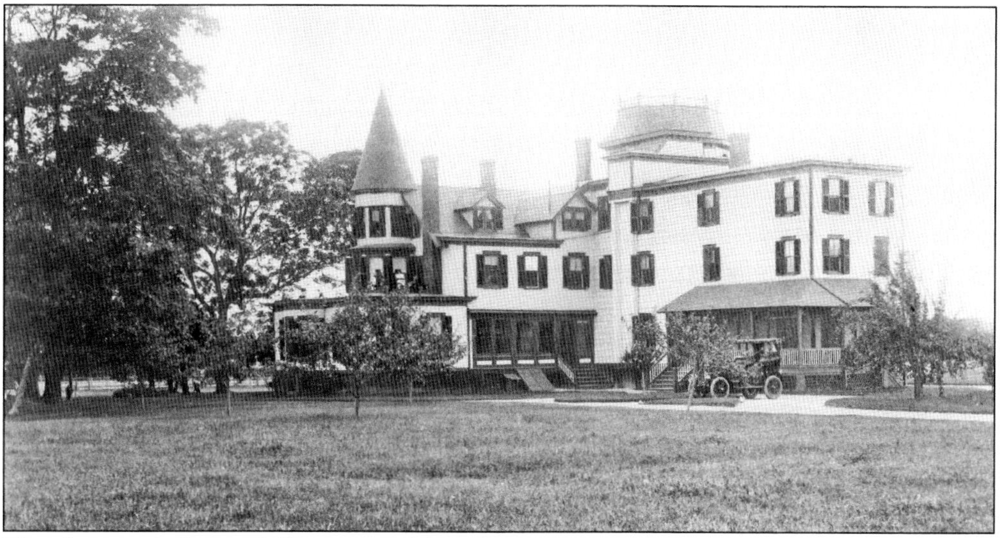

This photograph shows a different view of the Gilmore mansion, from the south side. Gilmore was an executive in the Arbuckle Brothers sugar refinery and coffee business and the director of the American Sugar Refining Company. (Courtesy Village of Babylon Historic and Preservation Society.)

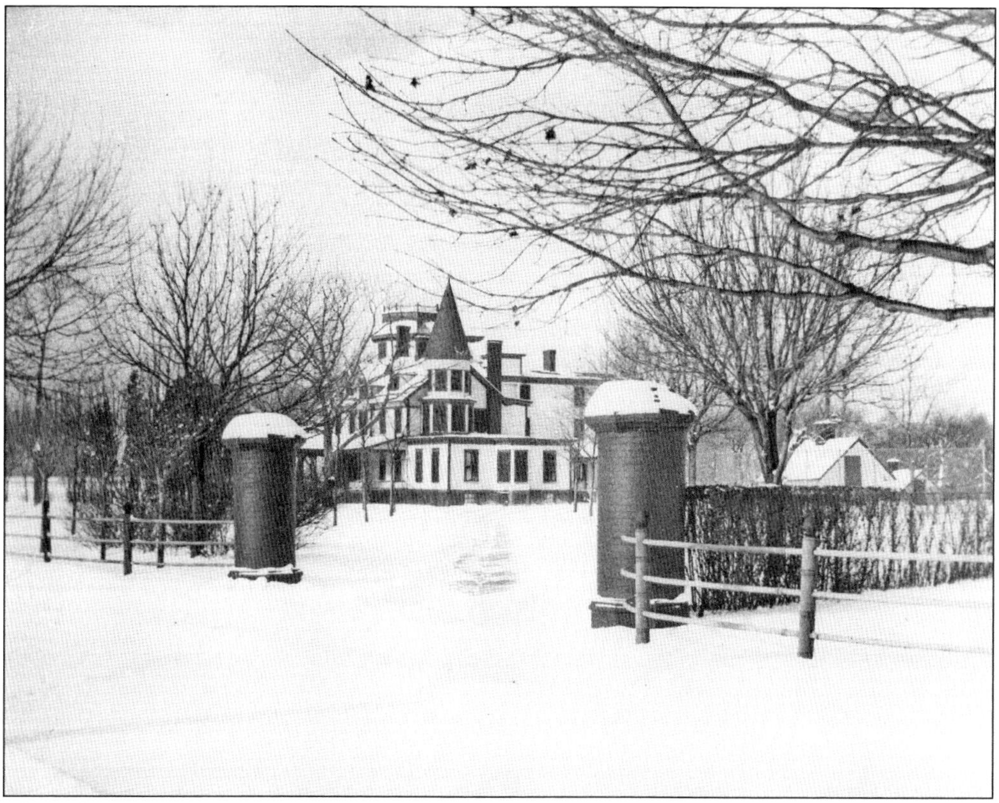

The Gilmore mansion sat abandoned for some time and was torn down in the 1950s. The Great South Bay Shopping Center, opened in 1957, now sits on the land. (Courtesy Village of Babylon Historic and Preservation Society.)

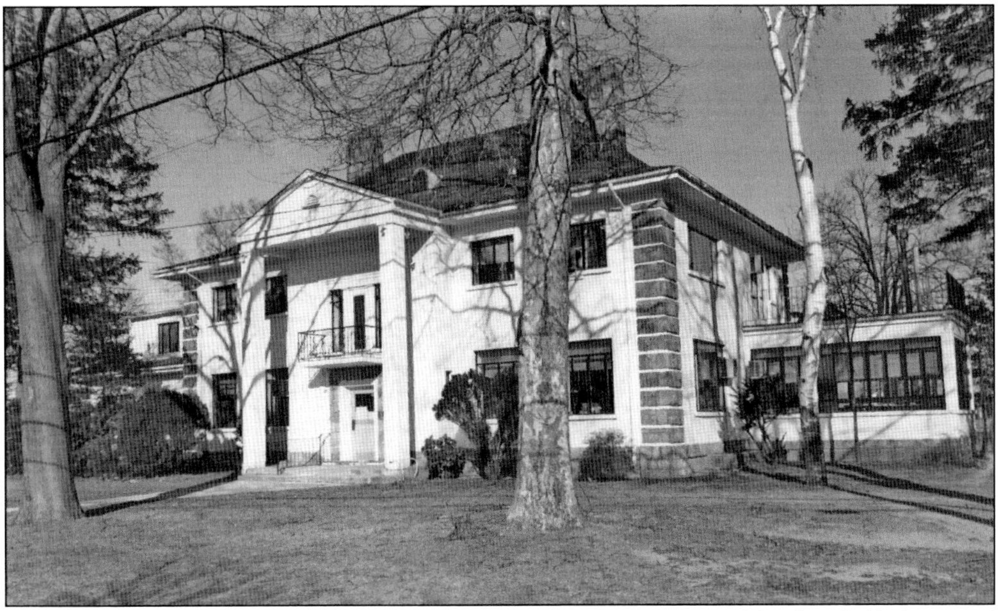

On this estate once stood the home of Royal Phelps. The estate was sold to baseball player and lawyer John Montgomery Ward (1860–1925). In 1941, it was sold to businessman David Schnur (1882–1948), who demolished it and built this 14-room French-style mansion that still stands. Today, the home is the Town of Babylon Parks Department headquarters and a public park. (Courtesy Collections of the Town of Babylon, Office of Historic Services.)

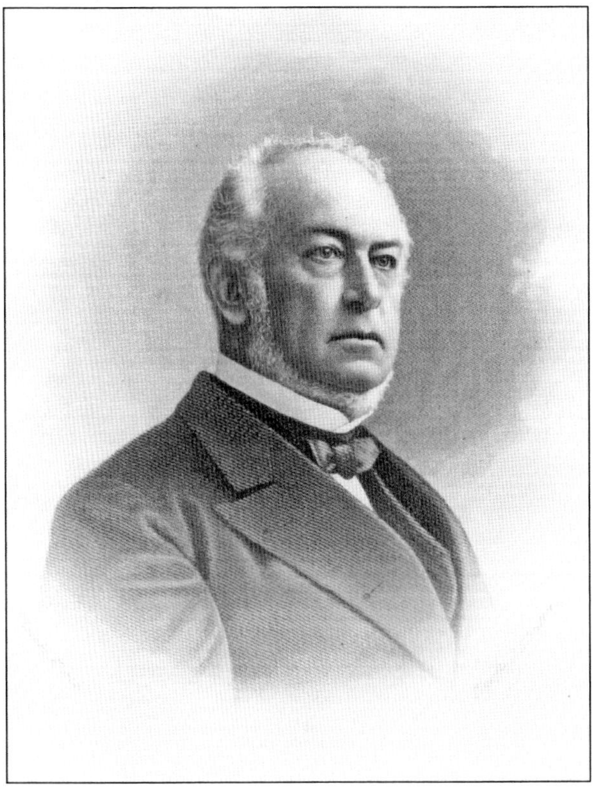

Royal Phelps (1809–1884) was an entrepreneur and politician. His original mansion sat next to the present Elda Lake and was once owned by the Rod and Reel Club. Phelps had a pond where he raised trout for fishing. (Courtesy Collections of the Town of Babylon, Office of Historic Services.)

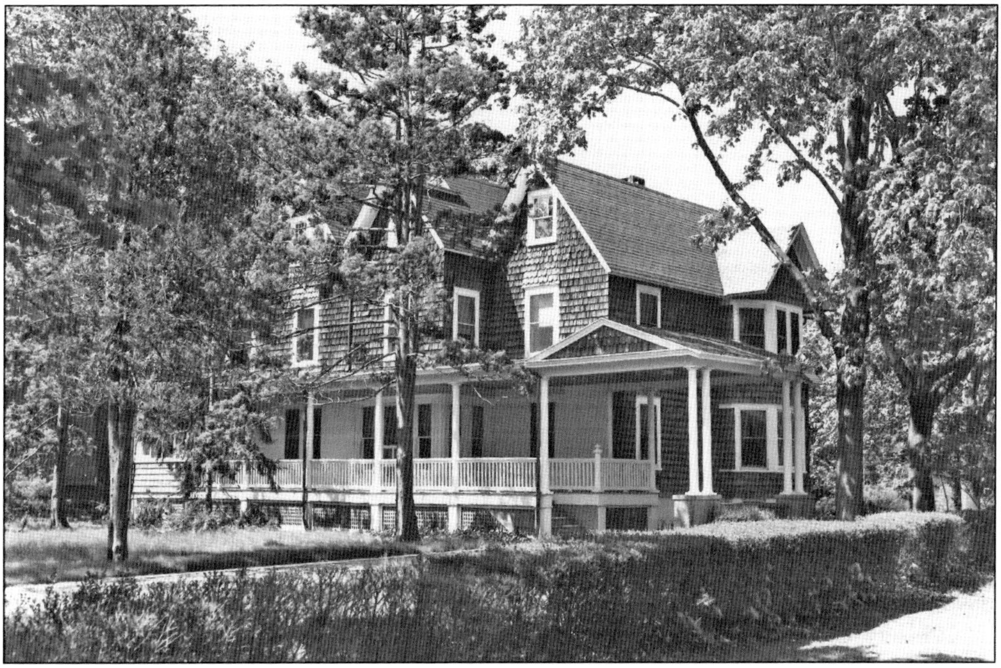

This Victorian house on Thompson Avenue was the home of Robert Moses. According to Suffolk County legislator Wayne Horsley, the house was burned down by an arson fire around 1968. Later, the C.M. Bergen home, which many believed to be the Moses home, was moved back one lot to make room for the current office building complex that sits on the site now. (Courtesy Village of Babylon Historic and Preservation Society.)

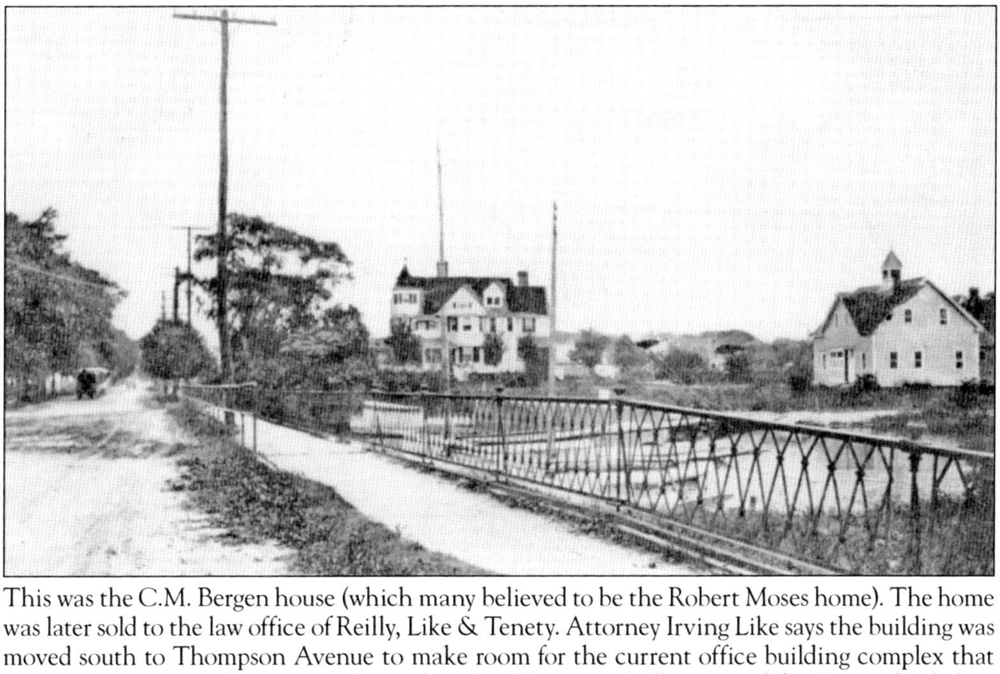

This was the C.M. Bergen house (which many believed to be the Robert Moses home). The home was later sold to the law office of Reilly, Like & Tenety. Attorney Irving Like says the building was moved south to Thompson Avenue to make room for the current office building complex that now sits on the site. The home still stands today. (Courtesy Collections of the Town of Babylon, Office of Historic Services.)

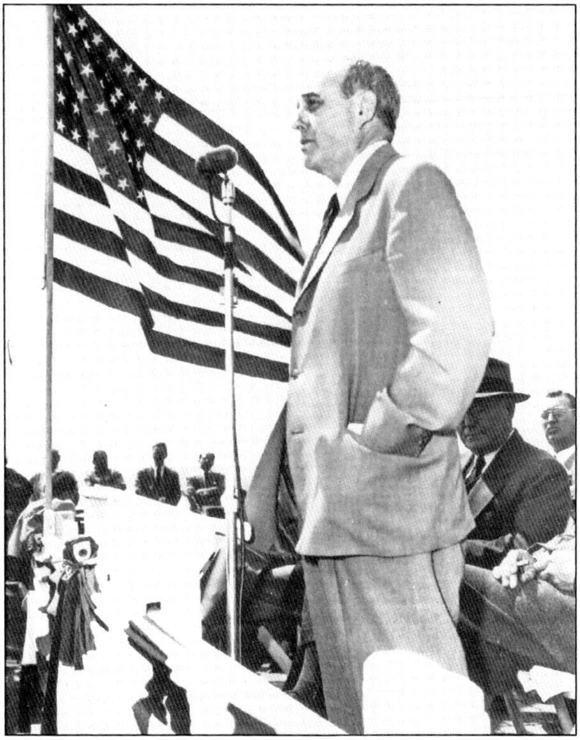

Robert Moses (1888–1981) was president of the Long Island State Park Commission from 1924 to 1963. Moses oversaw the building of 15 state parks on Long Island and 175 miles of parkways in Nassau and Suffolk Counties. He destroyed many of the mansions and private estates across Long Island, in some cases a controversial move at the time. (Courtesy Village of Babylon Historic and Preservation Society.)

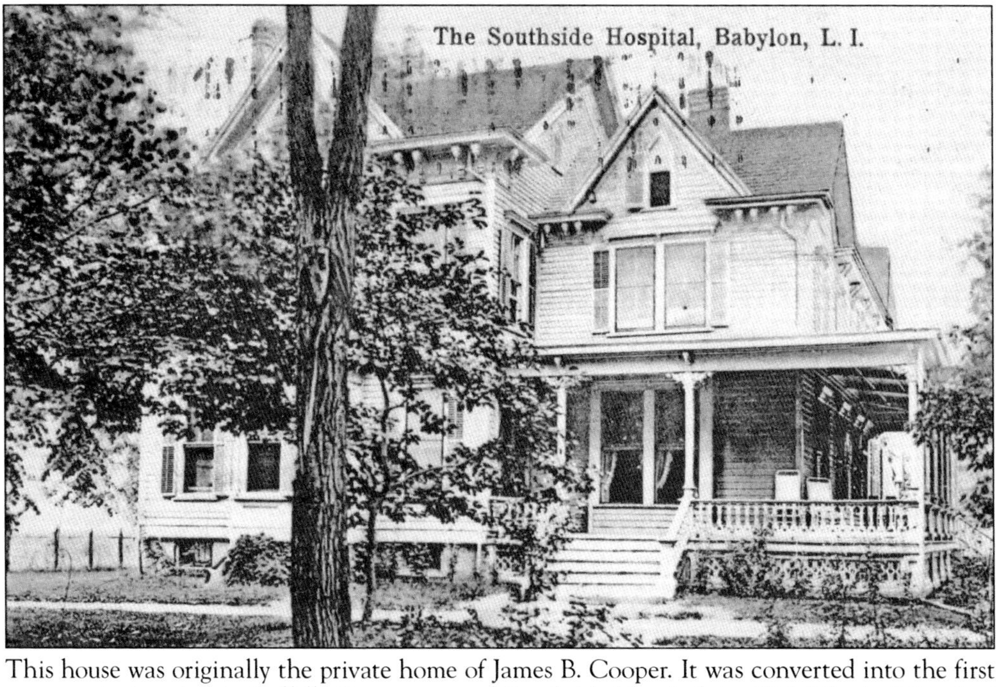

This house was originally the private home of James B. Cooper. It was converted into the first community hospital in Suffolk County, named Southside Hospital, in 1913. The building had 21 beds. Southside hospital was later moved to Bay Shore in 1923. The home no longer stands, and this is now the site of the Babylon Post Office. (Courtesy Village of Babylon Historic and Preservation Society.)

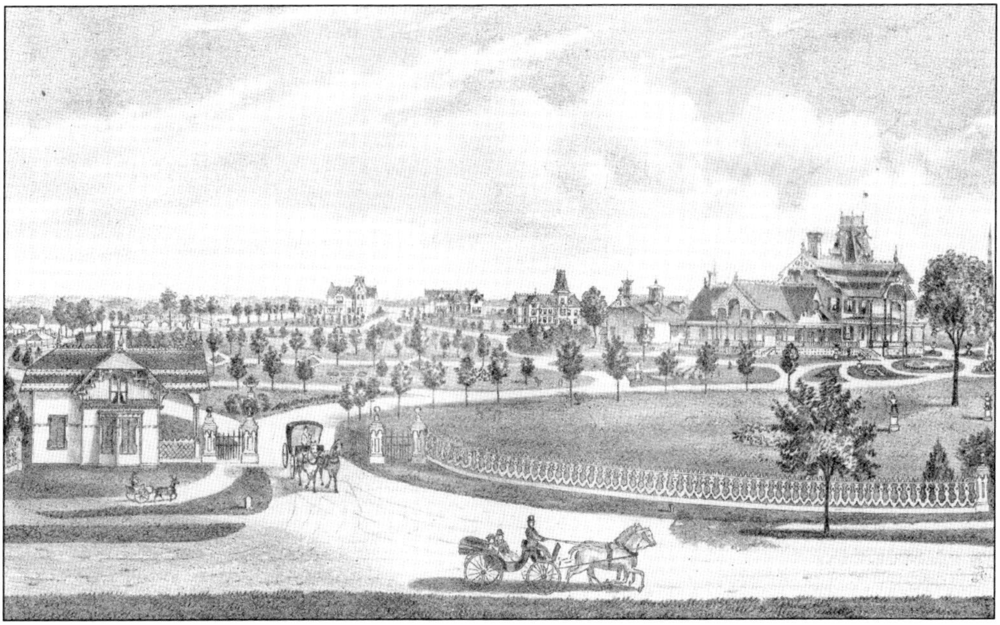

This scene depicts Effingham Park, what the area between Babylon and West Islip used to look like. The Effingham B. Sutton mansion is seen in the background. (Courtesy Collections of the Town of Babylon, Office of Historic Services.)

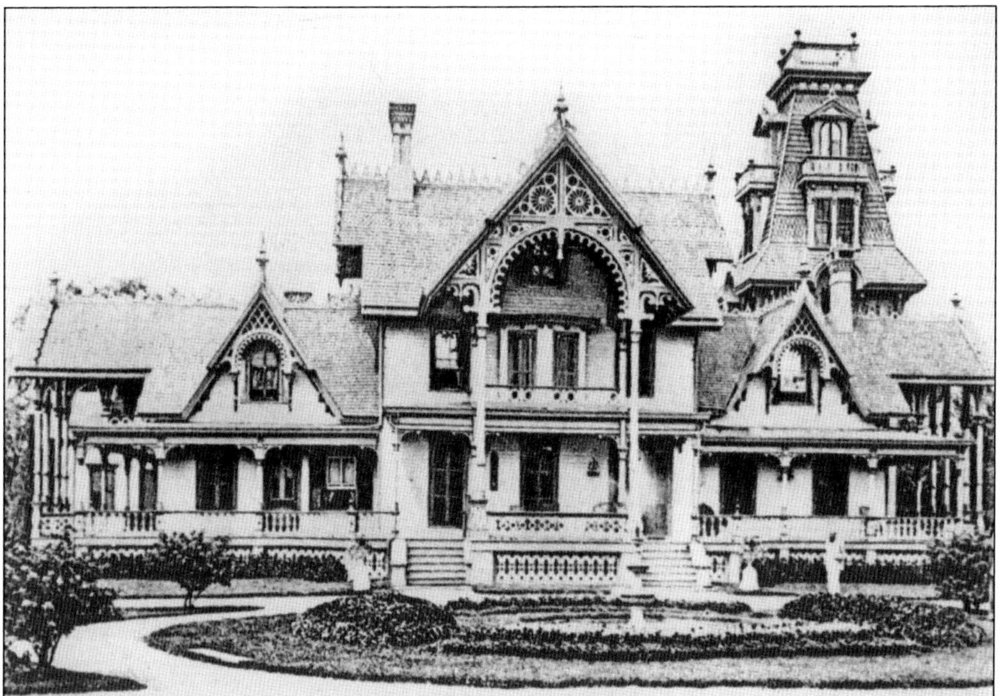

This estate, named Effingham Park, was built around 1870 by Effingham B. Sutton (1817–1891), shipping businessman and founder of the Sutton Line and Cromwell Steamship Line. In 1903, E.B. Sutton Jr. sold the mansion and property to Edwin Hawley, who demolished it. (Courtesy Collections of the Town of Babylon, Office of Historic Services.)

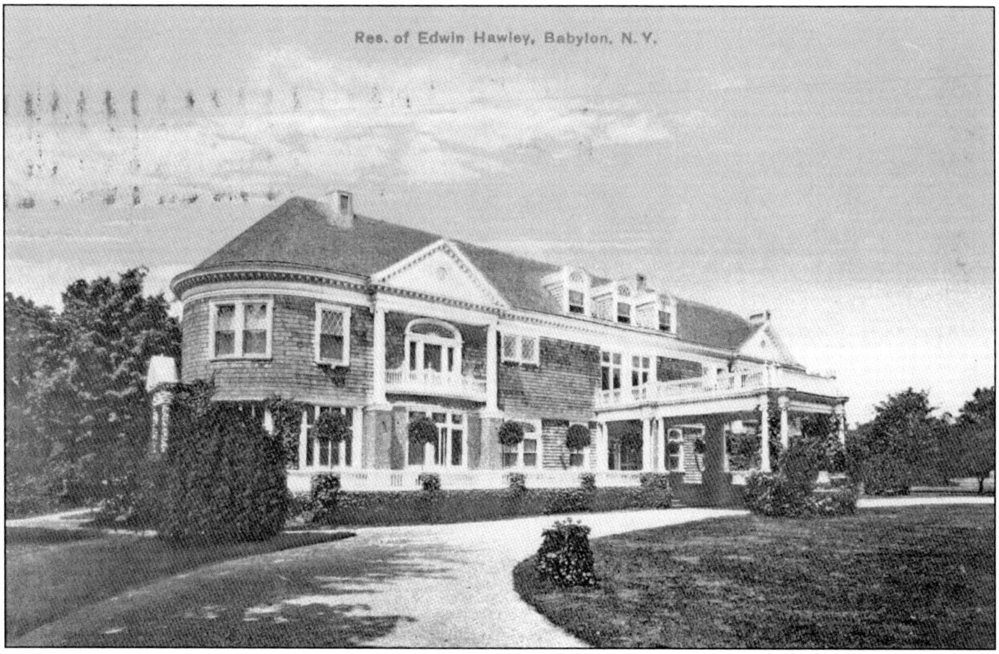

This Colonial-style mansion, named Effingham Towers, on Parkwood Road and George Street was built in 1898 by Edwin Hawley (1850–1912). At the time, it was one of the biggest houses in the area. It had 28 rooms, including 14 bedrooms; large dining, billiard, music, and living rooms; and a library. The mansion burned down in March 1958. (Courtesy West Islip Historical Society.)

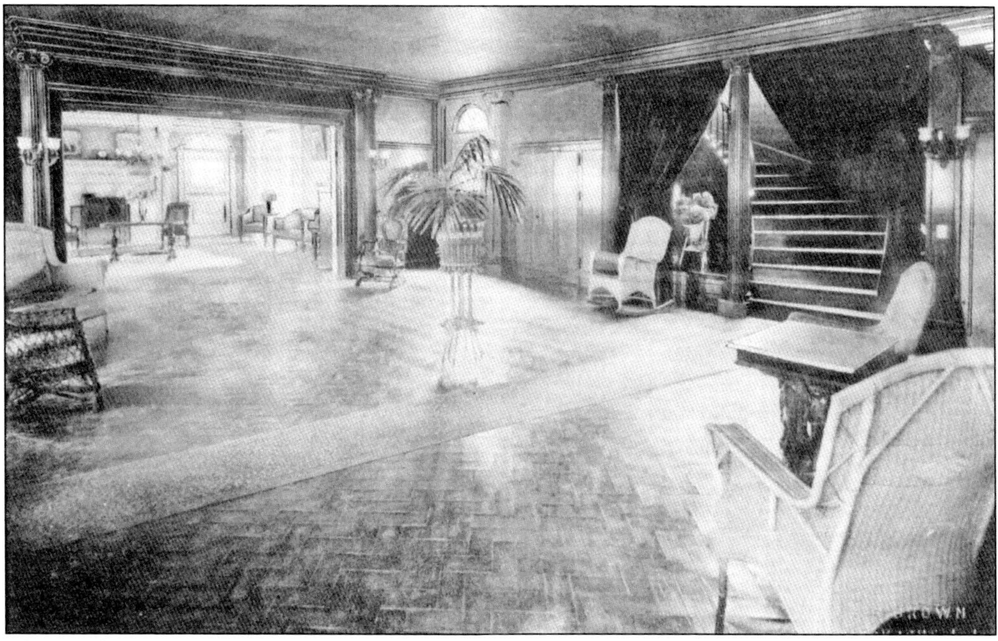

The Hawley Mansion was used as Haarmann's Parkwood Lake Mansion Restaurant and Inn from 1926 to 1938. After that, it became the Parkwood Lakes Private School until 1949. The mansion was then used in 1951 by the West Islip School District as a school for grades five and six for that year. This is a picture of the front entranceway. (Courtesy West Islip Historical Society.)

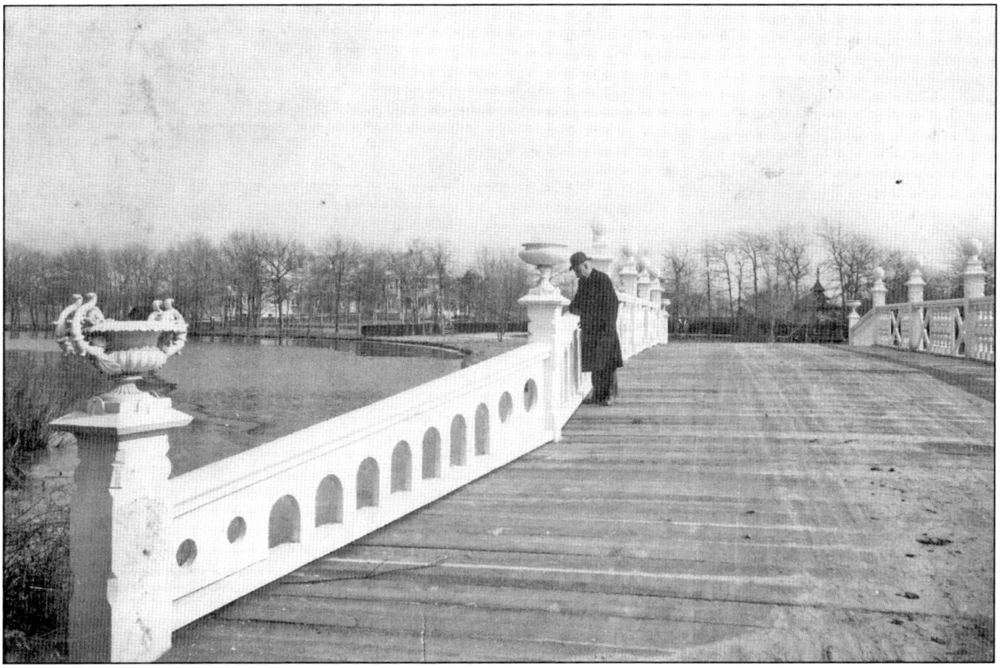

Edwin Hawley (1850–1912), seen here crossing the bridge on his estate, was a businessman and served as president or director of over 40 companies, including the Southern Pacific Railroad and the Pacific Mail Steamship Company. He was reported to be worth $25 million when he died in 1912. (Courtesy Village of Babylon Historic and Preservation Society.)

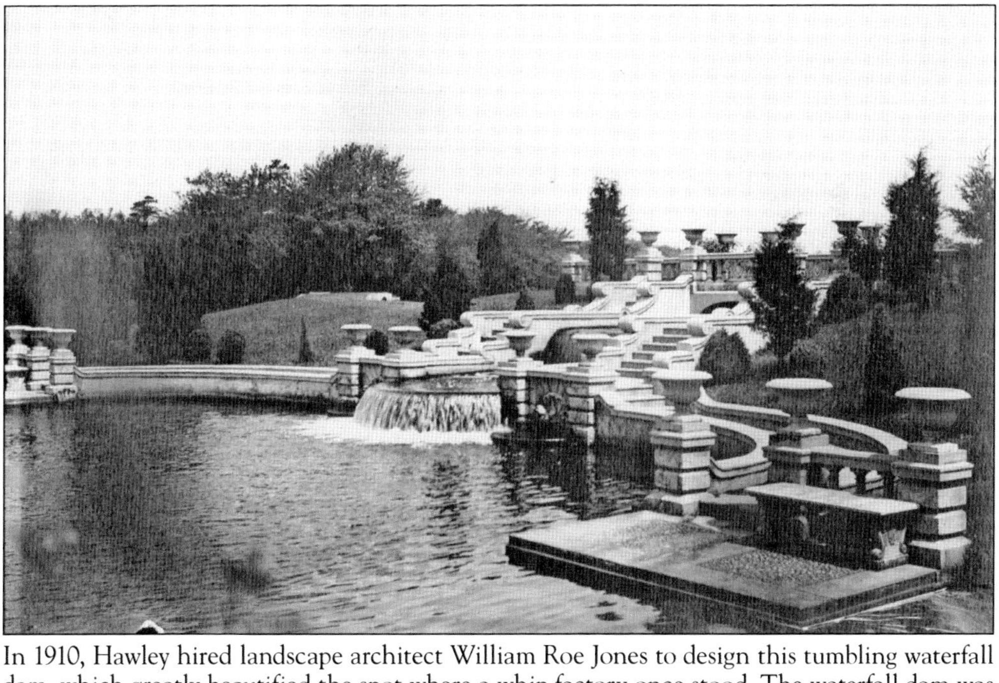

In 1910, Hawley hired landscape architect William Roe Jones to design this tumbling waterfall dam, which greatly beautified the spot where a whip factory once stood. The waterfall dam was destroyed with the construction of Route 231 and Montauk Highway in the 1960s. (Courtesy Village of Babylon Historic and Preservation Society.)

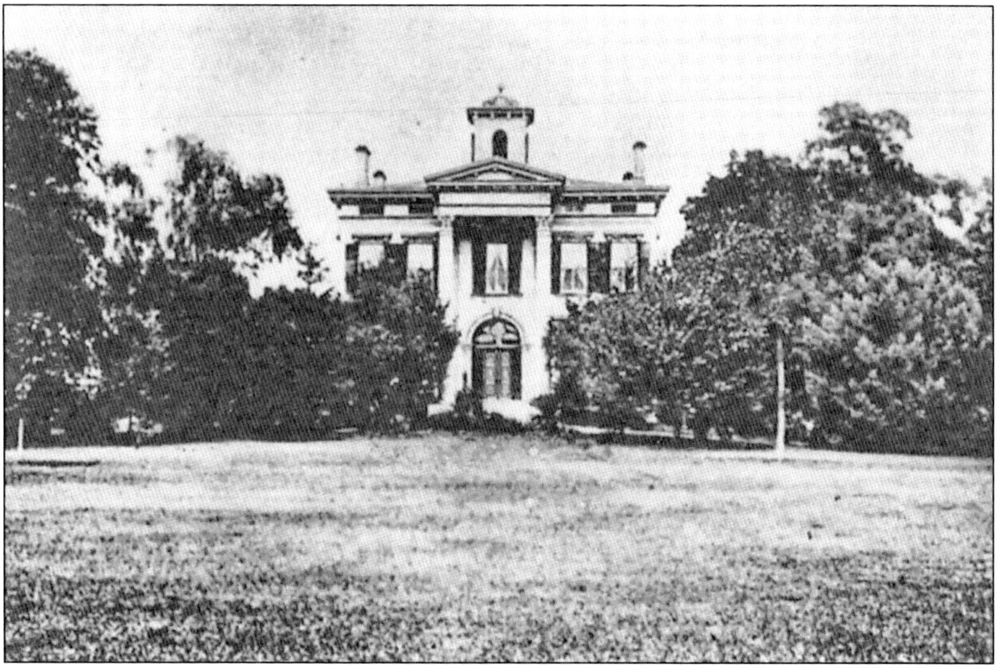

This Italianate-style estate, named Tahluah, was built around 1853 by Dr. Alfred Wagstaff Sr. (1804–1878). It had two 30-foot-high Corinthian columns supporting a veranda roof. It was sold at auction in 1904. The mansion no longer stands today. (Courtesy West Islip Historical Society.)

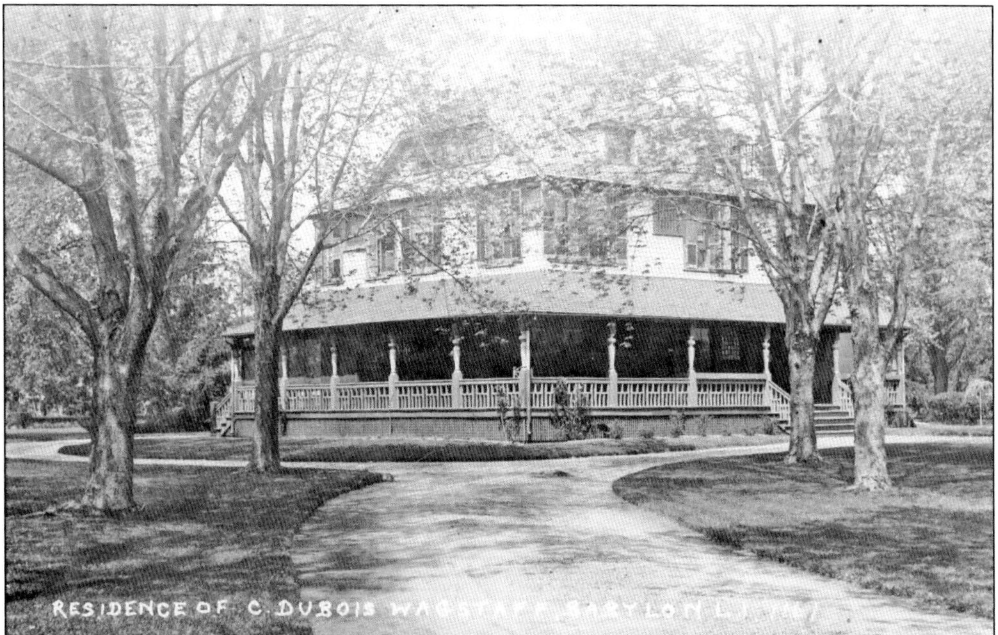

This was the home of Cornelius DuBois Wagstaff (1845–1919), the son of Dr. Alfred Wagstaff. Wagstaff married Amy Colt, the daughter of South Side Railroad president Robert Oliver Colt, who was mainly responsible for extending rail service to Babylon in 1867. The home no longer stands today. (Courtesy Village of Babylon Historic and Preservation Society.)

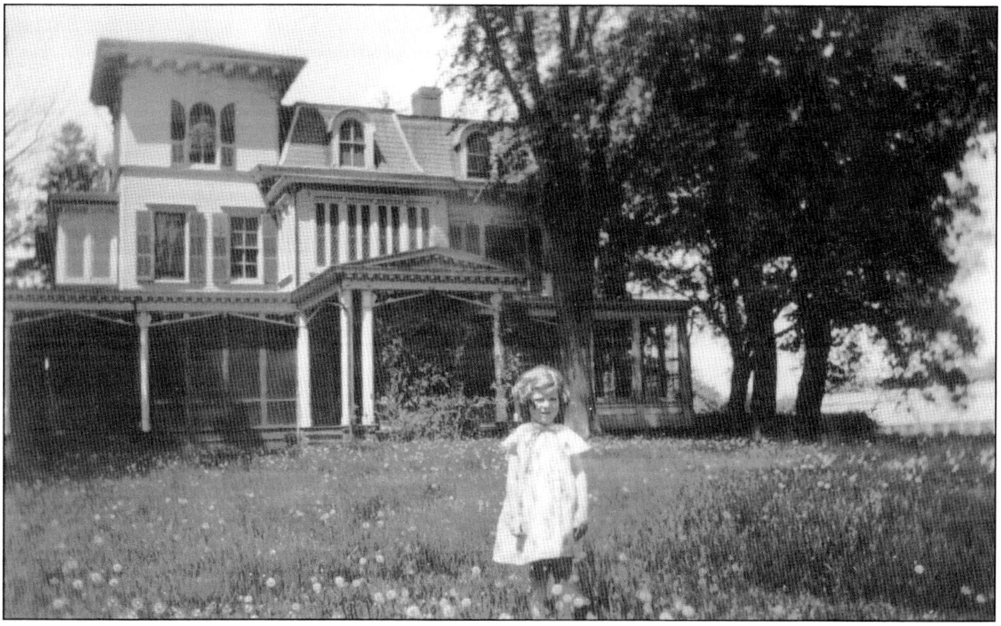

This mansion was the summer home of Minor C. Keith. Seen in front of the mansion is Katie (Whalen) Hafele. Hafele's father, Martin Whalen, was the superintendent of the estate. She lived on the estate for several years. "I remember living on the Keith estate; it was a beautiful experience," says Hafele. "It was a beautiful time to see all these mansions along Montauk Highway." The house was demolished around 1937. (Courtesy Katie Hafele.)

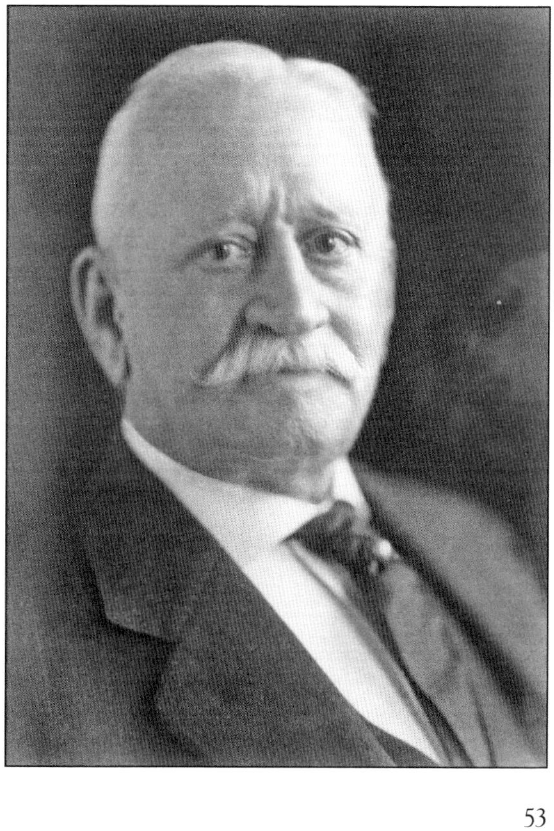

Minor C. Keith (1848–1929) was a railroad businessman. Keith built the first railroad in Costa Rica. He also owned United Fruit Line and was said to have introduced bananas to the United States by importing them from his banana plantations in Panama. (Courtesy Katie Hafele, West Islip Historical Society.)

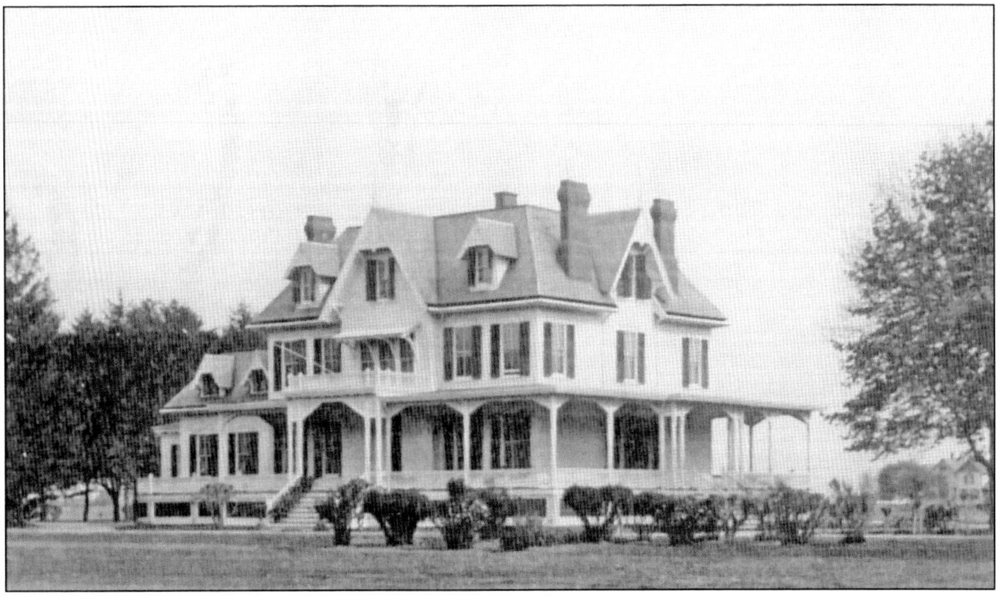

This shingle-style house, named Sunnymead and located on South Country Road, was built by philanthropist John Vandeveer (1868–1941). The home was demolished in 1953 and is now the site of Good Samaritan Hospital. The gardener's cottage still stands and is used for a hospital office. (Courtesy West Islip Historical Society.)

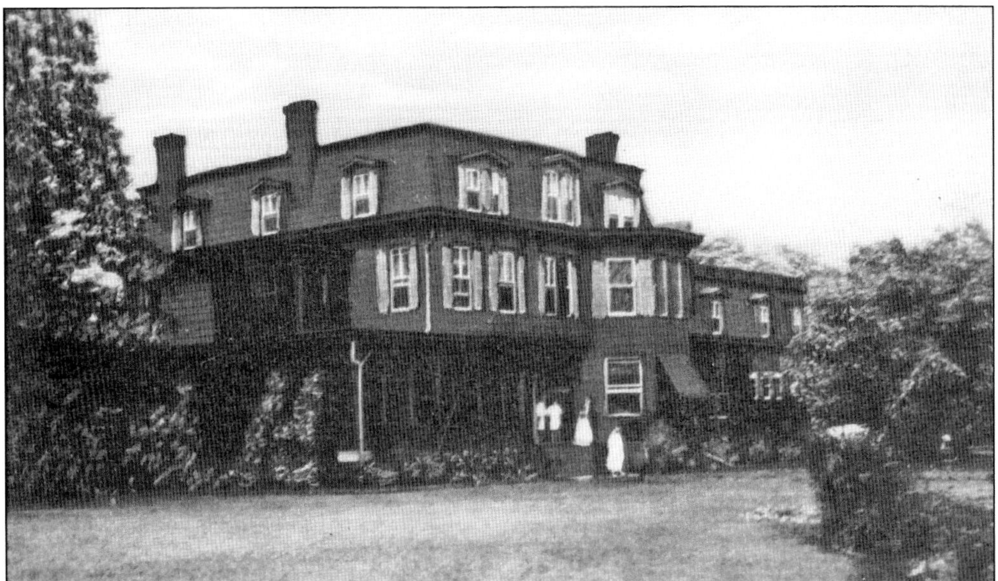

This 30-room estate on South Country Road was built in 1879 by Mutual Life Insurance general manager and South Side Hospital Association president Robert H. McCurdy (1860–1932). In 1925, the 10-acre estate was purchased with a $300,000 bequest from Emily Bourne to create a place were nurses could rest called the Nurse's House. (Courtesy Village of Babylon Historic and Preservation Society.)

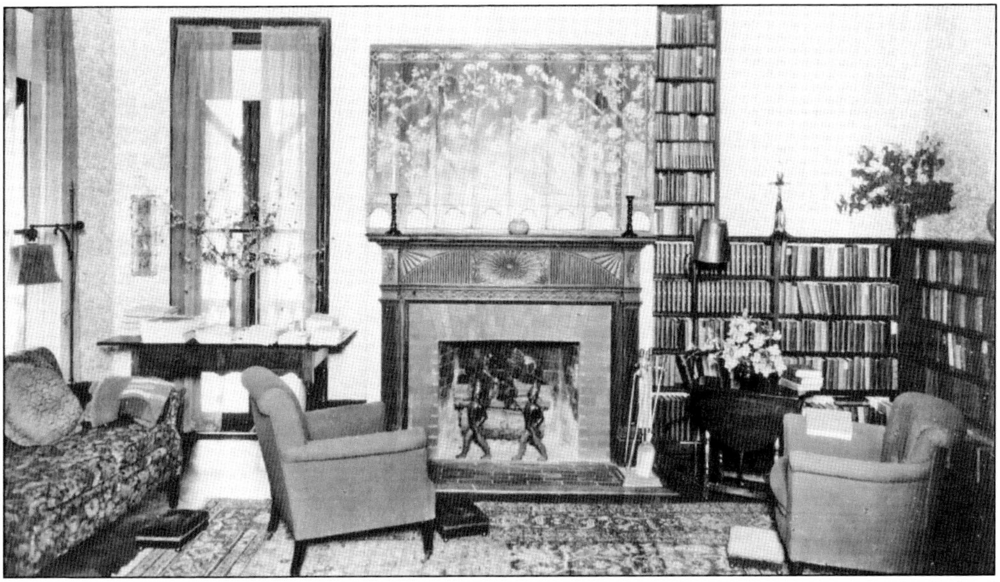

This picture shows the interior of the McCurdy house, later the Nurse's House, which had 30 rooms. This picture shows a living room area. (Courtesy Village of Babylon Historic and Preservation Society.)

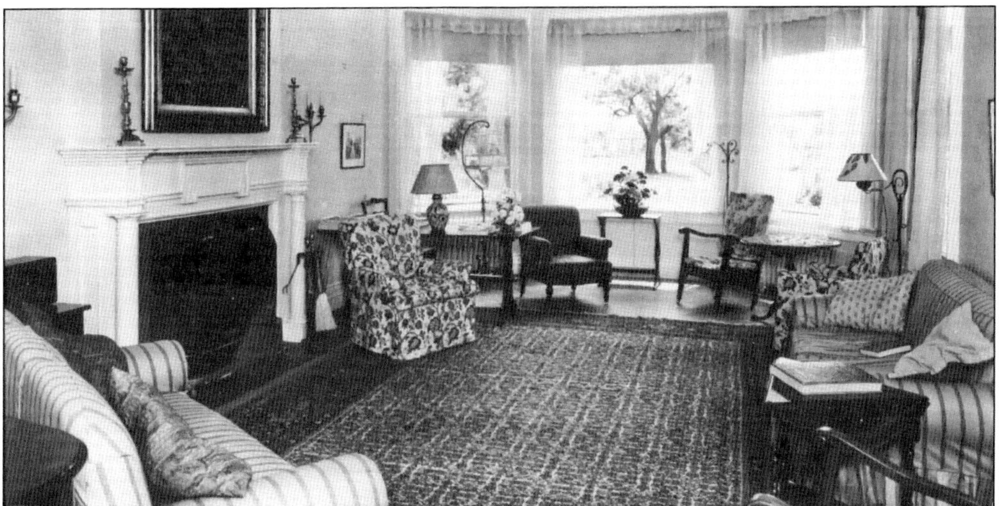

The Nurse's House was intended to be a place where nurses from all around Long Island could go to vacation and rest. It was torn down in the 1950s. A CVS pharmacy now sits on the land where the house once stood. (Courtesy Village of Babylon Historic and Preservation Society.)

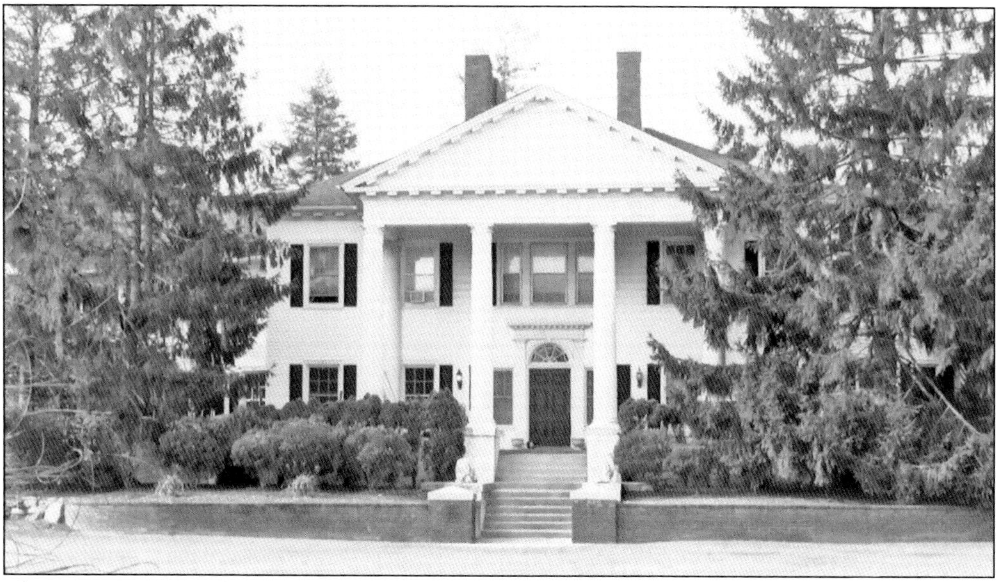

This Georgian Revival–style mansion, named Clovelly, on South Country Road was built in 1906 by Annie Stuart Cameron Arnold (died 1945). Arnold willed the mansion to the Dominican Fathers of the Provence of St. Joseph. The mansion still stands as an apartment building. (Photograph by Christopher Collora.)

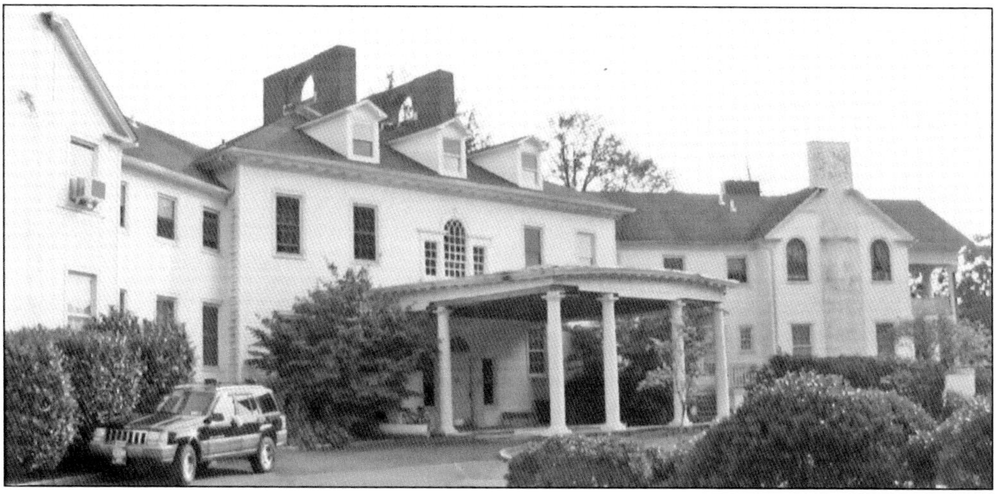

Here is a rear view of the Arnold Mansion. The home is subdivided as apartment buildings today. In 1948, the church sold it to Cadman H. Frederick, who subdivided the property for a housing development. (Photograph by Christopher Collora.)

Five

Bay Shore, Brightwaters, and Islip

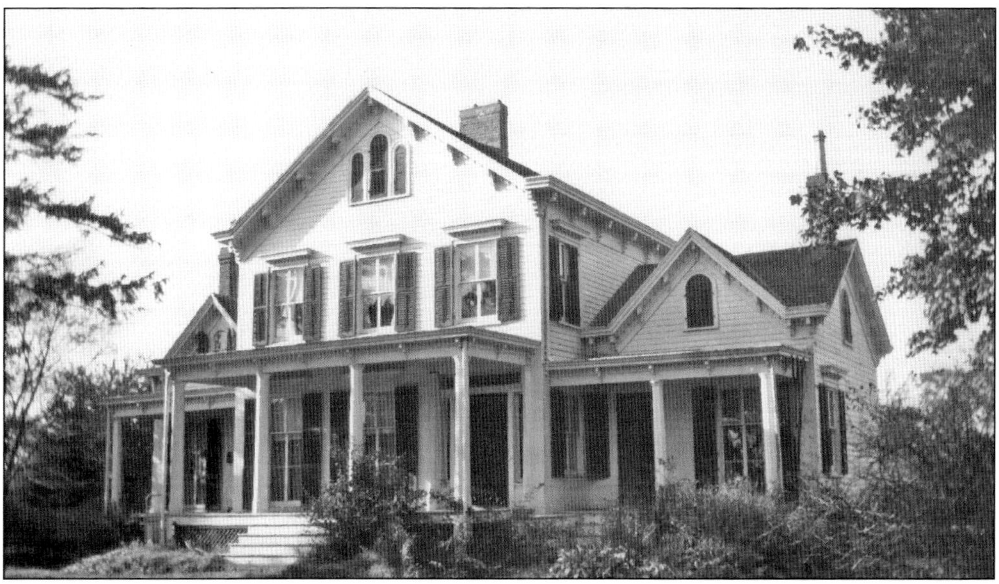

The Mowbray-Tuttle House was completed in 1858. This was the home of Dr. Jarvis Mowbray, grandson of Bay Shore's founder, John Mowbray (died 1720). In 1701, John Mowbray purchased the land from the Secatogue tribe. In 1708, Queen Anne of England issued Mowbray a patent for the land he called Aweeksa. The town was called Mechanicsville in 1831 and changed to Penataquit in 1849 before being changed once more to Bay Shore in 1868. After retiring from his medical practice, Dr. Jarvis Mowbray (1820–1886) served as supervisor for the Town of Islip. (Courtesy Barry Dlouhy, Bay Shore Historical Society.)

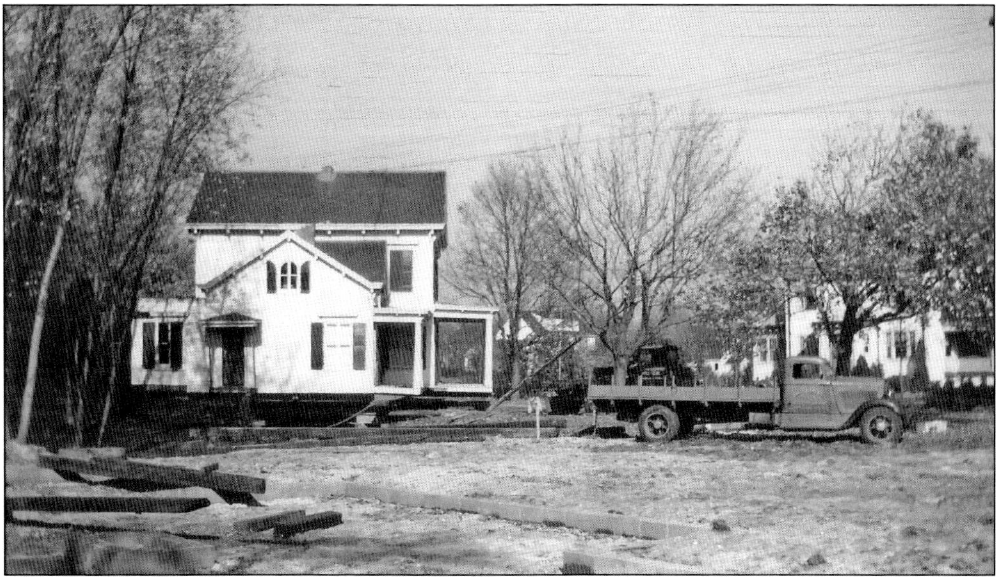

In 1945, the land the Mowbray house sat on was sold, and Walter Tuttle (Jarvis Mowbray's grandson), who inherited the home, had it moved from its original location on Main Street to its present location on Mowbray Avenue. The house still stands today as a private residence owned by Bay Shore Historical Society president Barry Dlouhy and his wife, Joan. (Courtesy Barry Dlouhy, Bay Shore Historical Society.)

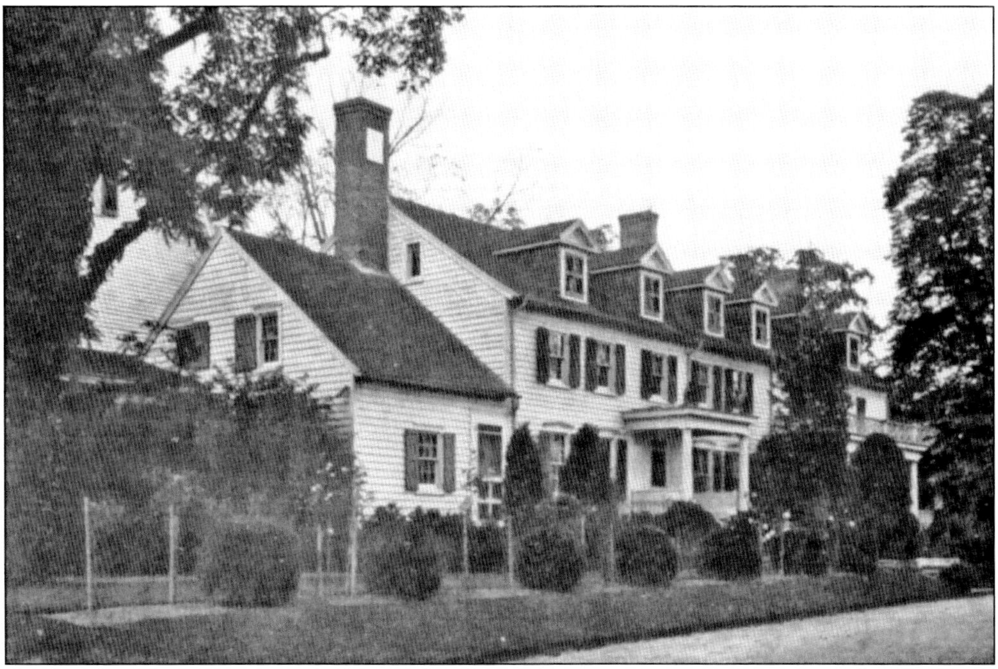

Sagtikos Manor is the oldest house in the town of Islip. The first section was built in 1697. It was originally the home of Stephanus Van Cortlandt, who purchased the land from the Secatogue Indians in 1692. Jonathan Thompson bought the house in 1758. Sagtikos Manor was eventually deeded to his son Isaac and Issac's wife, Mary Gardiner-Thompson. They expanded the mansion, adding nine rooms. (Courtesy George Weeks Library, West Islip.)

Judge Isaac Thompson was a prominent member of Islip town government before and after the American Revolution and was later a member of the New York State Assembly. (Courtesy Suffolk County Parks Department.)

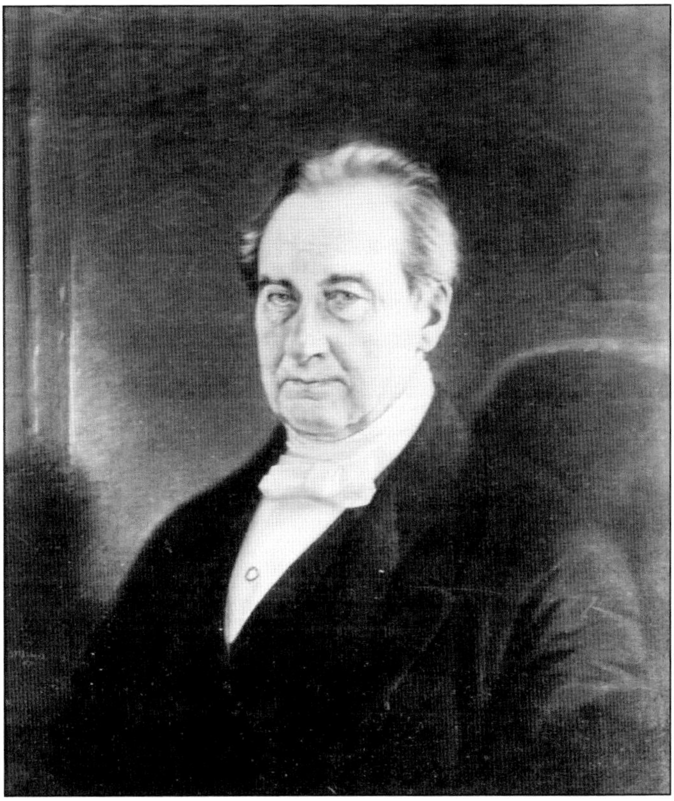

On April 21, 1790, Pres. George Washington spent the night at Sagtikos Manor during his tour of Long Island. Legend has it that Washington was originally offered the master bedroom to stay in, but upon learning that it was once the room of the British general Sir Henry Clinton, quartered there during the American Revolution, Washington opted for this guest room instead. (Courtesy George Weeks Library, West Islip.)

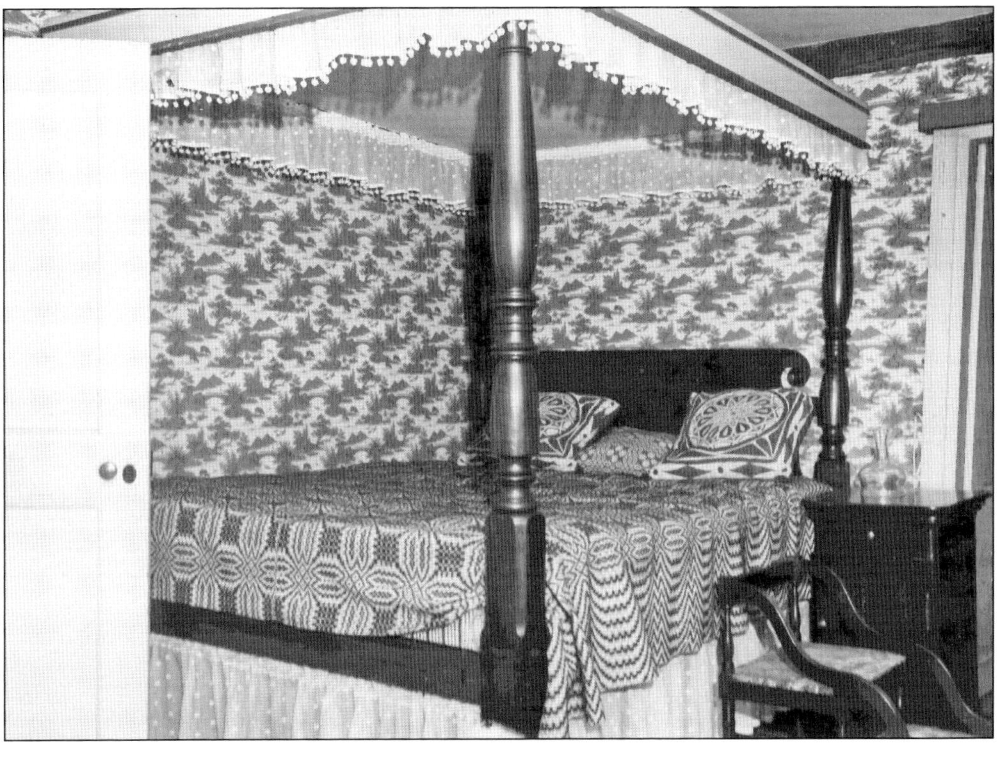

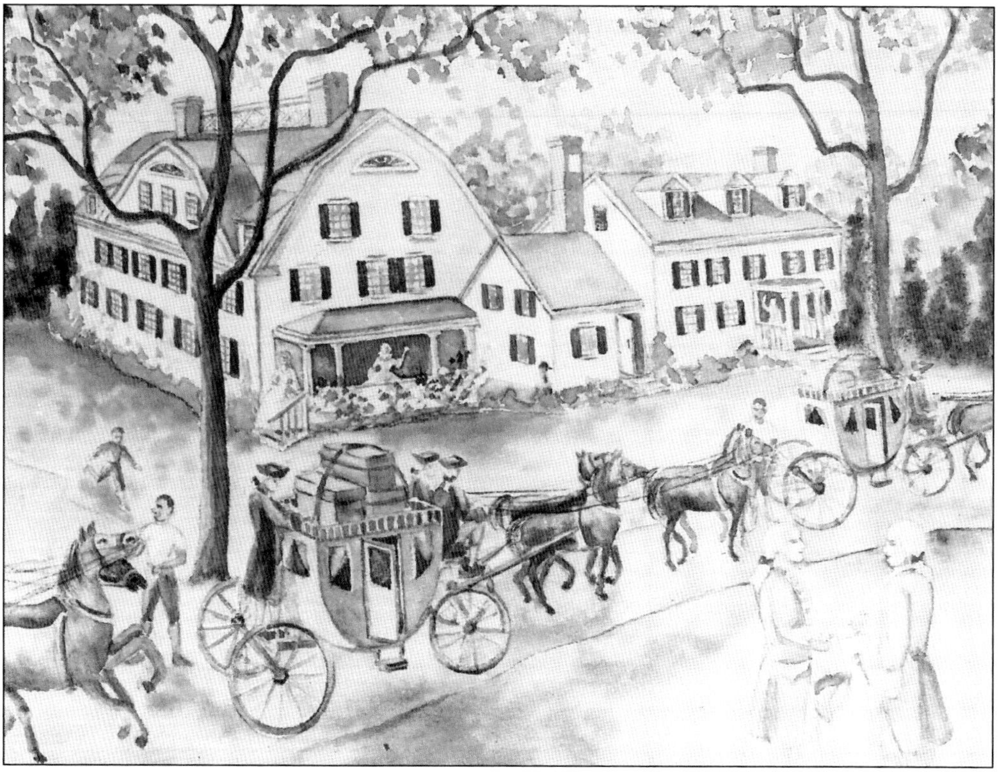

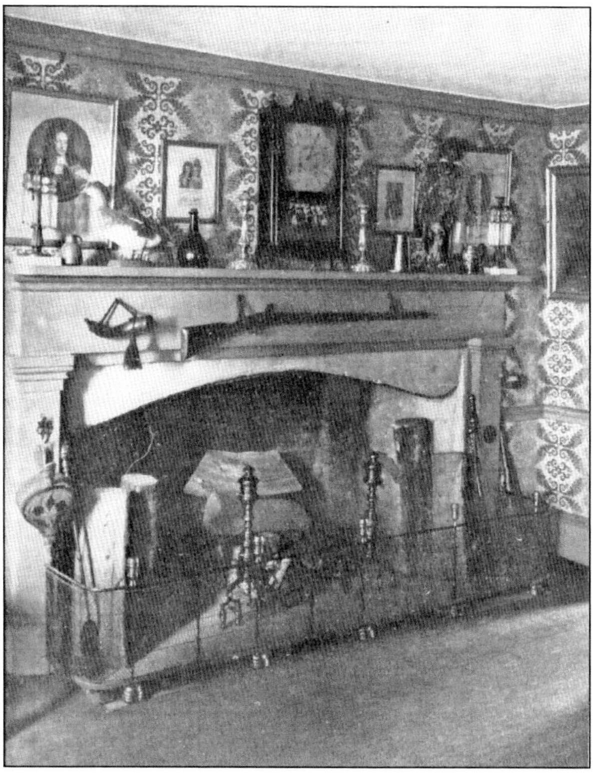

This sketch depicts Washington's visit to Sagtikos Manor in 1790. Washington previously had dinner at the Ketchem Inn in Amityville. After his stay at Sagtikos, he proceeded farther east to the Green Home in West Sayville, then onto Patchogue and Brookhaven before heading to the North Shore. (Courtesy George Weeks Library, West Islip.)

This interior shot of the older part of Sagtikos Manor shows the living room area. The home is open today for public tours as a museum managed by the Sagtikos Manor Historical Society and overseen by the Suffolk County Parks Department. (Courtesy George Weeks Library, West Islip.)

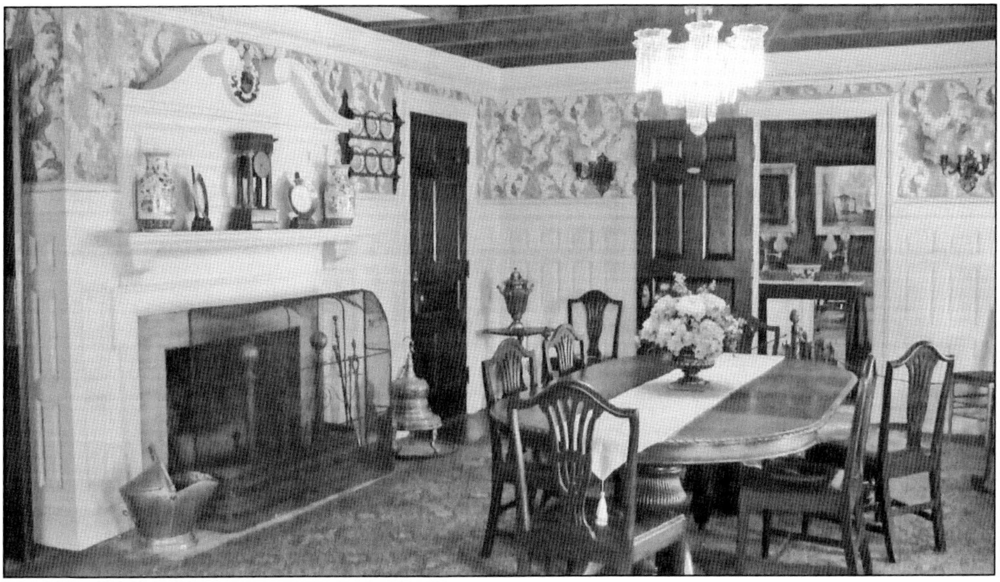

The dining room area, shown here, is in one of the newer parts of Sagtikos Manor. (Courtesy George Weeks Library, West Islip.)

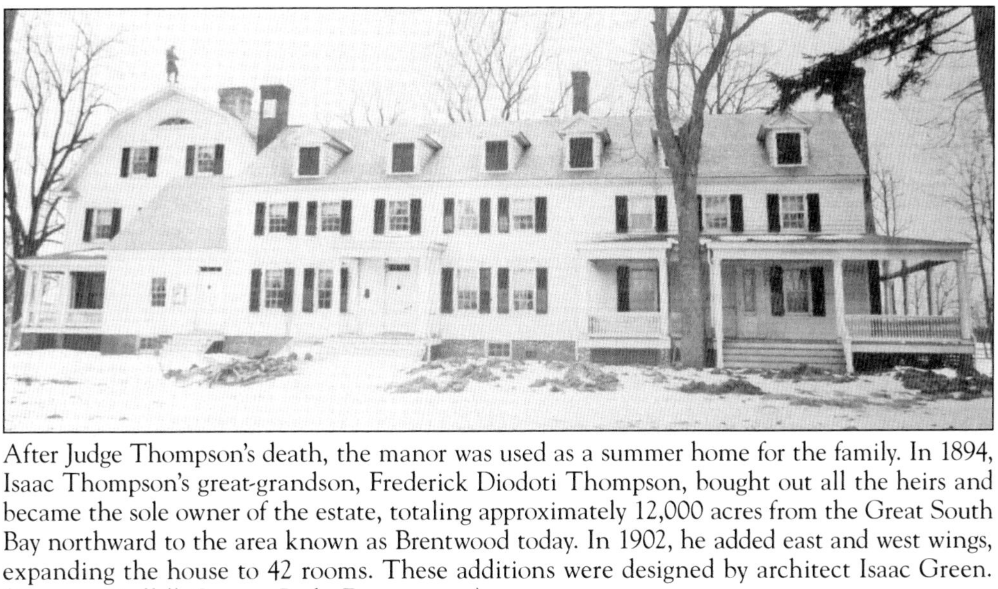

After Judge Thompson's death, the manor was used as a summer home for the family. In 1894, Isaac Thompson's great-grandson, Frederick Diodoti Thompson, bought out all the heirs and became the sole owner of the estate, totaling approximately 12,000 acres from the Great South Bay northward to the area known as Brentwood today. In 1902, he added east and west wings, expanding the house to 42 rooms. These additions were designed by architect Isaac Green. (Courtesy Suffolk County Parks Department.)

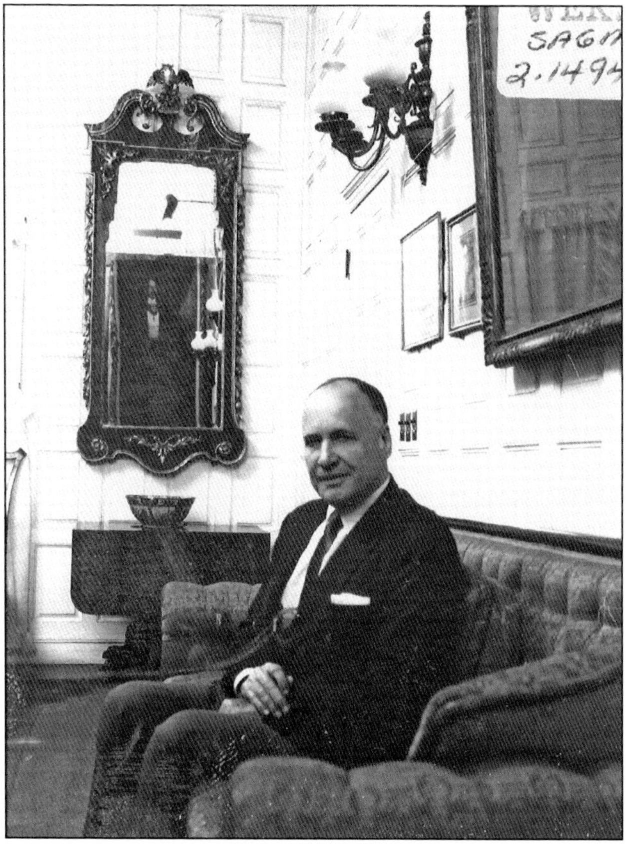

Robert David Lion Gardiner was the last family member to live in Sagtikos Manor. He owned the property until 1985. He slowly sold the land for development and established the Gardiner Manor Mall on Sunrise Highway. In 2002, Suffolk County purchased the remaining 10 acres and manor house with outer buildings. (Courtesy George Weeks Library, West Islip.)

The Guastavino Tile House, seen here, is a Mediterranean villa–style home constructed in 1912 by Rafael Guastavino Jr. (1872–1950), owner of the Guastavino Tile Company, architect, inventor, and builder. It still exists as a private residence. (Courtesy Bay Shore Historical Society.)

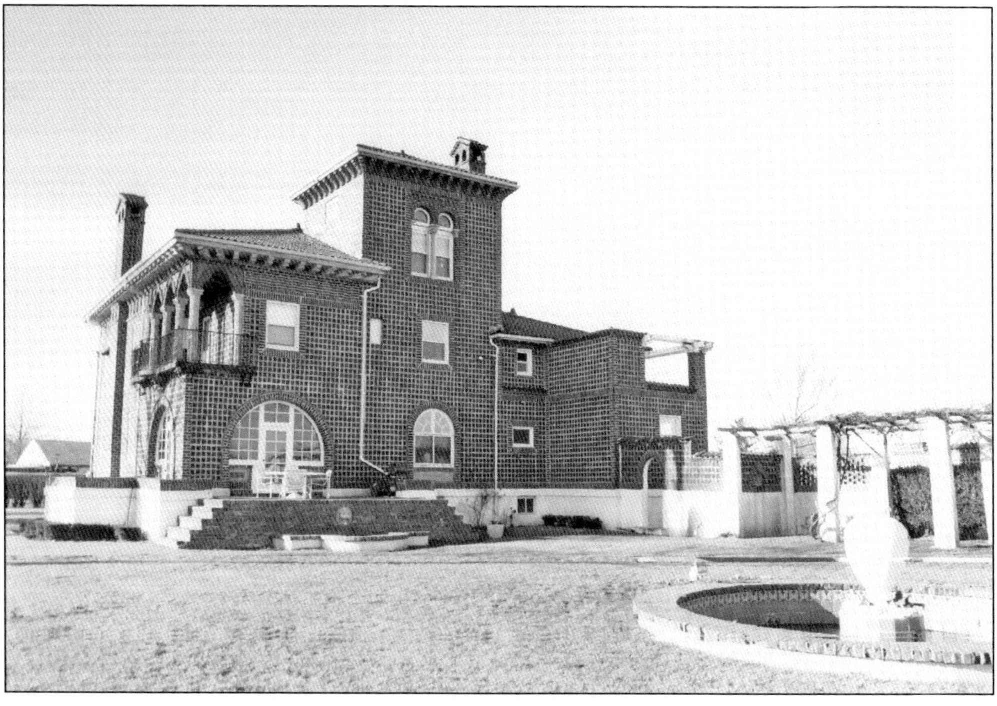

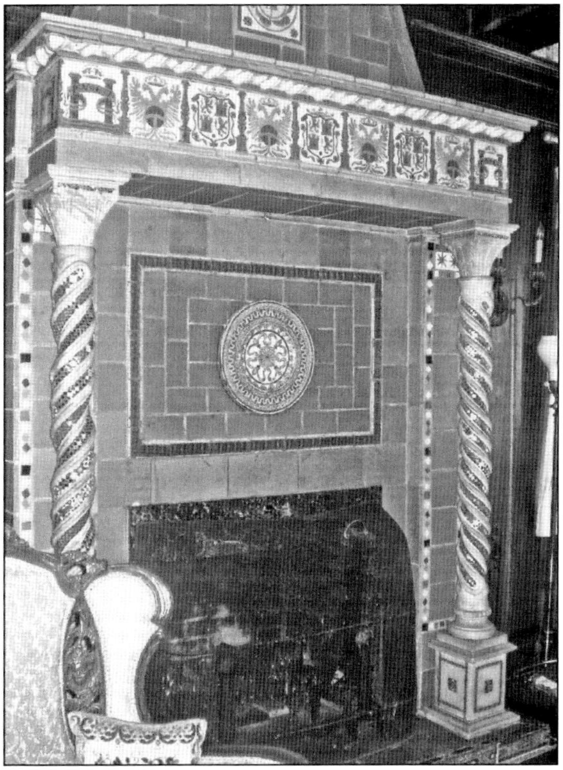

The Guastavino Tile House contains 16 rooms and sits on 1.2 acres on Awixa Avenue. This is a picture of one of the beautiful tile fireplaces inside the home. (Courtesy Bay Shore Historical Society.)

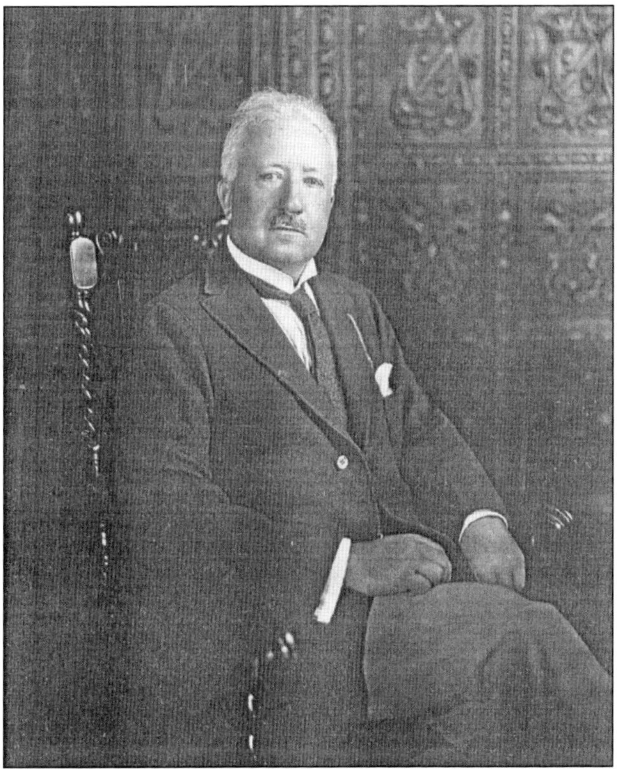

Guastavino constructed over 1,000 domes, vaulted ceilings, and spiral staircases in North America, 383 in Manhattan. The company manufactured its own tiles and cement. Guastavino donated tile work to St. Patrick's Church in Bay Shore. Guastavino Tiles also worked on Riverside Church in Manhattan, Grant's Tomb, the Oyster Bar in Grand Central Terminal, the ceiling of Vanderbilt Hall, and the ceiling of the Grand Hall on Ellis Island. (Courtesy Bay Shore Historical Society.)

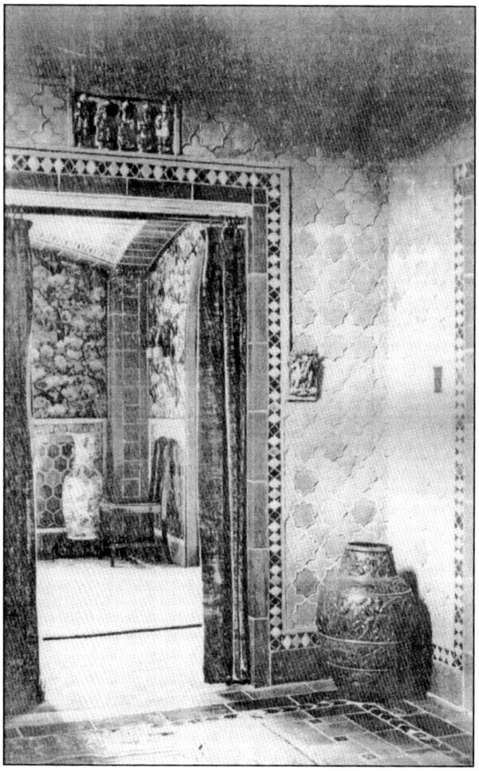

These rare photographs show the inside of the home, constructed from Guastavino's own personal tile collection from all over the world. The home still stands today as a private residence. (Both, courtesy Bay Shore Historical Society.)

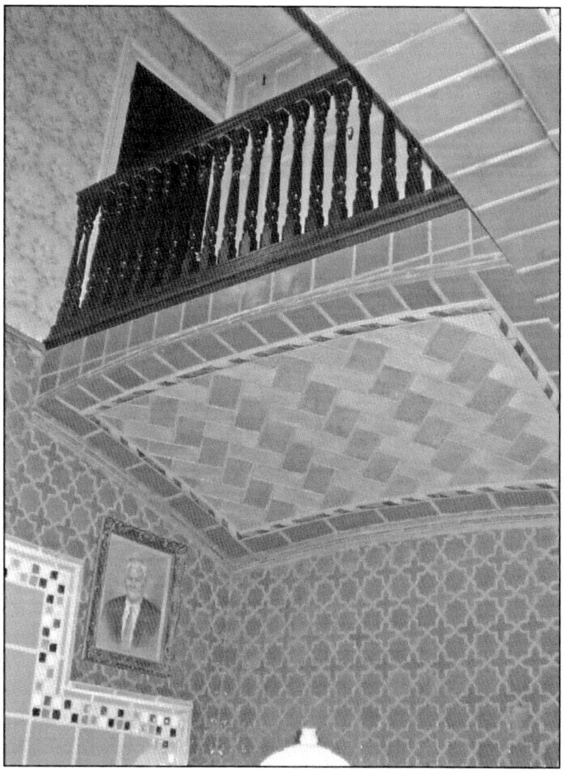

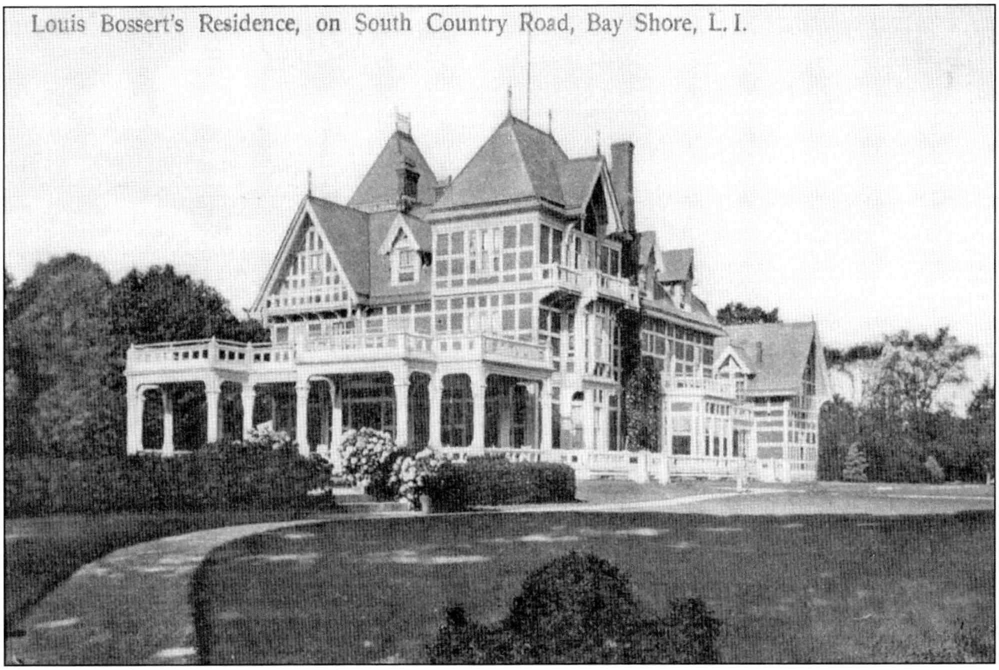

This 40-room mansion, The Oaks, was built around 1876 by Henry Baldwin Hyde (1834–1899), president of the Equitable Life Assurance Society. The estate contained an aviary with birds from around world. The mansion was inherited by James Hazen Hyde (1876–1959). It was sold to Louis Bossert (1843–1913) in 1901. Part of the mansion stands as the clubhouse for the Southward Ho Country Club. (Courtesy Bay Shore Historical Society.)

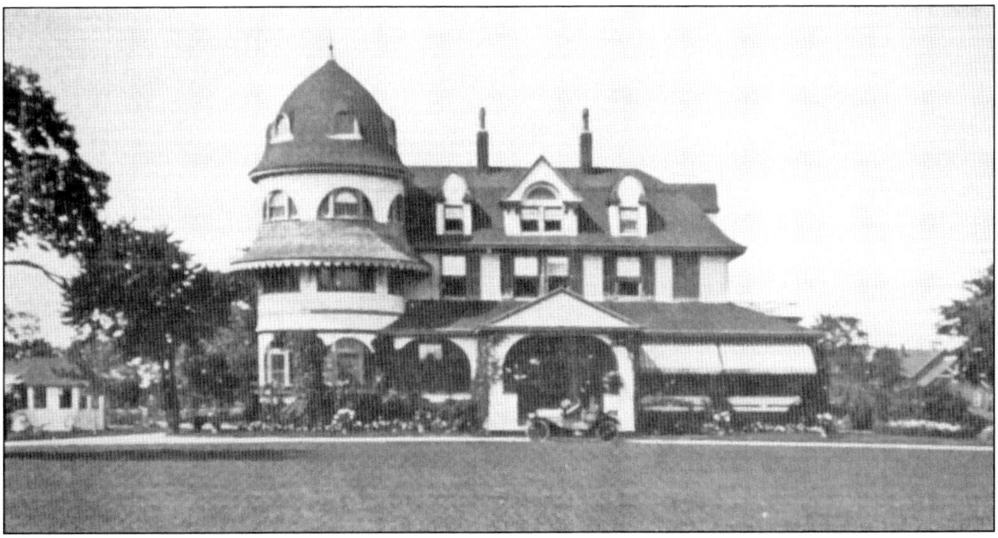

This shingle-style home was built in 1895 by vaudeville theater entrepreneur Richard Hyde. It was designed by architect Clarence K. Birdsall. The house no longer stands, but the clubhouse for his private golf course, the first golf course in Bay Shore, is still in existence. (Courtesy Bay Shore Historical Society.)

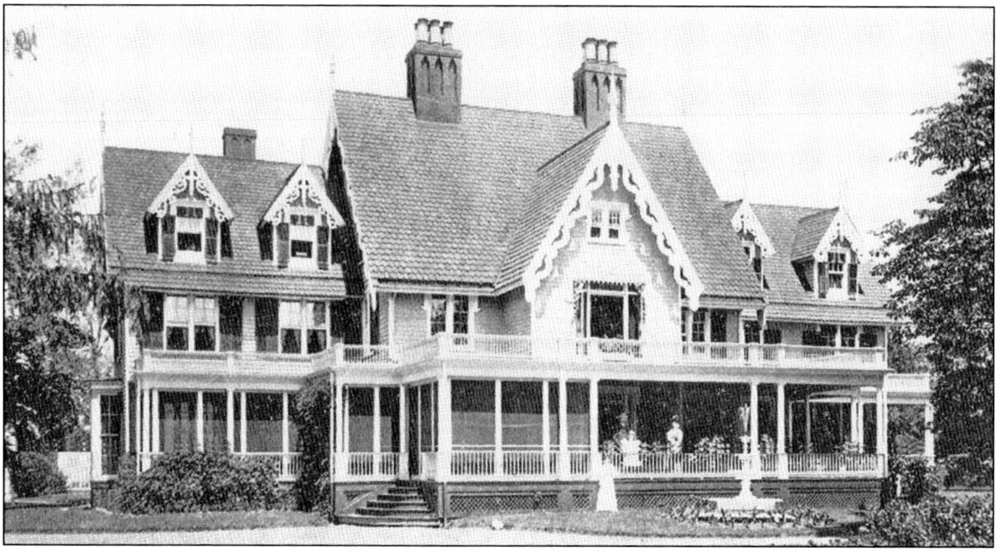

This High Victorian Gothic–style mansion, named Sans Souci, on South Country Road was built around 1860 by attorney and financier Bradish Johnson Sr. (1811–1892). Johnson is said to be the first summer resident of Bay Shore, nicknamed the "Dean of the South Shore Residents." The house was eventually inherited by his son Henry Meyer Johnson. The house no longer stands today. (Courtesy Bay Shore Historical Society.)

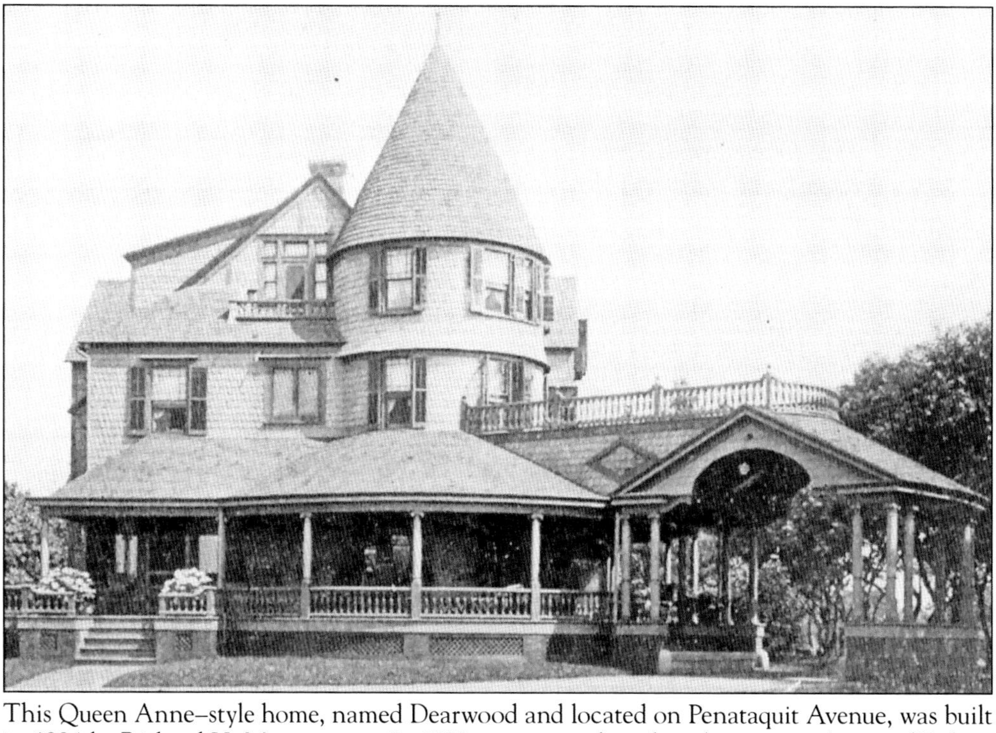

This Queen Anne–style home, named Dearwood and located on Penataquit Avenue, was built in 1884 by Richard H. Montgomery. In 1899, it was purchased as the summer home of Robert Allan Pinkerton Sr. (1848–1907). Pinkerton was president of the Pinkerton National Detective Agency (founded by his father, Allan Pinkerton, who protected Pres. Abraham Lincoln during his inauguration). The house no longer stands today. (Courtesy Bay Shore Historical Society.)

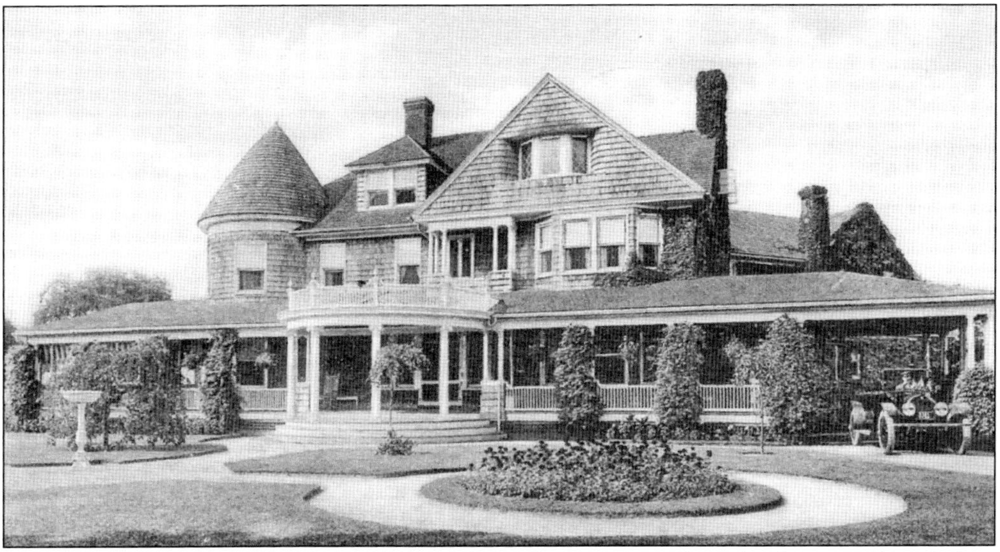

Fairlawn was built by George P. Baker, president of First National Bank of New York and close financial ally of J.P. Morgan, who held a controlling interest in Chase National Bank. The house no longer stands today. (Courtesy Bay Shore Historical Society.)

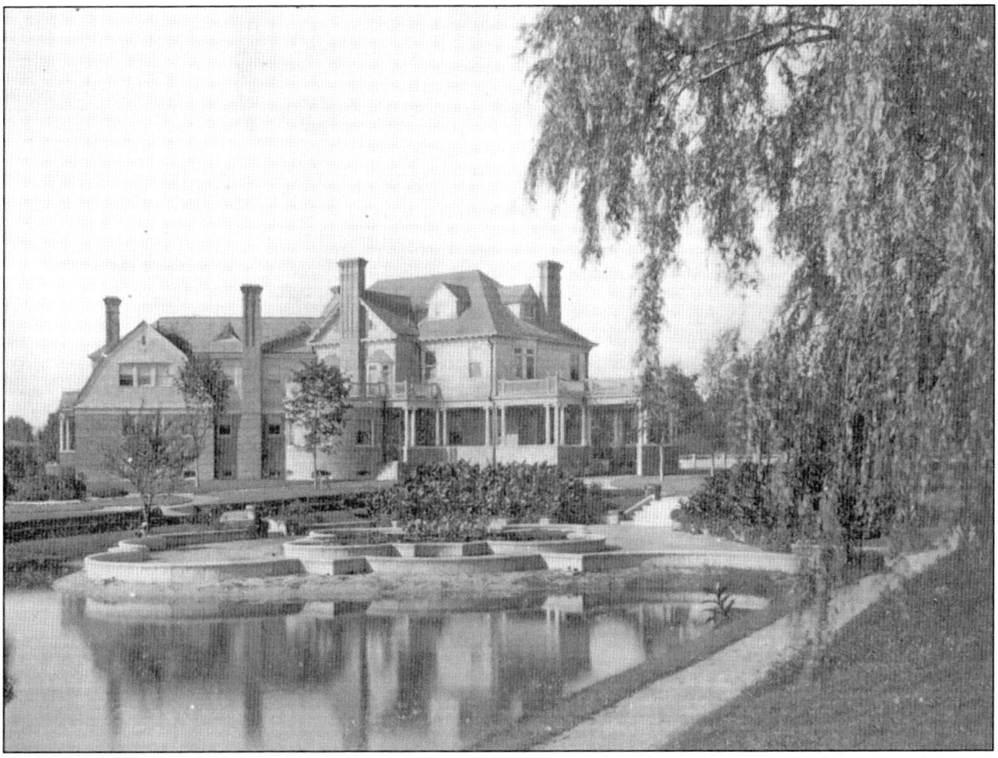

This shingle-style mansion, Homeport, was built on Awixa Avenue in 1899 by John Adolph Mollenhauer (1857–1926). Mollenhauer was vice president of the Mollenhauer Sugar Refining Company. He was active in Bay Shore as a trustee of South Side Hospital and donated land on Main Street for the Soldiers and Sailors Memorial Building. The house stands today as a private residence, now called Awixa Castle. (Courtesy Bay Shore Historical Society.)

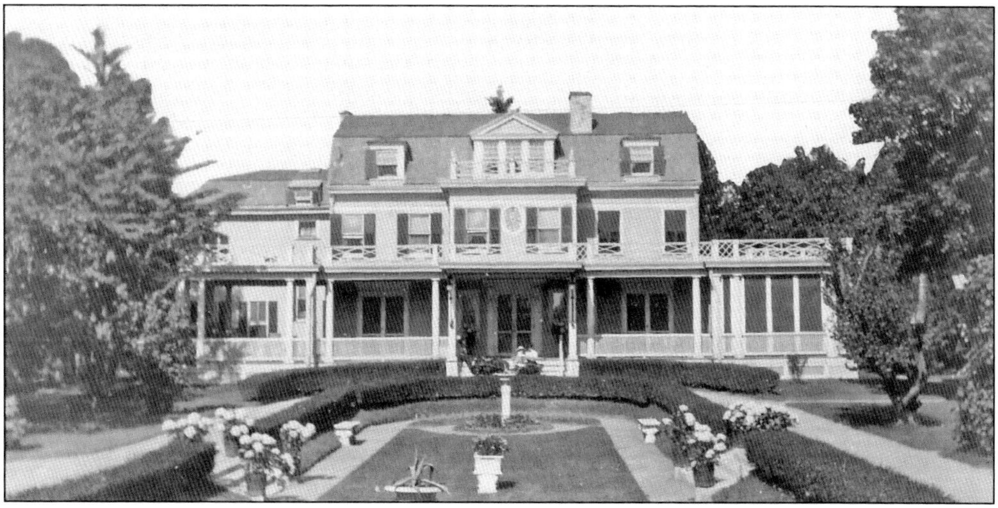

This shingle-style home, named Evergreens, was built for US Army general William Graves Bates (1860–1944). The home was demolished and no longer stands today. (Courtesy Bay Shore Historical Society.)

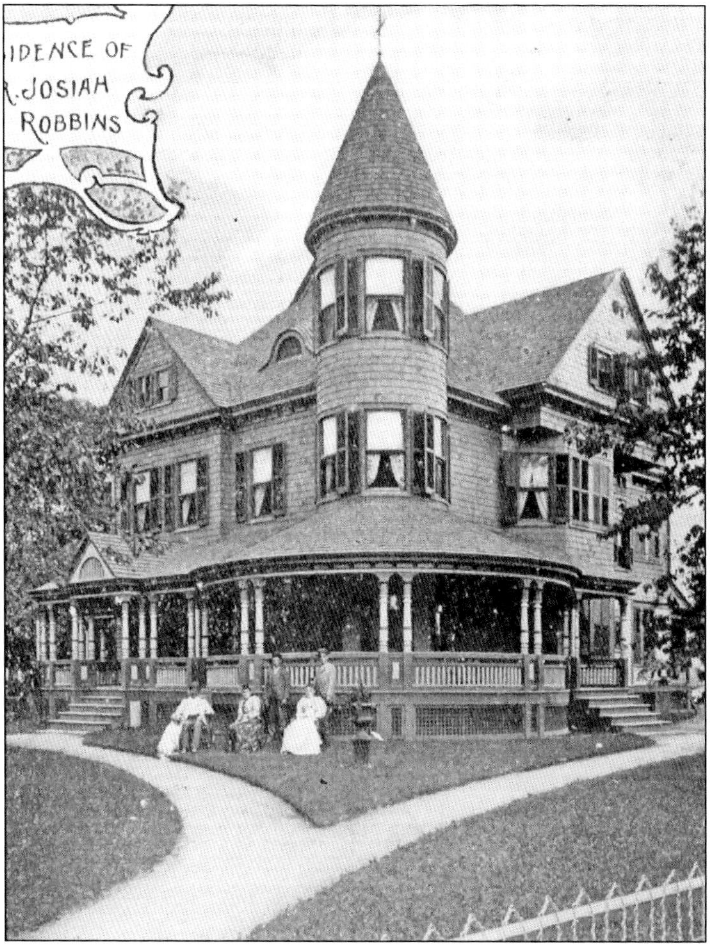

This Victorian-style home on South Country Road was built around 1903 by politician Josiah Robbins. The house is no longer standing today. (Courtesy Bay Shore Historical Society.)

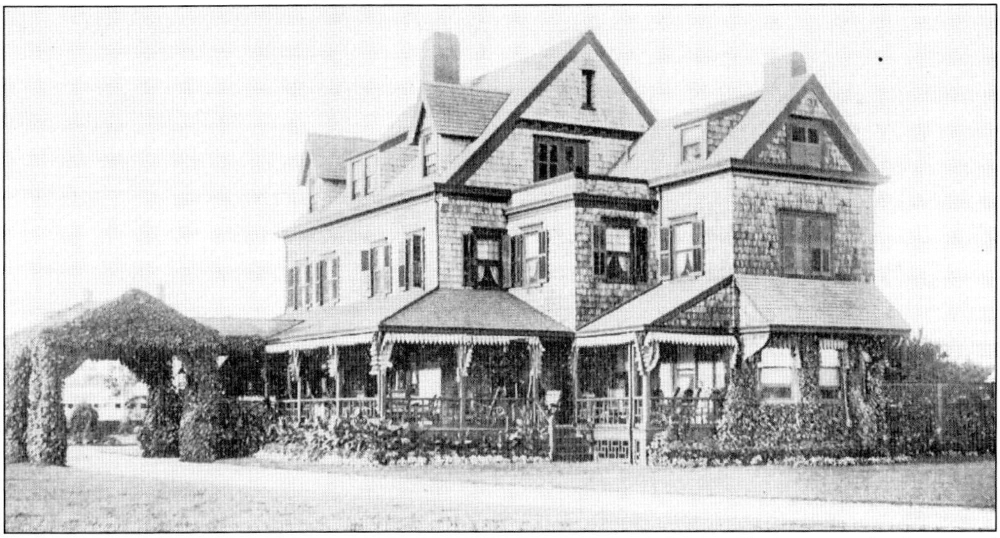

This Colonial Revival–style mansion, named Breeze Lawn, on Ocean Avenue was built around 1889 by Brooklyn parks commissioner Leander Waterbury (died 1889). The home was later owned by Howard Gibb (1855–1905), president of Frederick Loeser & Co. It was purchased by Henry Timmerman in 1898 and eventually passed on to his daughter Grace Toby. The house is no longer standing today. (Courtesy Bay Shore Historical Society.)

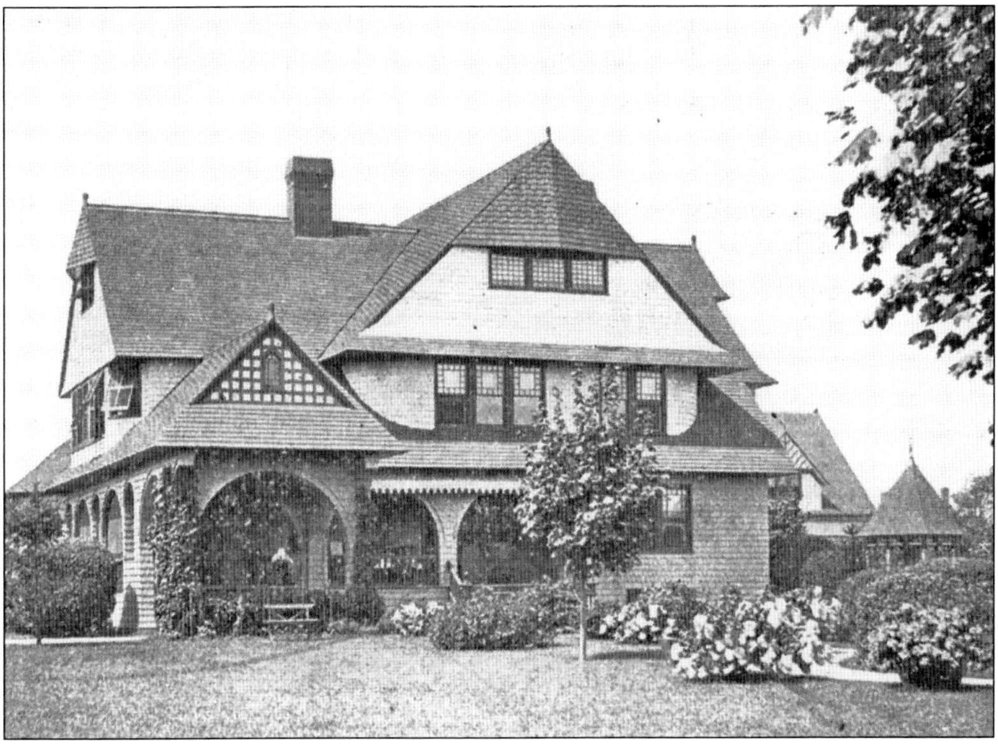

This Shingle–style home on Awixa Avenue was built in 1893 by John Mollenhauer (1827–1904), founder of Mollenhauer Sugar Refining Company (later called the National Sugar Refining Company). Mollenhauer was also president of Dimes Savings Bank of Williamsburg. The house still stands as a private residence. (Courtesy Bay Shore Historical Society.)

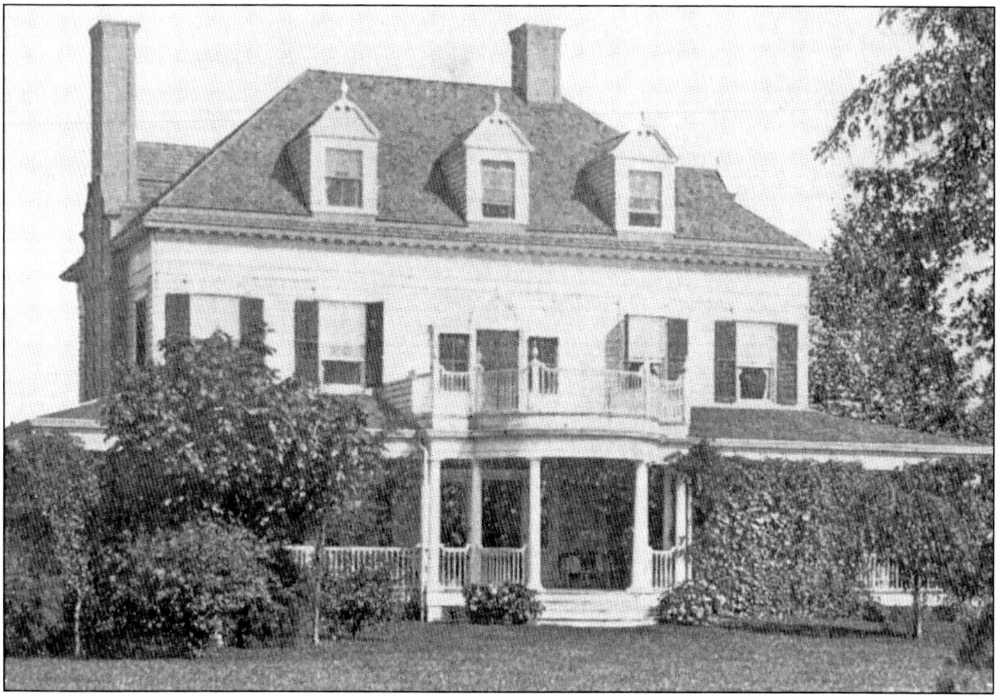

This Neo-Georgian-style estate, named Scrub Oaks, on South Country Road was built around 1900 by Henry W. Maxwell (1850–1902). Maxwell was director of several railroad companies and an associate of Long Island Railroad president Austin Corbin of Babylon. He was noted for his philanthropy and civic activism. Maxwell reportedly donated to numerous educational, medical, and charitable causes. (Courtesy Bay Shore Historical Society.)

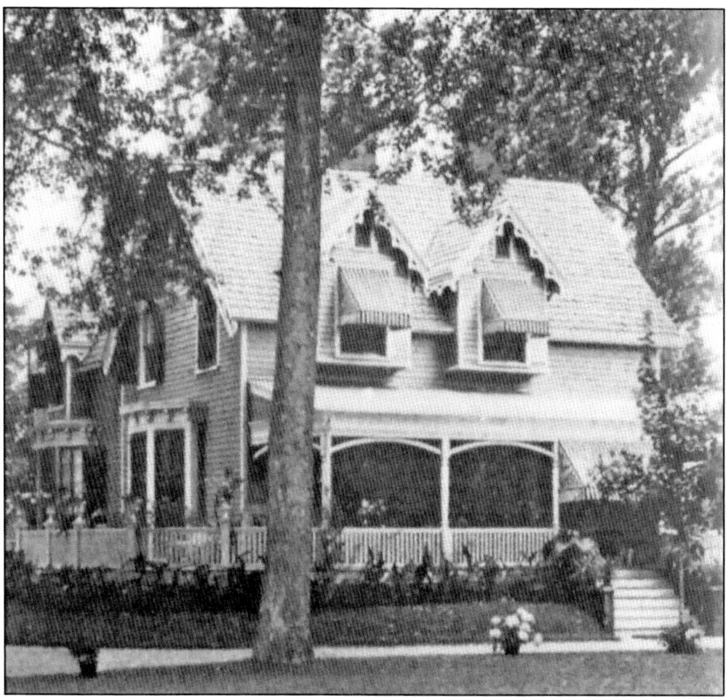

This Mediterranean villa–style estate, named Admore, on South Country Road was built around 1905 by Thomas Adams Jr. (1846–1926), president of the Adams & Sons chewing gum company. The house still stands and is part of the Southward Ho Country Club. (Courtesy Bay Shore Historical Society.)

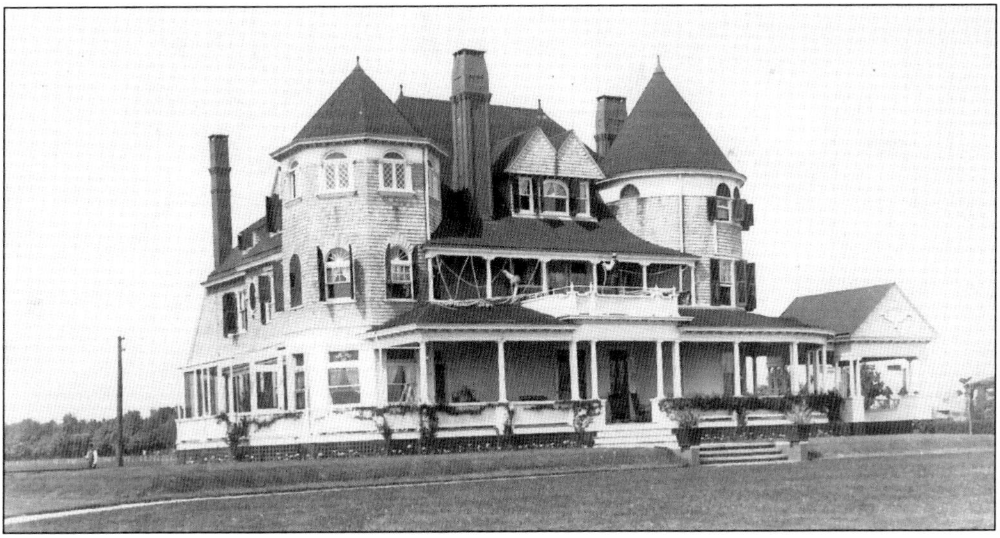

This Queen Anne–style estate on Awixa Avenue was built in 1894 by Marine Insurance Firm president Emil H. Frank Sr. (1843–1919). In 1904, it was purchased by financier Julian Douglas Fairchild (1850–1926). The house no longer stands today. (Courtesy Bay Shore Historical Society.)

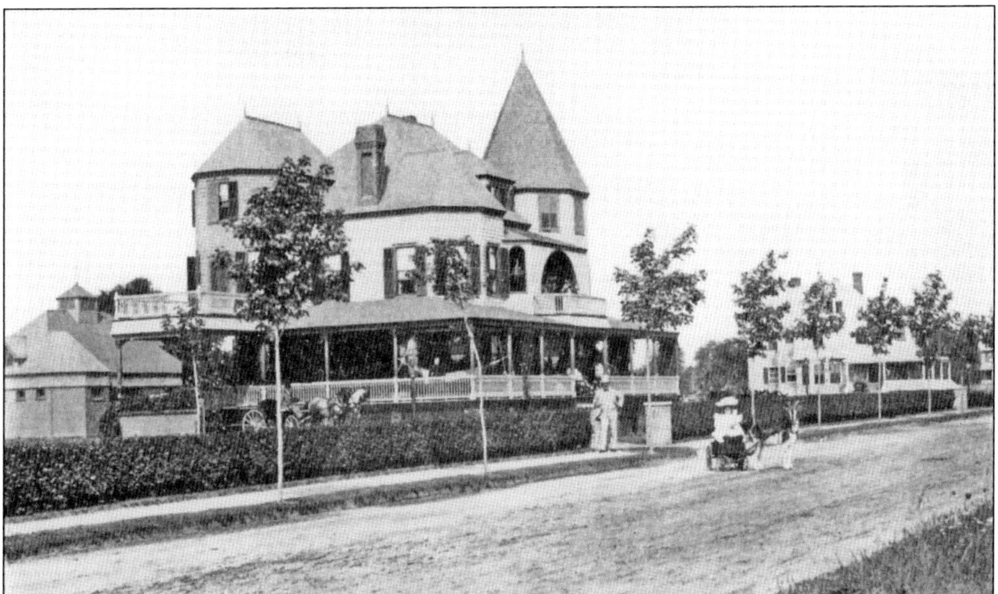

This Queen Anne–style estate, named Nether Bay, on Clinton Avenue was built around 1890 and was the home of Charles Gulden Sr. (died 1916), director of the Bank of the City of New York and founder of Gulden's Mustard Company. The home still stands as the Open Gate Nursing Home. (Courtesy Bay Shore Historical Society.)

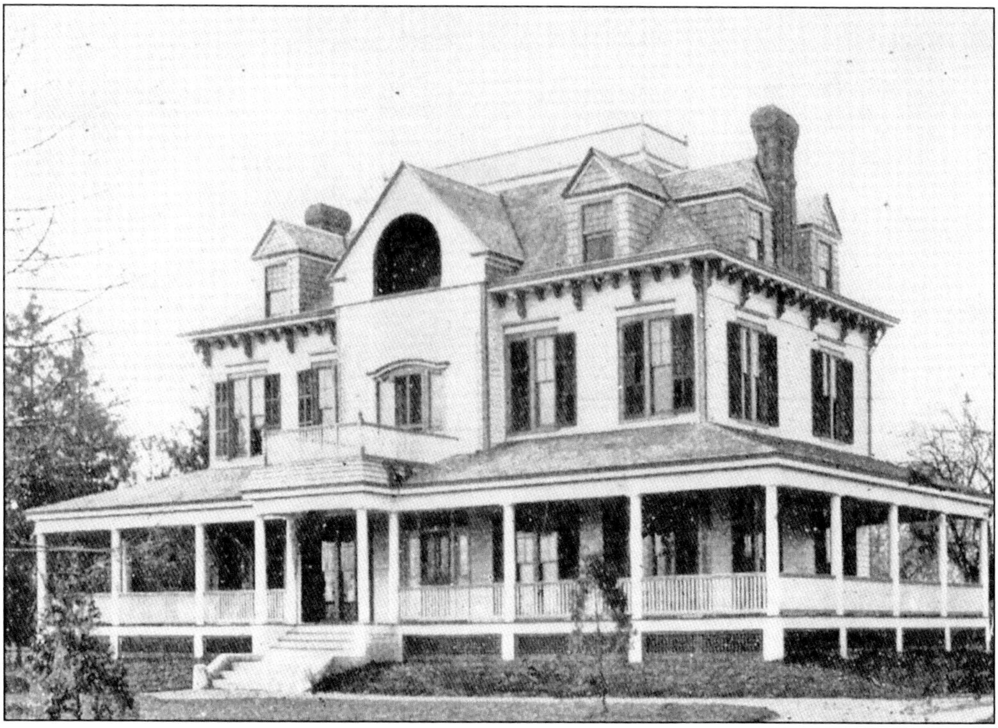

This Victorian estate, named Elysian Views, was built around 1900 by the Reverend William Warren Hulse (1838–1929). Hulse was a member of the Suffolk County Board of Supervisors. During World War I, the house was used as a canteen for pilots training to fly. The house later became the first St. Patrick's School. It is no longer standing. (Courtesy Bay Shore Historical Society.)

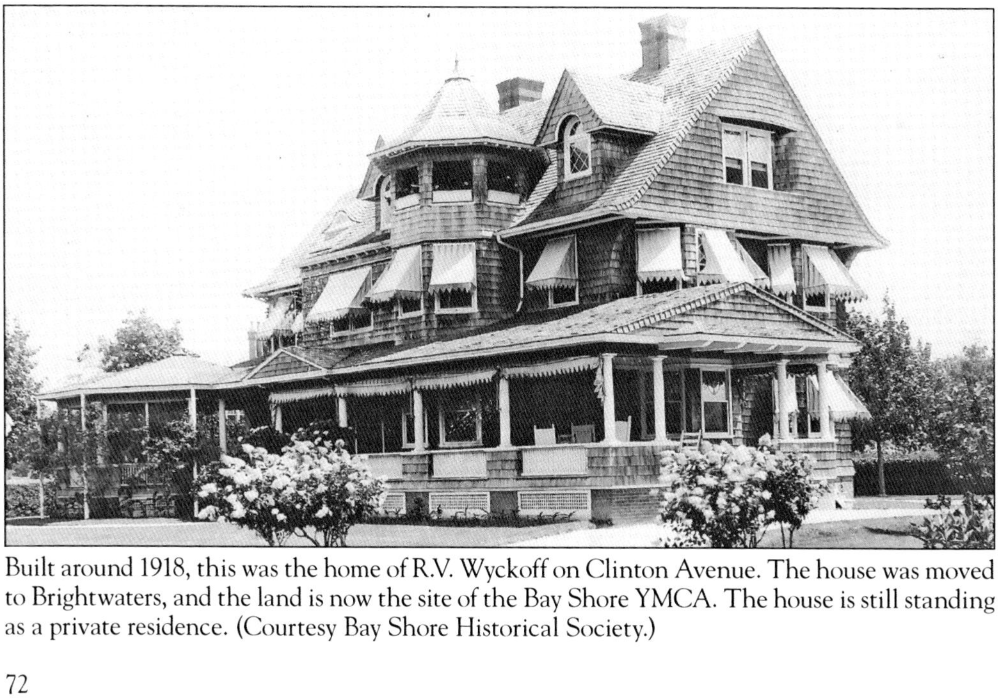

Built around 1918, this was the home of R.V. Wyckoff on Clinton Avenue. The house was moved to Brightwaters, and the land is now the site of the Bay Shore YMCA. The house is still standing as a private residence. (Courtesy Bay Shore Historical Society.)

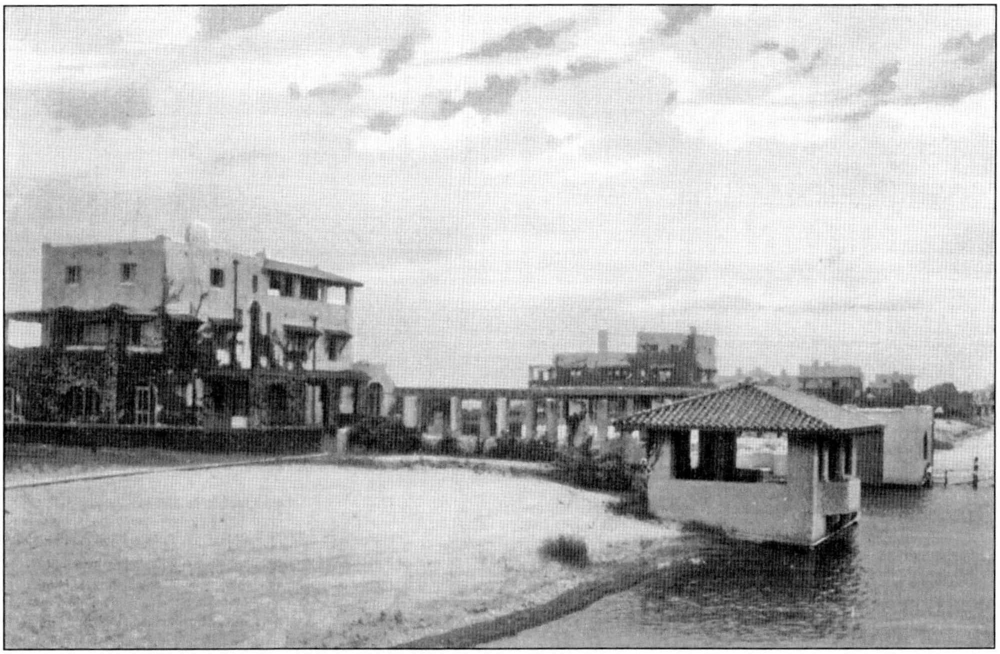

This Moorish-style estate, named Bayberry Point, was completed in 1900. It was designed by architect Grosvenor Atterbury for Henry Osborne Havemeyer (1847–1907). It was part of a planned community. (Courtesy Bay Shore Historical Society.)

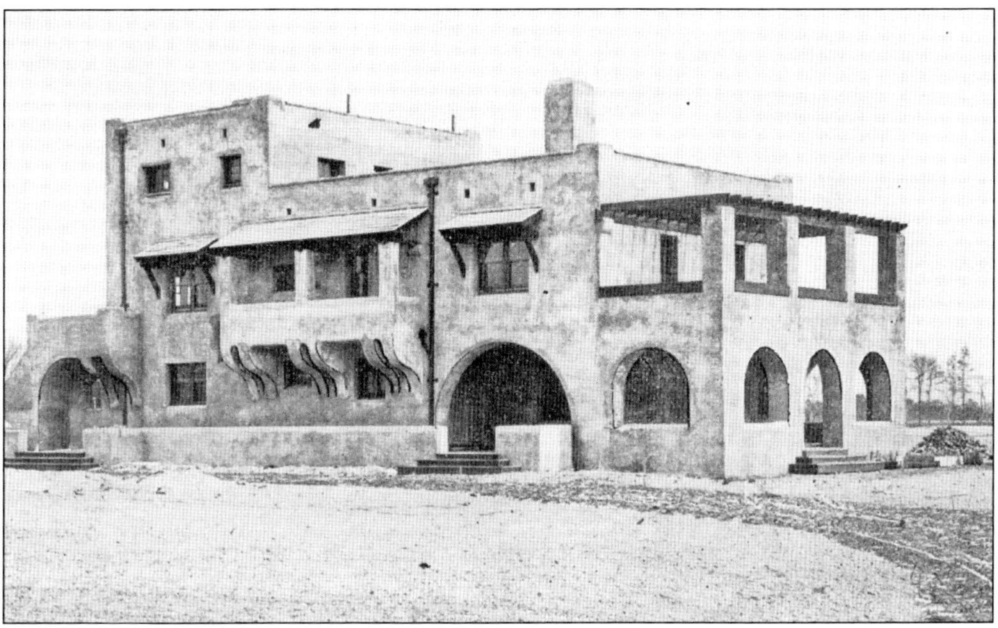

The Havemeyer home is one of the most interesting architectural designs in the area. The house still stands as a private residence. Legend has it that the idea for the Moorish architecture for the planned community was suggested by Louis Comfort Tiffany. (Courtesy Bay Shore Historical Society.)

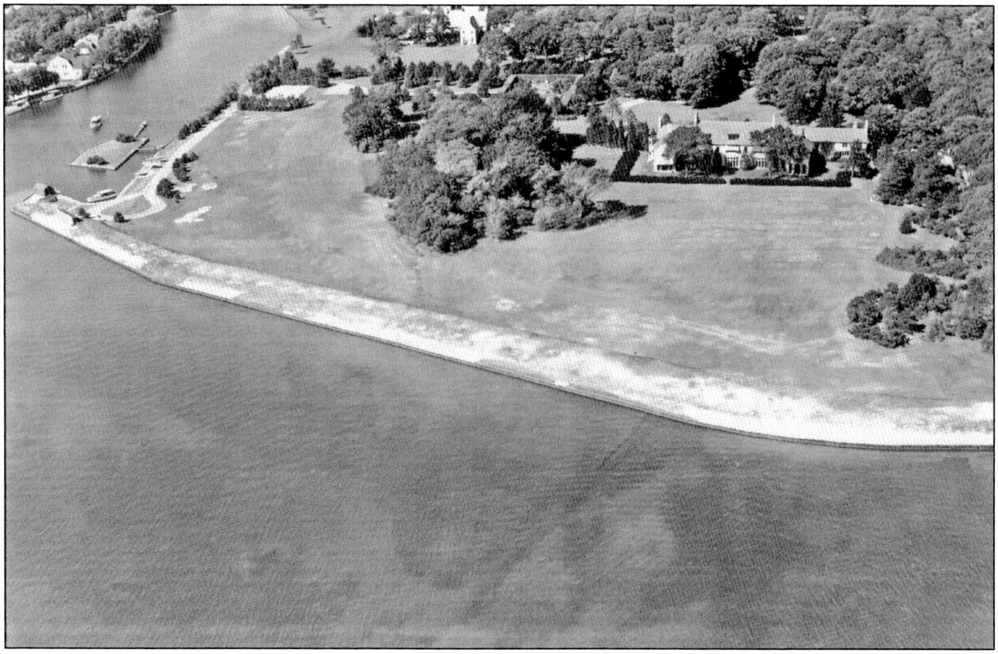

This Cotswold-style estate, named Olympic Point, on Saxon Avenue was completed in 1919 by Horace Havemeyer Sr. (1886–1956). Havemeyer was president of Havemeyers & Elder (a sugar refinery). The home was demolished in 1948 to build a smaller Colonial-style house for the Havemeyer family. (Courtesy Bay Shore Historical Society.)

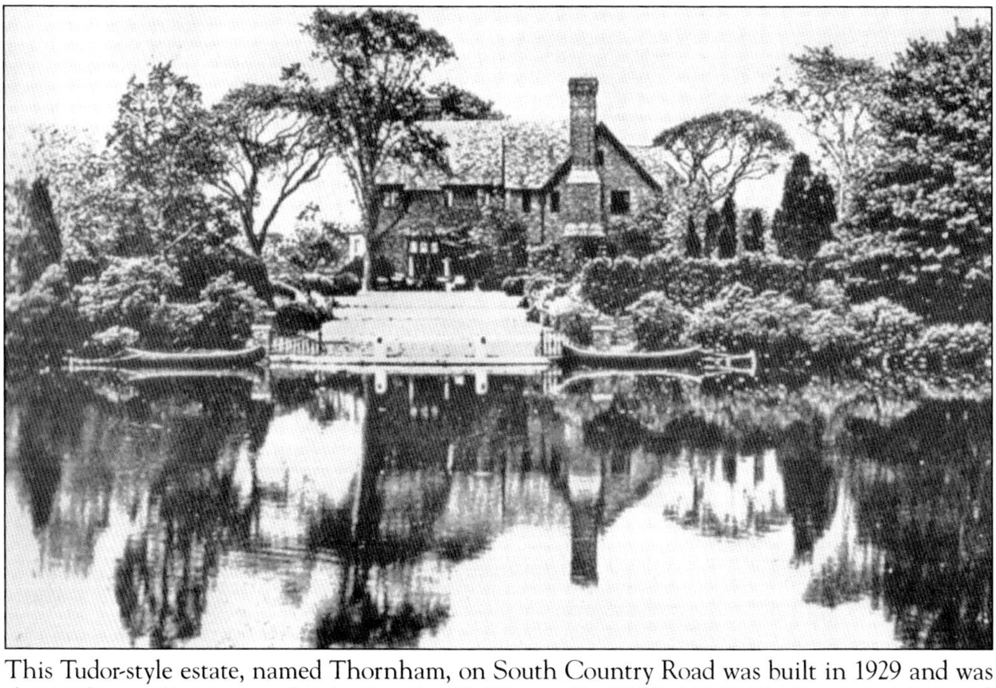

This Tudor-style estate, named Thornham, on South Country Road was built in 1929 and was the residence of investment banker Landon K. Thorne Sr. (1888–1964). The home was designed by architect William F. Dominick. It was demolished in 1976. The land is now the Admiralty. (Courtesy Bay Shore Historical Society.)

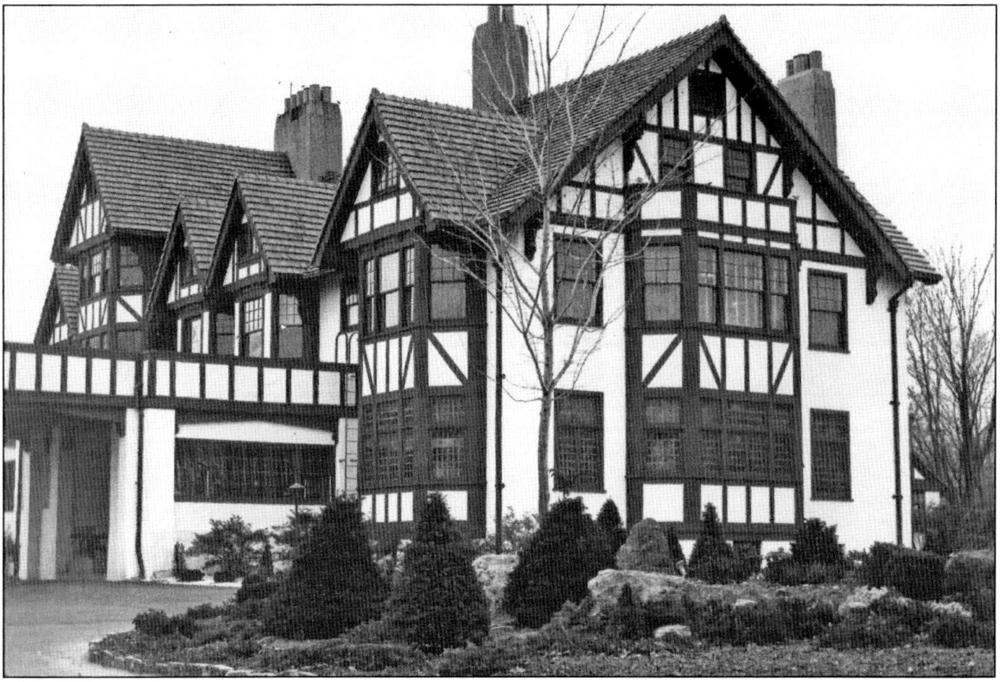

This Neo-Tudor-style estate, named Woodlea, on South Country Road was built around 1902 by Dr. Alfred Ludlow Carroll. It was later purchased by John Dunbar Adams (1849–1934), president of the American Chicle Company, a chewing gum manufacturer. John Dunbar was also the younger brother of Thomas Adams Jr. The estate became Mimi's Awixa Pond Restaurant in 1950 before burning down in 1955. (Courtesy Bay Shore Historical Society.)

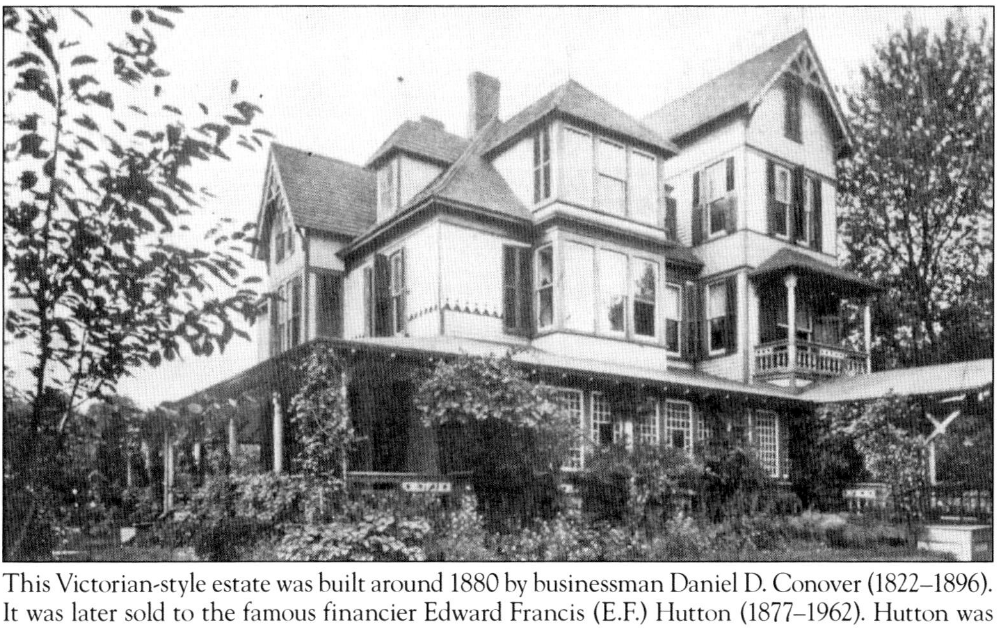

This Victorian-style estate was built around 1880 by businessman Daniel D. Conover (1822–1896). It was later sold to the famous financier Edward Francis (E.F.) Hutton (1877–1962). Hutton was chairman of several companies, including Coca-Cola, Chrysler, and General Foods Corporation. He was also married to the famous Marjorie Merriweather Post of the Post Cereal Company. The house was demolished in 1932. (Courtesy Bay Shore Historical Society.)

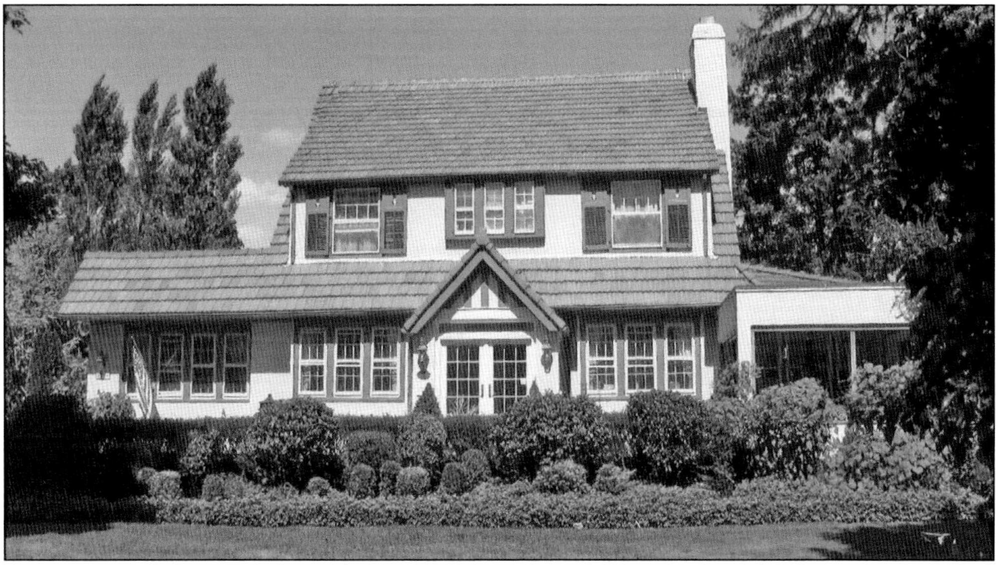

This Colonial-style home, Sweet Violet, was built in 1916 by silent film actress Anita May Stewart (1895–1961). Stewart began her acting career in 1911 and starred in such films as an early adaptation of *A Tale of Two Cities* and *The White Feather*. She also became one of the earliest female producers. The house was moved to Brightwaters and still stands today on Windsor Avenue. (Photograph by Christopher Collora.)

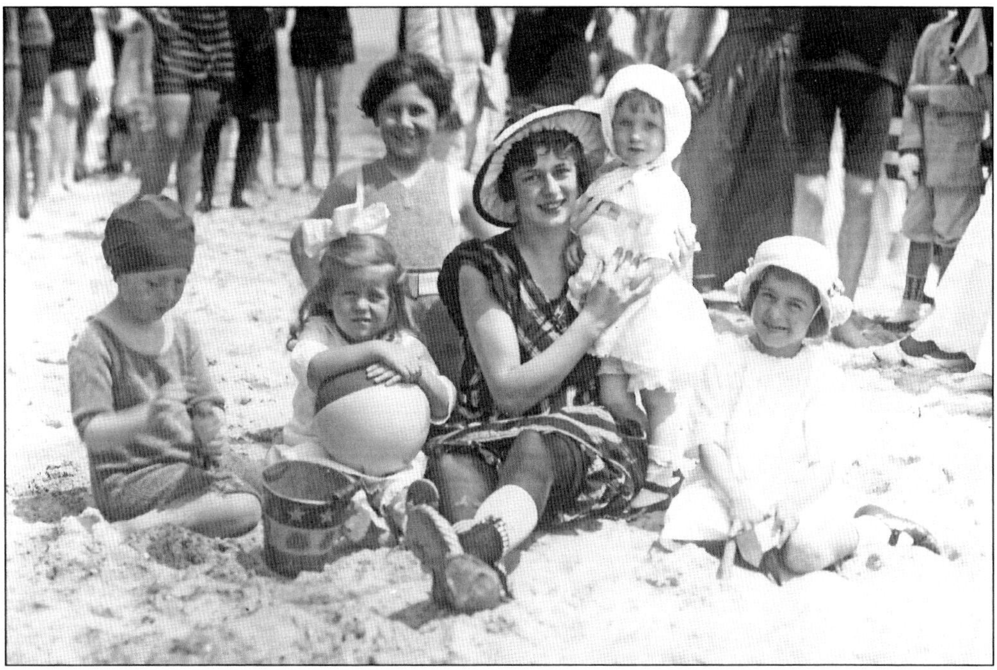

Actress Anita May Stewart, seen here on the beach, is said to have enjoyed summering in Bay Shore and Brightwaters. She would eventually sell the home and move to California. (Courtesy Bay Shore Historical Society.)

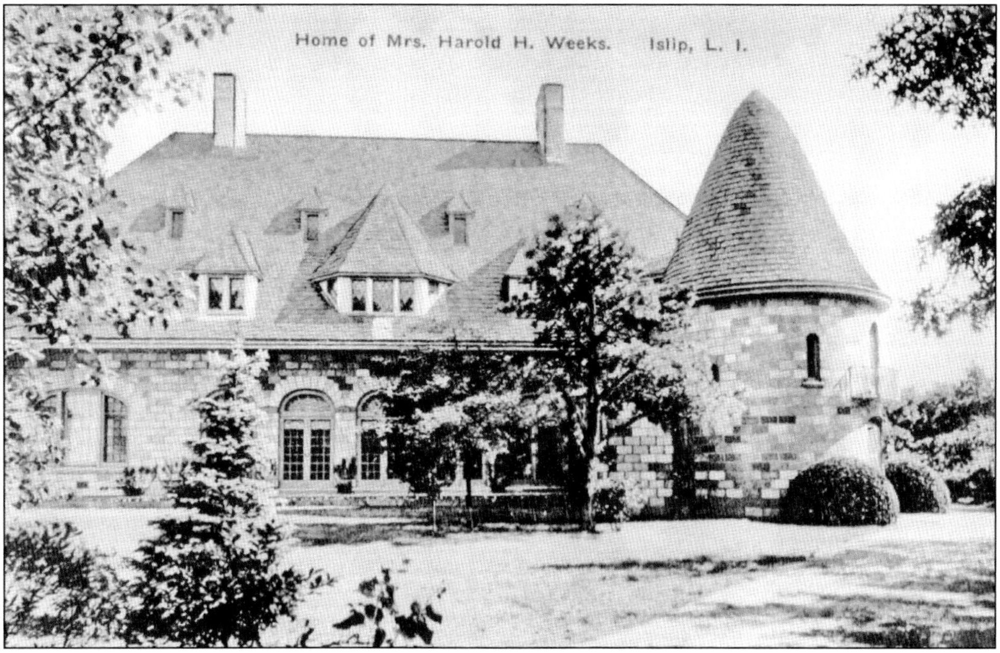

This French chateau–style mansion, named Wereholme, was built in 1917 by Harold Hathaway and Lousine Peters-Weekes. It was designed by architect Grosvenor Atterbury. It was inherited by their daughter Adeline, who married Charles B. Scully. In 1984, she willed the property to the National Audubon Society. In 2004, Suffolk County purchased the mansion. It is now the Suffolk County Environmental Interpretive Center. (Courtesy Islip Hamlet Historical Society.)

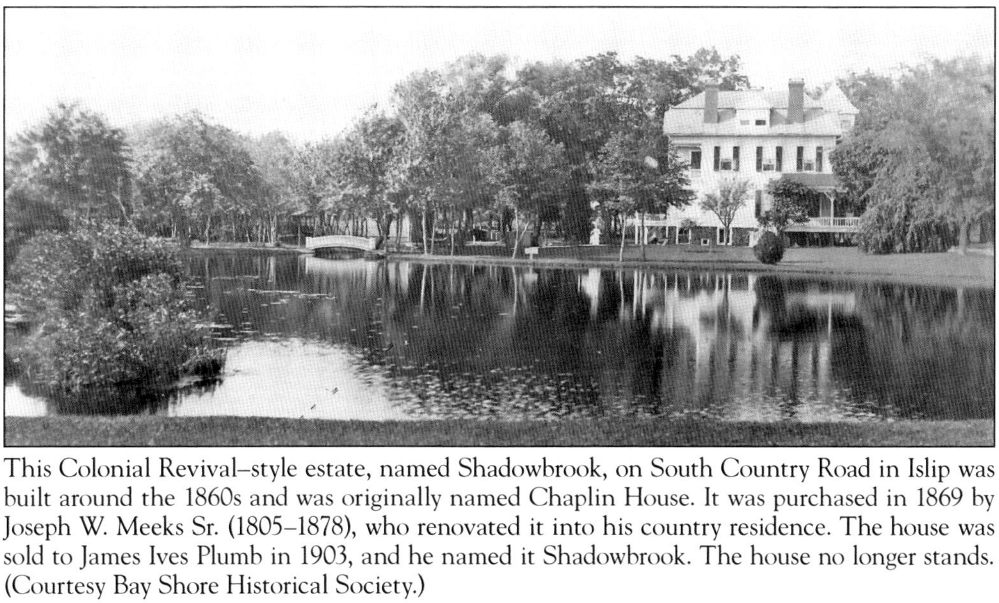

This Colonial Revival–style estate, named Shadowbrook, on South Country Road in Islip was built around the 1860s and was originally named Chaplin House. It was purchased in 1869 by Joseph W. Meeks Sr. (1805–1878), who renovated it into his country residence. The house was sold to James Ives Plumb in 1903, and he named it Shadowbrook. The house no longer stands. (Courtesy Bay Shore Historical Society.)

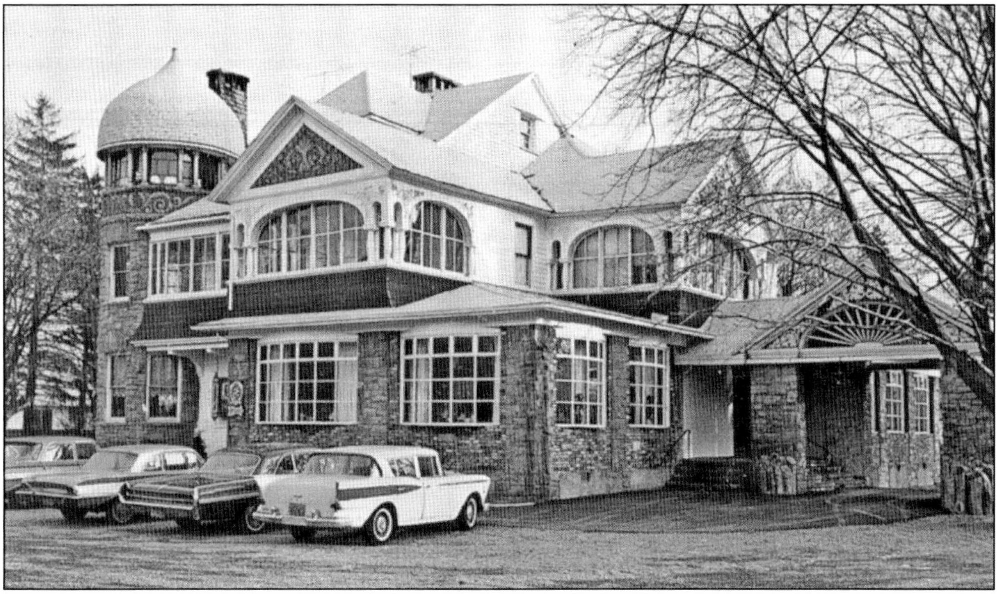

This Queen Anne–style mansion was built by sheriff and businessman Frank D. Creamer Sr. (died 1913). The home still stands today as a business building. (Courtesy Islip Hamlet Historical Society.)

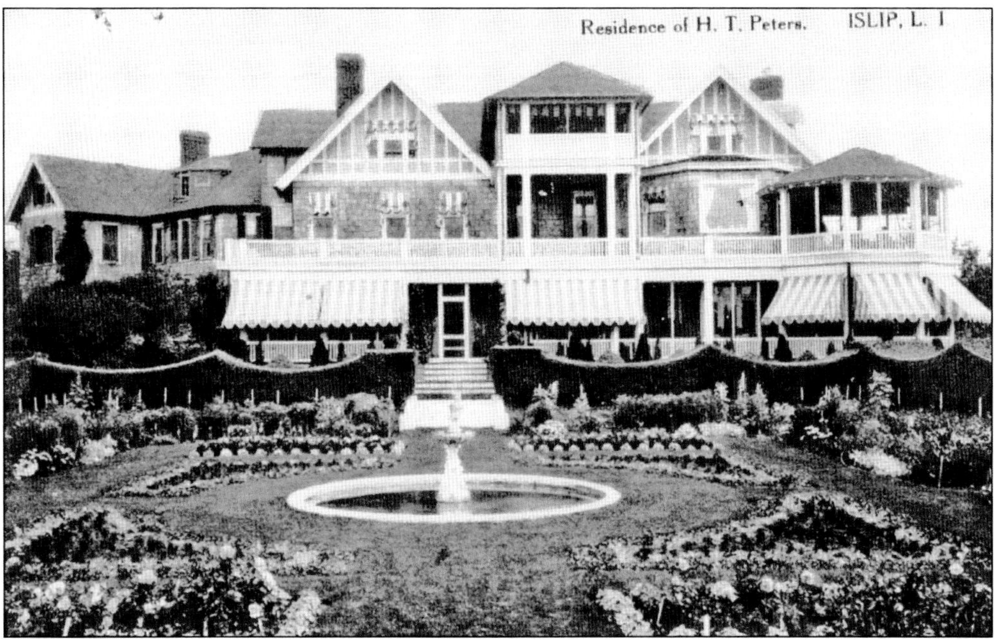

This shingle-style mansion, named Nearholm, on St. Marks Lane in Islip, was built in 1910 by coal industry businessman and author Harry Twyford Peters (1881–1948). The home no longer stands. (Courtesy Islip Hamlet Historical Society.)

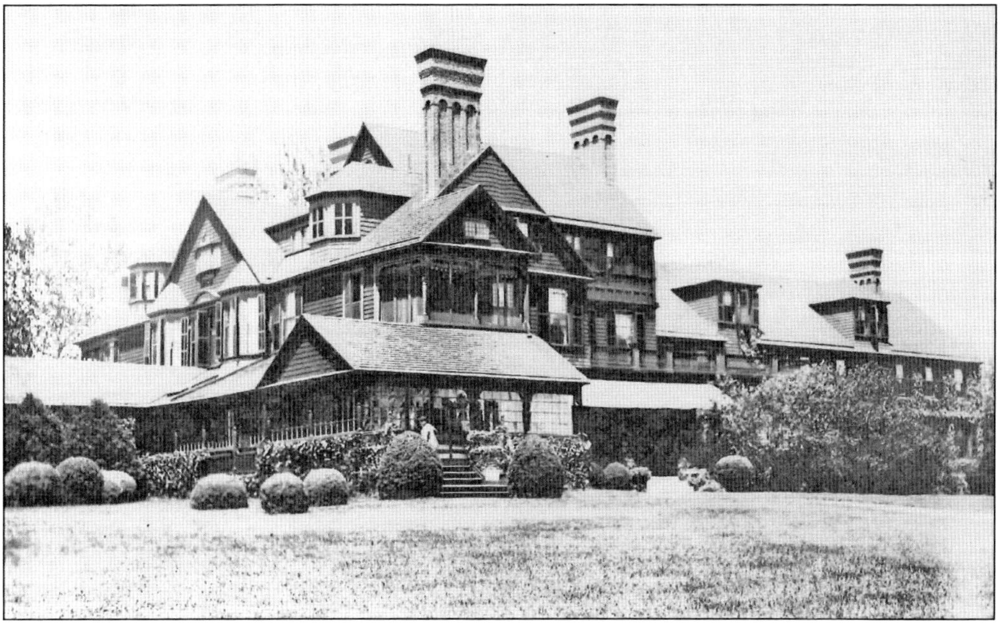

This shingle-style mansion, named Windholm Farm, was built in 1850 by John Prince. It was later purchased by Samuel Twyford Peters (1854–1921), who had it redesigned by architect Alfred Hopkins in 1910. The house and farm were demolished in the 1950s. (Courtesy Islip Hamlet Historical Society.)

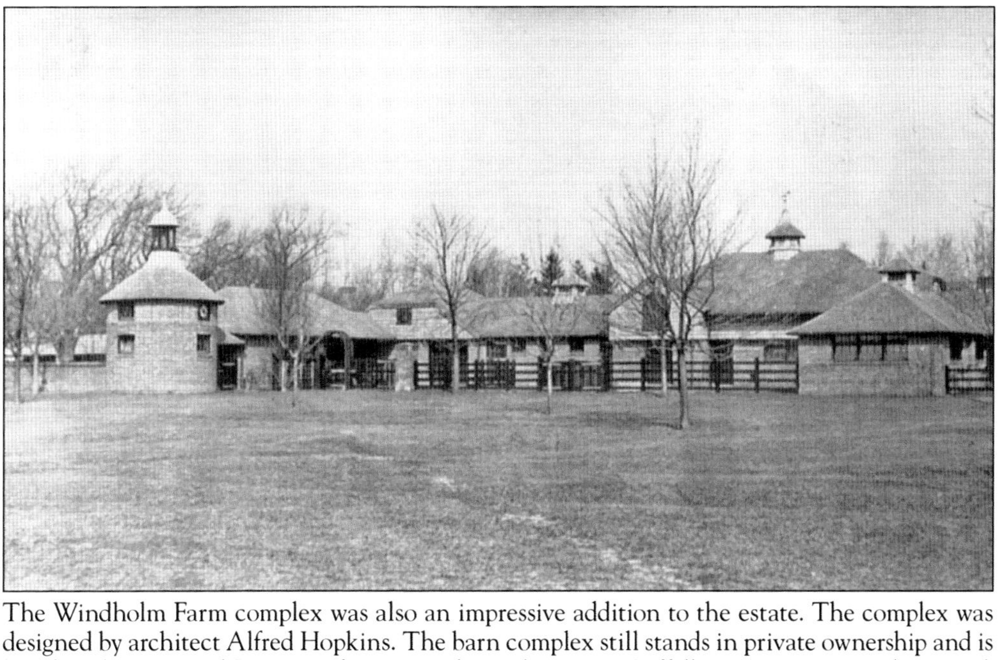

The Windholm Farm complex was also an impressive addition to the estate. The complex was designed by architect Alfred Hopkins. The barn complex still stands in private ownership and is listed in the National Register of Historic Places. (Courtesy Suffolk County Historical Society.)

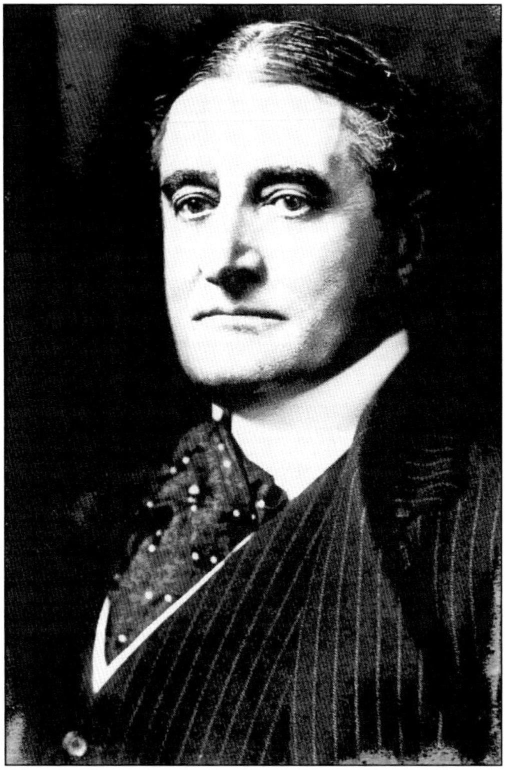

Samuel Twyford Peters (1854–1921) was a coal industry businessman and financier. He was also a collector of art, including Chinese porcelain and jade specimens. He was a trustee of the Metropolitan Museum of Art. After summering on Long Island, he purchased and redesigned Windholm in 1910. (Courtesy Islip Hamlet Historical Society.)

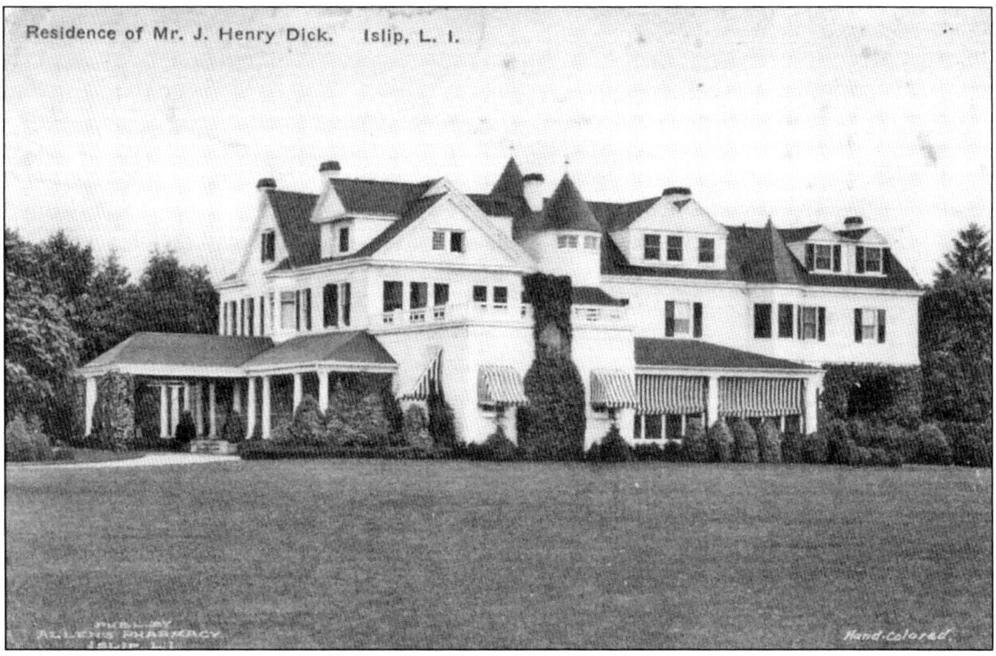

This Victorian–style mansion, named Allen Winden Farm, was built around 1880 by Charles Tucker. It was later purchased by banker and sugar refining company director William Dick (1823–1912). The home was designed by architect Isaac Henry Greene. It was demolished around 1960. (Courtesy Dowling College Library Archives and Special Collections.)

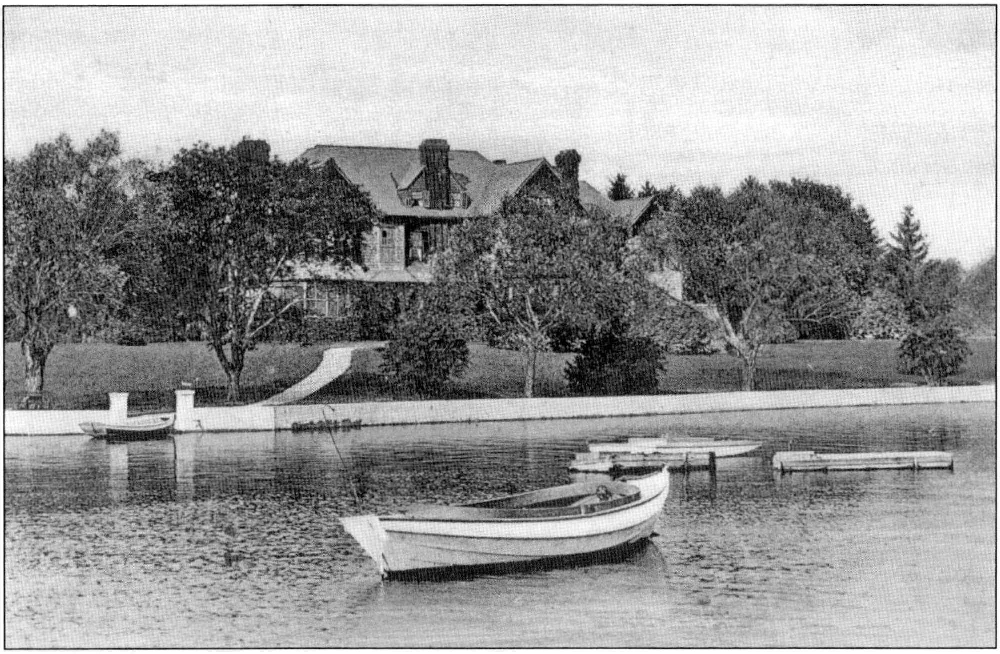

This shingle-style mansion, named Whileaway, was built around 1881 by businessman Schuyler Parsons Sr. (1852–1917). The home sat on 40 acres on Champlain Creek. (Courtesy East Islip Historical Society.)

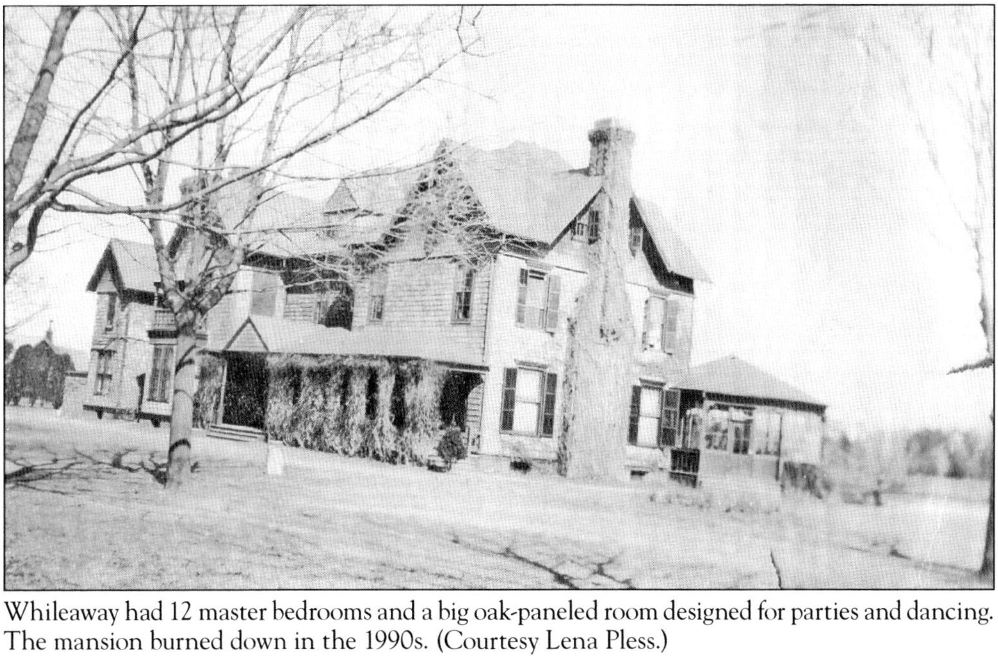

Whileaway had 12 master bedrooms and a big oak-paneled room designed for parties and dancing. The mansion burned down in the 1990s. (Courtesy Lena Pless.)

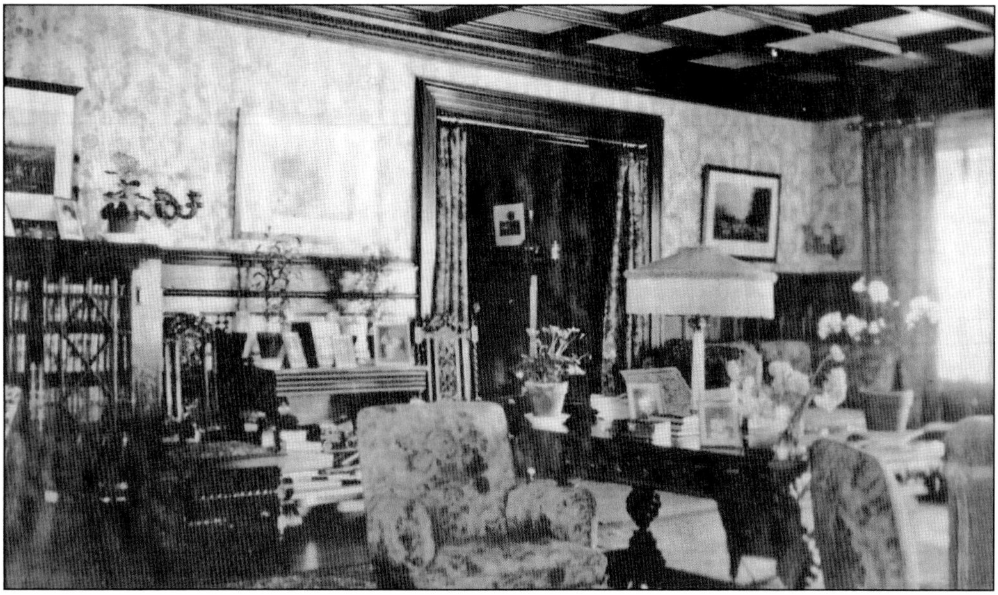

This rare interior shot of Whileaway from the family photo album shows a living room area around 1910. (Courtesy Lena Pless.)

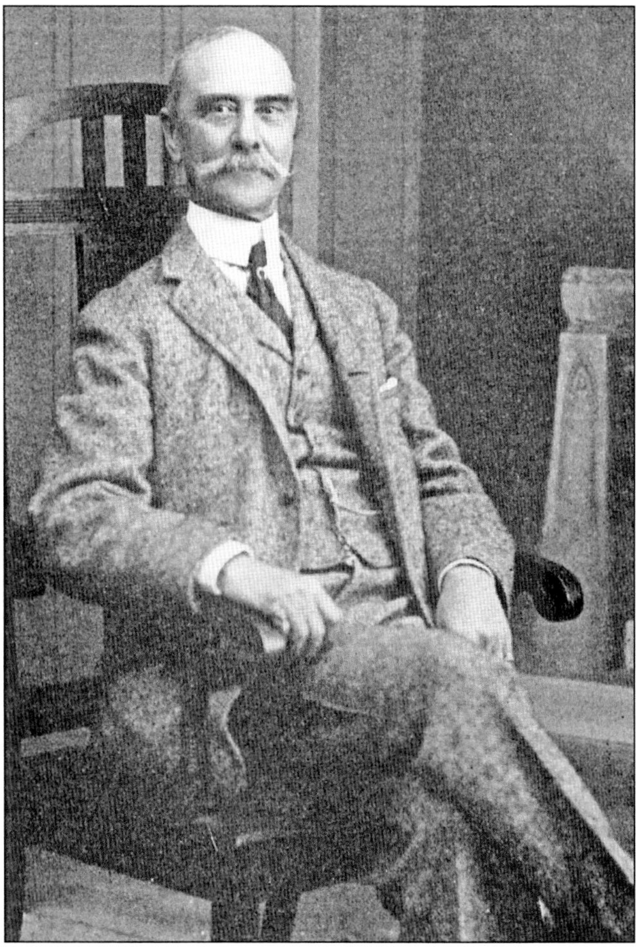

Schuyler Parsons Sr. (1852–1917) was president of a wholesale chemical company. He was friends with William K. Vanderbilt Sr. When they were deciding what to name their estates, they both liked the name Idlehour; a coin toss decided the matter. (Courtesy Jackie Ruffino.)

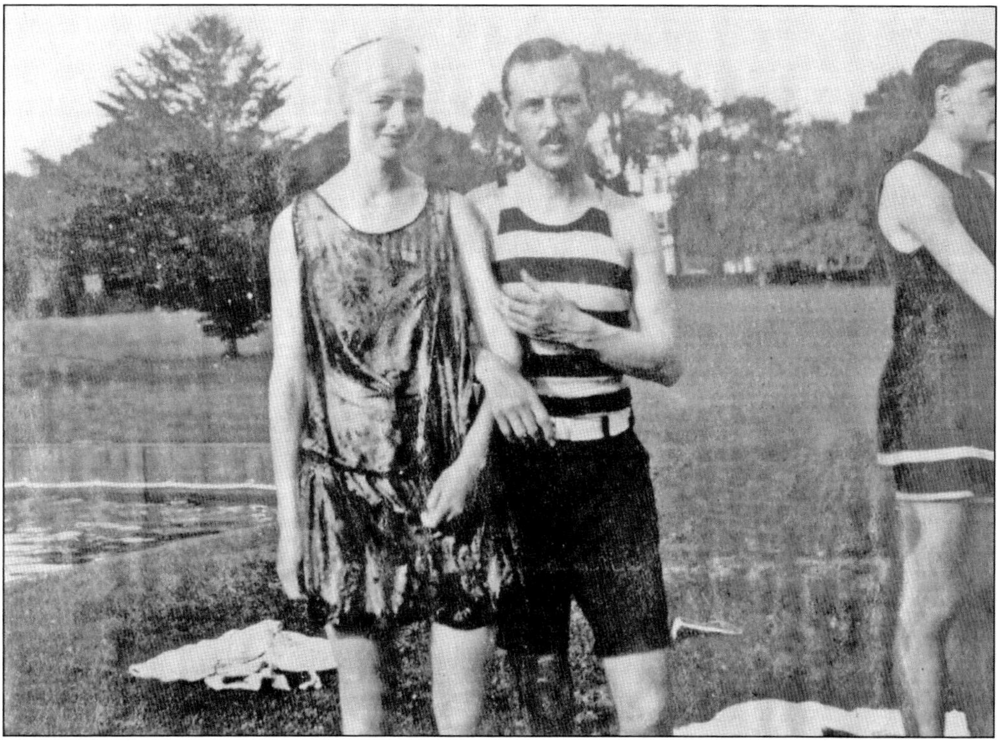

Schuyler Parsons Jr. (1892–1967), seen here with his sister Helena, lived at Pleasure Island and could have been called a South Shore Gatsby. He was a well-known personality in the 1920s. Frequent party guests to Pleasure Island from 1924 to 1928 included Charlie Chaplin, Gertrude Lawrence, Rudolph Valentino, Beatrice Lillie, Cole Porter, Helen Hayes, Noël Coward, Douglas Fairbanks, Diana Manners, George Gershwin, and Charles Lindbergh. (Courtesy Lena Pless.)

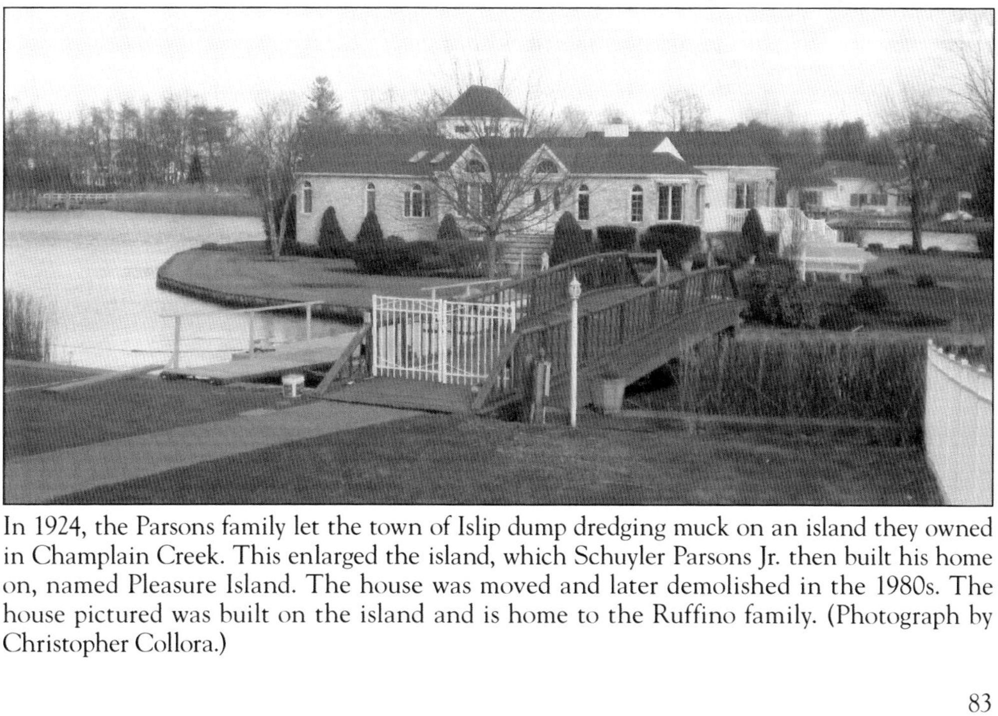

In 1924, the Parsons family let the town of Islip dump dredging muck on an island they owned in Champlain Creek. This enlarged the island, which Schuyler Parsons Jr. then built his home on, named Pleasure Island. The house was moved and later demolished in the 1980s. The house pictured was built on the island and is home to the Ruffino family. (Photograph by Christopher Collora.)

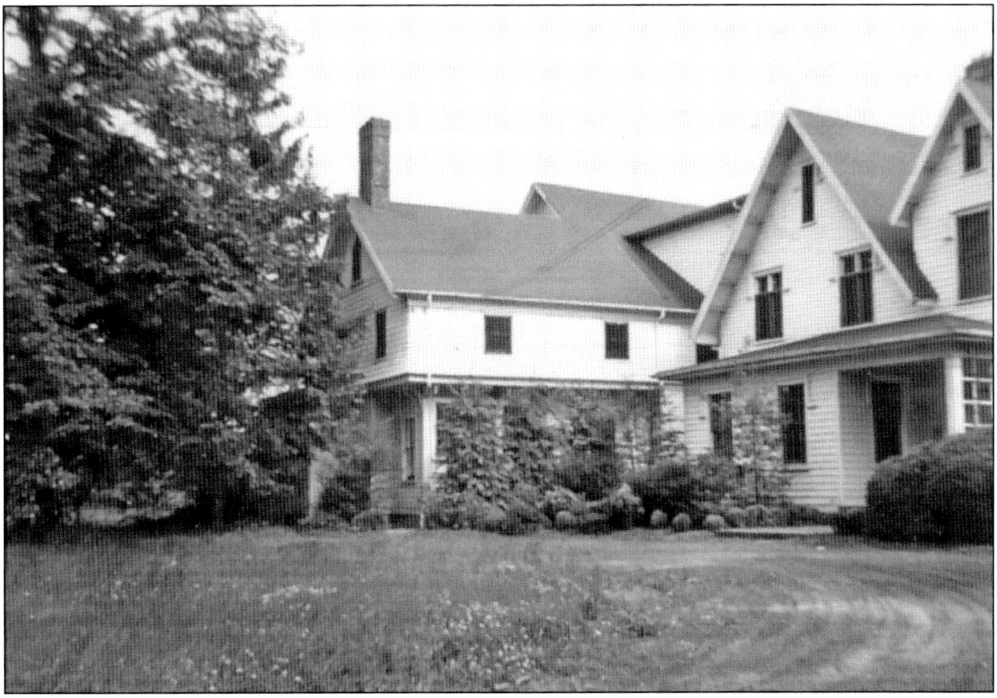

This Gothic Revival–style home was once owned by dancer Fred Astaire (1899–1987). It was built in 1847 by John Johnson. The house was purchased in 1887 by the Livingstons and then by the Bull family. In 1931, Phyllis Livingston Potter met Fred Astaire at a party at Idlehour. They married and used the home as a summer residence. Fred Astaire's sister Adele also lived there for a while. (Courtesy Ellen Egelman.)

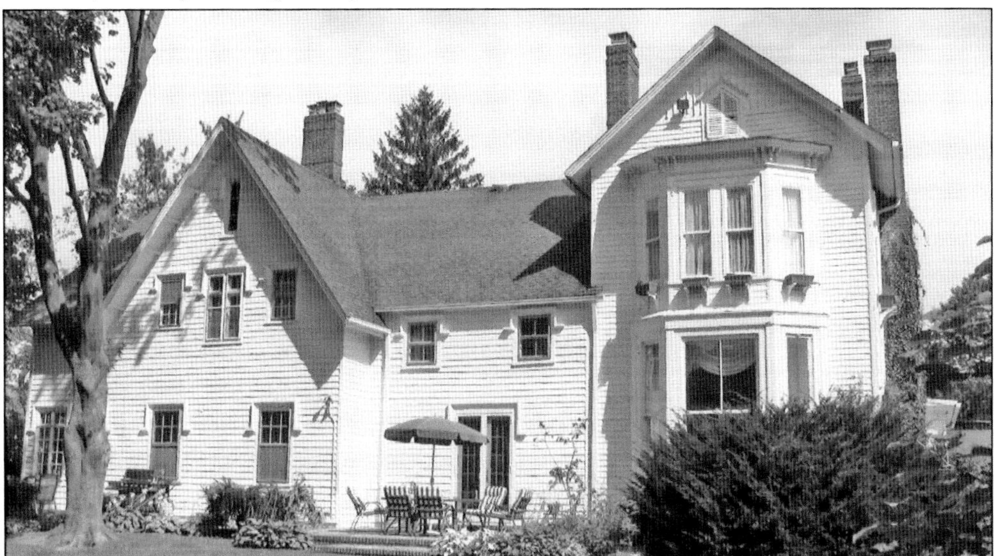

The Astaire house, seen here from the rear, still stands as a private residence owned by Russ and Lynda Moran. The home has 25 rooms, including seven bedrooms. Astaire performed with his sister Adele at the 1927 Venetian Fete fundraiser for South Side Hospital and was well known in the community. (Photograph by Christopher Collora.)

Six

East Islip and Great River

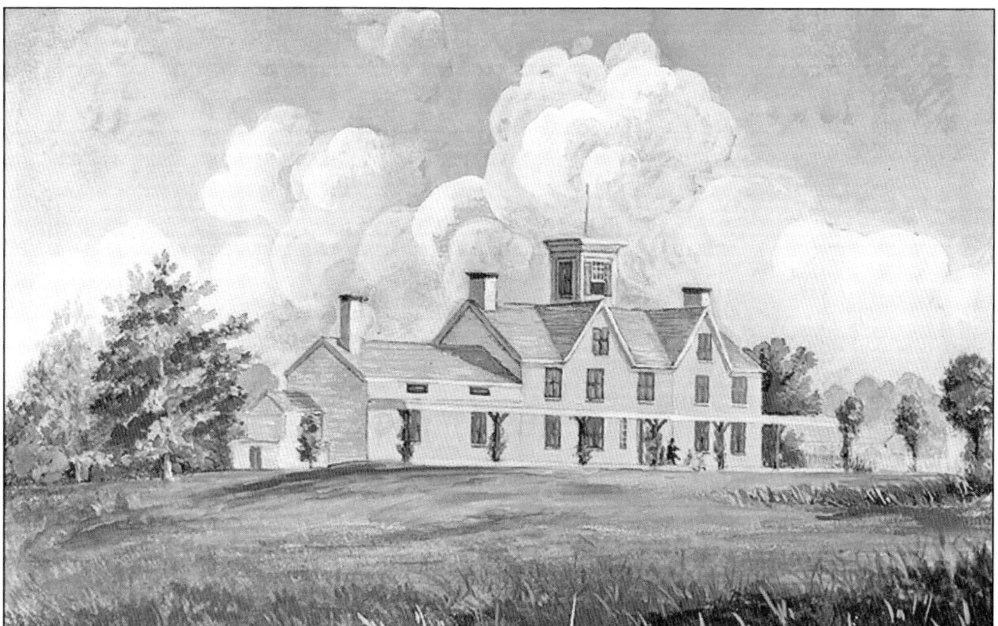

This Colonial-style mansion, named Islip Grange, was built around 1710 by Islip founder William Nicoll (1657–1723). The house and land remained in the family for several generations. Legend has it that this is the second house he built. The first house is said to have been located two miles farther east. Artifacts were found and returned to the Nicoll family that suggest there was an earlier home built. Islip Grange was demolished in 1910. Some salvaged pieces appeared in subsequent local mansions. It was partially excavated in the 1980s. The mansion was located in what is now Heckscher State Park. (Courtesy East Islip Historical Society.)

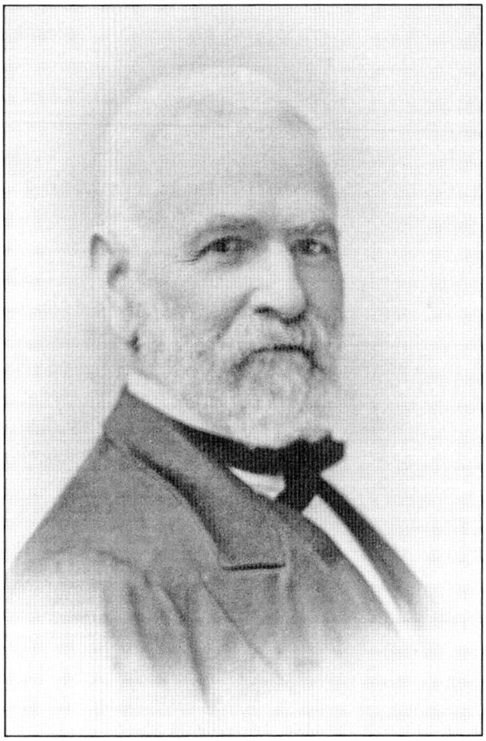

William Nicoll VII (1820–1900) was descended from William Nicoll (1657–1723), who was the founder of Islip town. In 1683, founder William Nicoll purchased the land that became Islip from the sachem of the Connetquot tribe. William Nicoll named his home Islip Grange after his hometown in England. The Nicoll family owned the land until William Nicoll VII sold off the Nicoll holdings. (Courtesy East Islip Historical Society.)

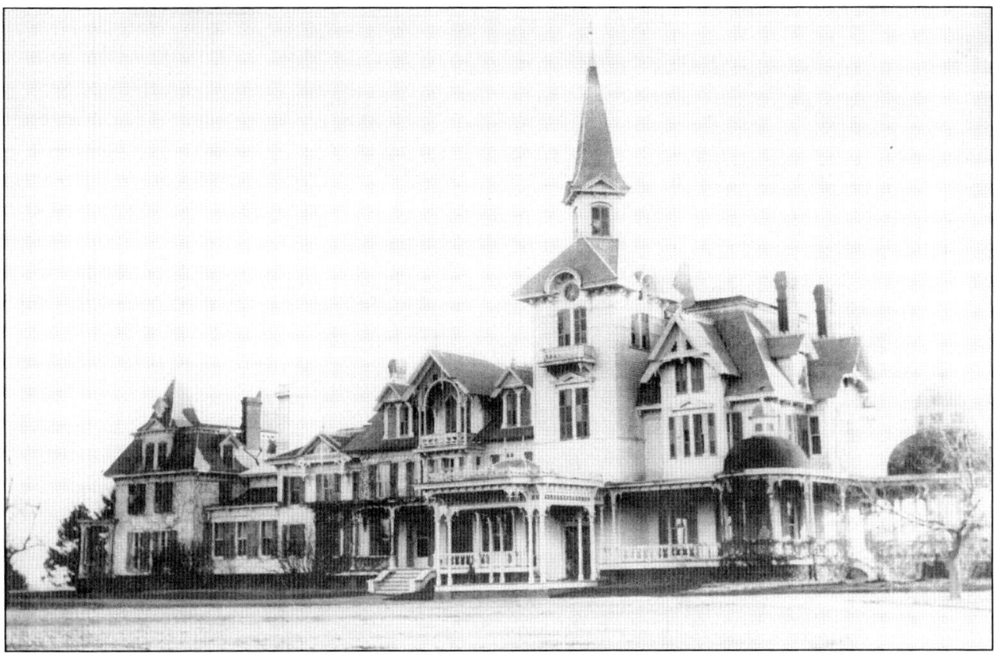

Deer Range Farm was built by Edwin Johnson around 1850. In 1872, it was purchased by Sarah Ives Plumb (died 1877). Her husband, James Neal Plumb, then made architectural alterations. In 1899, Plumb murdered the administrator of his wife's trust; Plumb later died of erysipelas in jail. The estate was inherited by James Ives Plumb, who sold it to George Taylor. It was later demolished. (Courtesy East Islip Historical Society.)

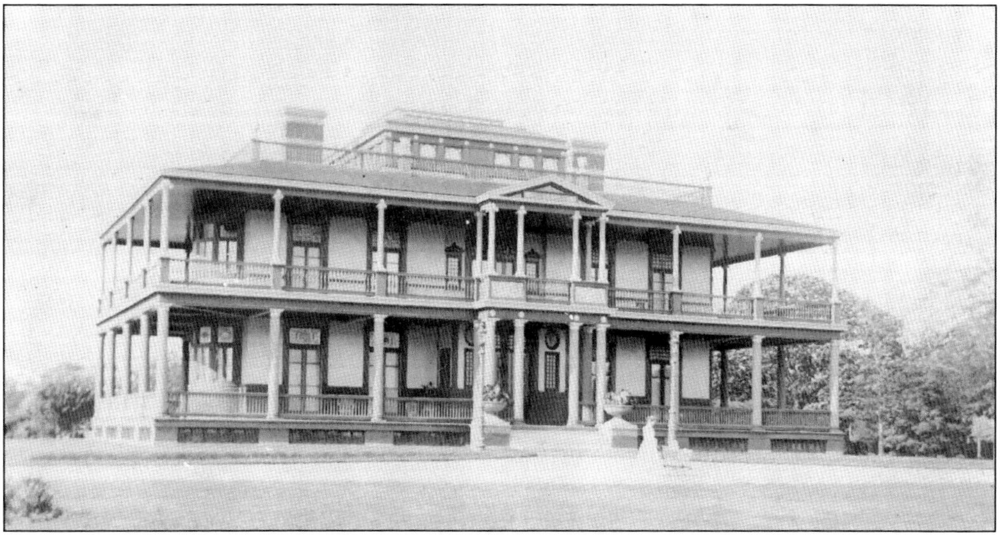

This mansion, on the site of Islip founder William Nicoll's land, was built in 1885 by diplomat George Campbell Taylor (1835–1908). The house was the center of controversy involving Long Island State Parks commissioner Robert Moses, who used eminent domain to annex and demolish the house in 1933 to create Heckscher State Park despite lawsuits and local resident objections. (Courtesy East Islip Historical Society.)

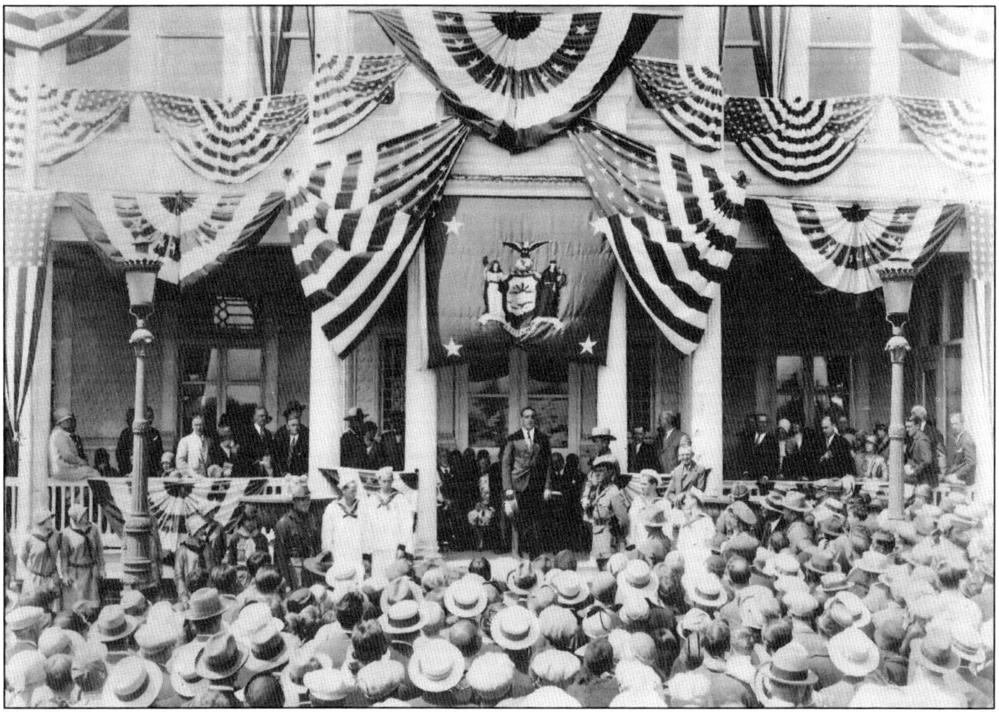

Here is Robert Moses speaking at the opening of Heckscher State Park in East Islip in 1929. This was a controversial decision at the time. The case traveled to the Supreme Court of the United States and involved 25 appellate proceedings. A campaign was waged by citizens fighting the plans by Long Island State Parks commissioner Robert Moses. (Courtesy Village of Babylon Historic and Preservation Society.)

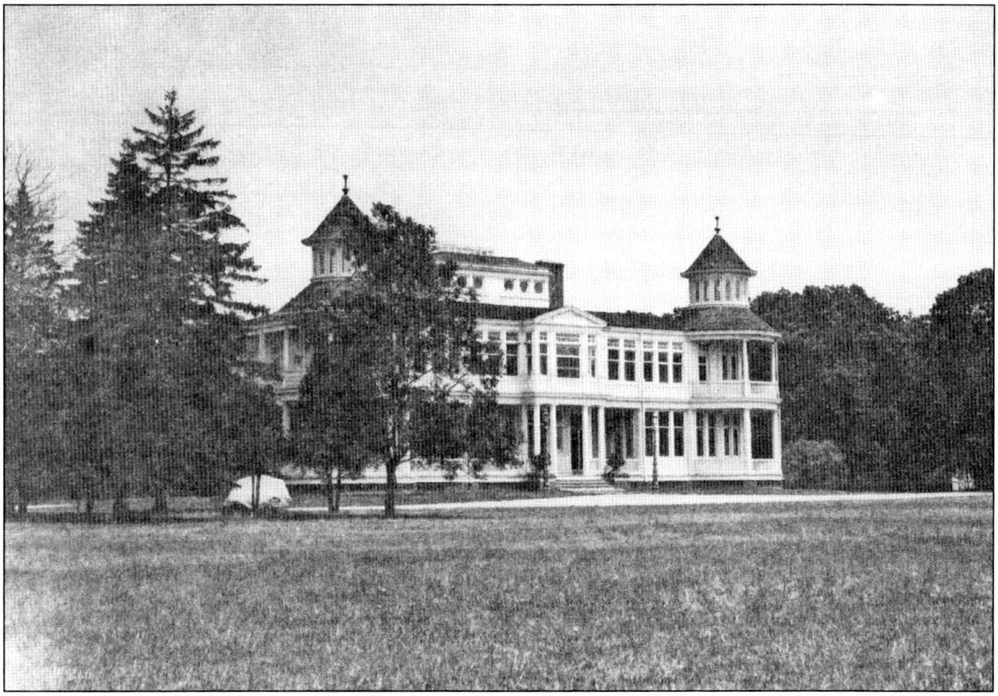

Taylor had the outside of the mansion redesigned from its original structure. It is said that all the rooms in the mansion were frescoed and finished with different colored woods. This is how it looked before it was demolished in 1933. (Courtesy East Islip Historical Society.)

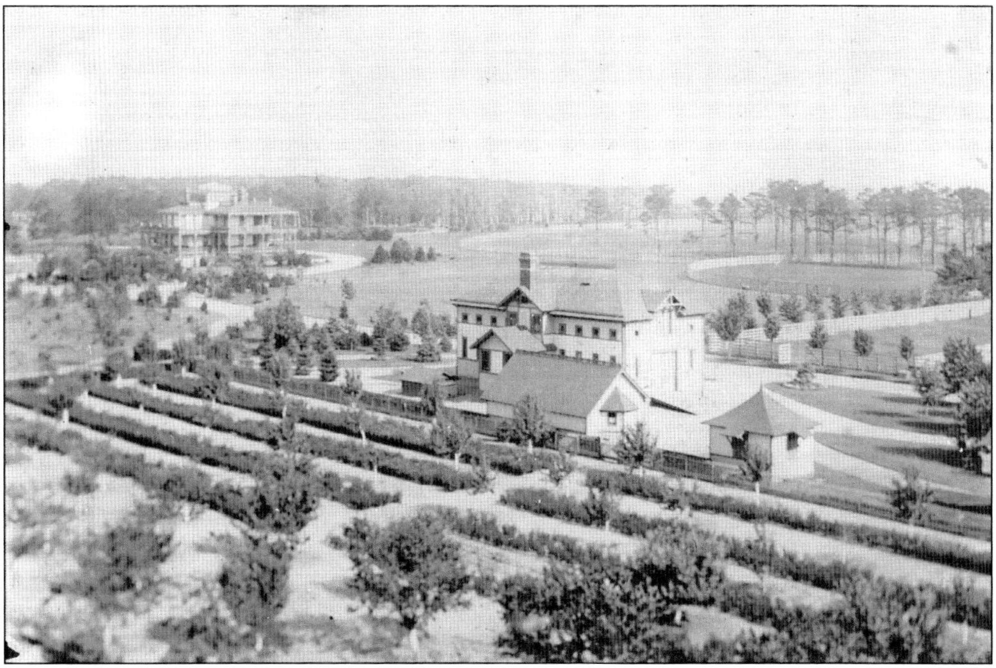

In 1903, Taylor increased the size of the estate to 1,500 acres by purchasing the adjoining Plumb estate. The estate had 30 outbuildings. The barn in the center of this picture still stands. (Courtesy East Islip Historical Society.)

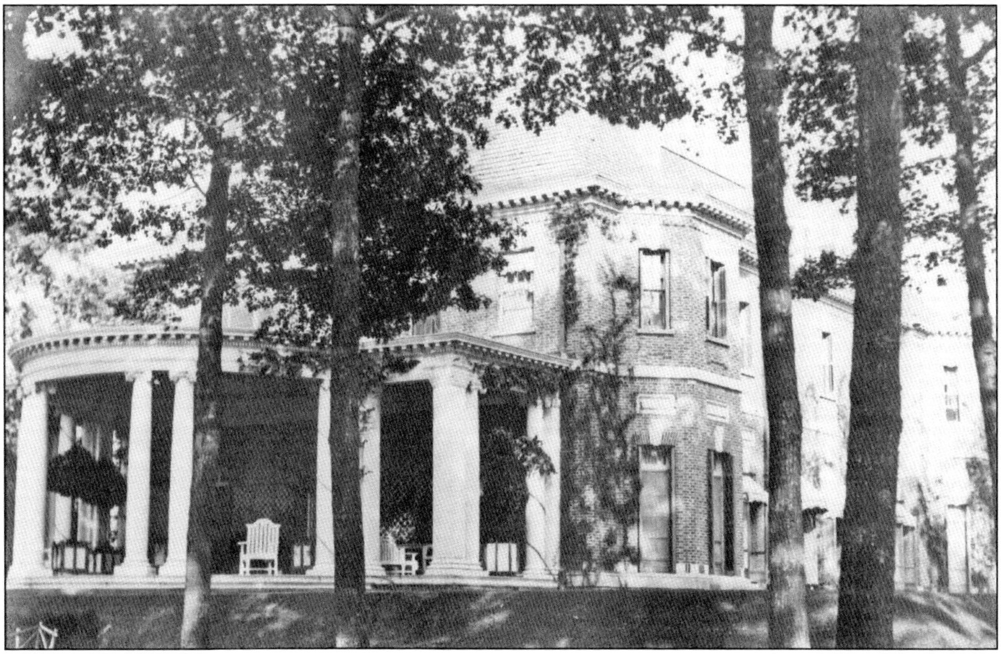

This 41-room Georgian Revivial-style mansion, named Brookwood Hall, was designed by architects Delano and Aldrich and built in 1903 by Harry Knapp. In 1929, the mansion was sold to Francis Thorne. In 1942, the Thorne family sold it to the Orphan Asylum Society of Brooklyn. The Town of Islip bought it in 1967. Today, it is home to the Islip Arts Council, the Islip Arts Museum, and the Town of Islip Parks, Recreation, and Cultural Affairs Departments. (Courtesy East Islip Historical Society.)

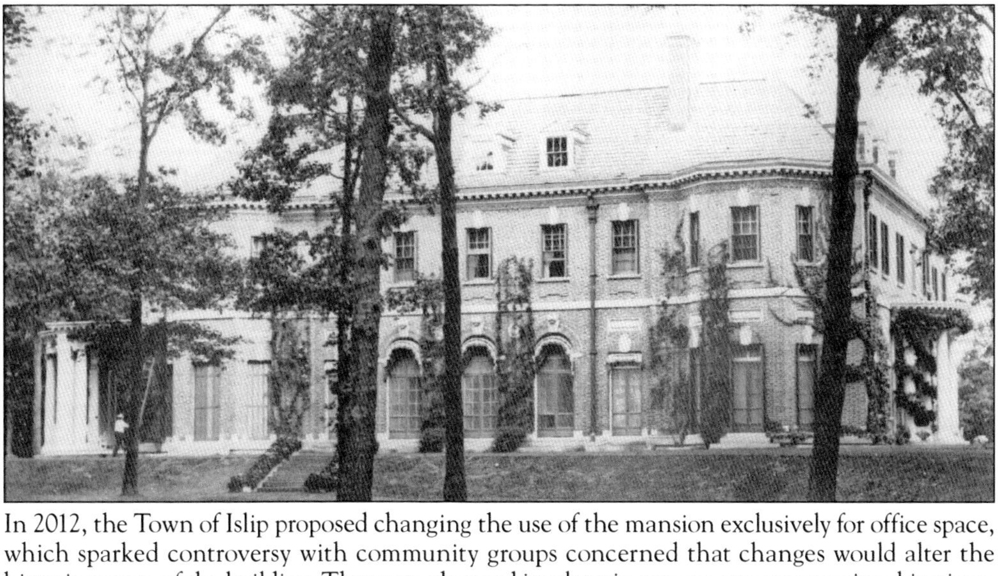

In 2012, the Town of Islip proposed changing the use of the mansion exclusively for office space, which sparked controversy with community groups concerned that changes would alter the historic nature of the building. The town changed its plans in response to community objections. Brookwood Hall remains one of few historic South Shore mansions that can be accessed by the public as a cultural center. (Courtesy East Islip Historical Society.)

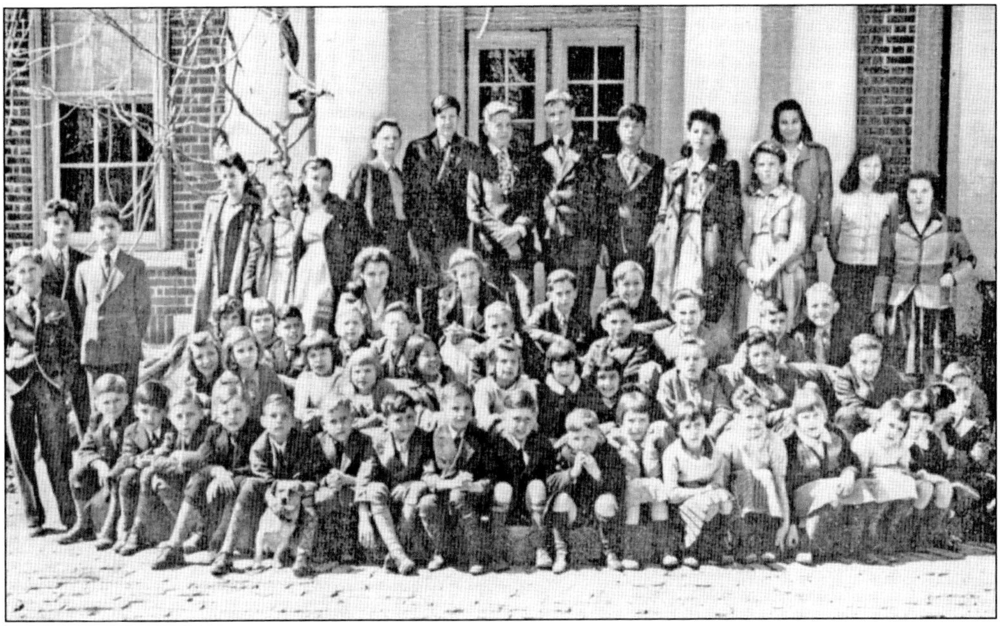

A group picture shows the first orphan children who came to the Brookwood mansion in 1942, when it was used by the Orphan Asylum Society of Brooklyn. (Courtesy East Islip Historical Society.)

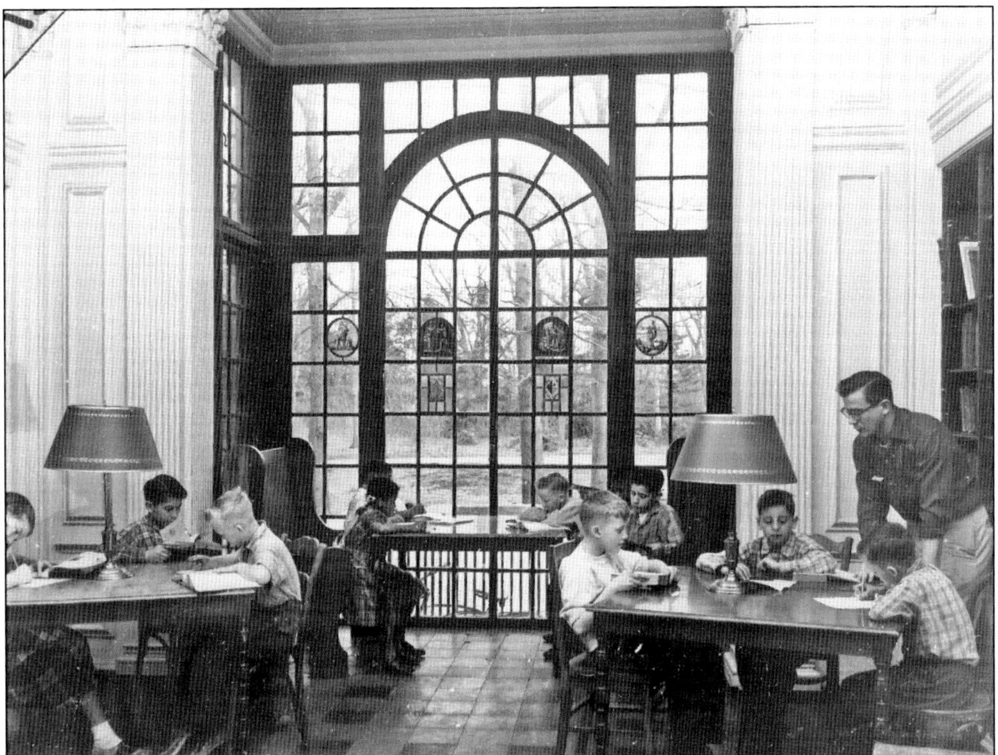

Some of the orphans who grew up in the mansion said it was a truly magnificent home to grow up in. This is the library, which is jointly used as town offices and by the Islip Arts Council. (Courtesy East Islip Historical Society.)

Frank Szemko is one of the orphans who grew up at Brookwood Hall. He is pictured here at age 13 in 1948. Szemko says he has fond memories of the mansion, including ice skating on the pond and the annual Christmas tree tradition that the orphans enjoyed, started by the Knapp family and carried on through the time the mansion was used as the orphans' home. (Courtesy East Islip Historical Society.)

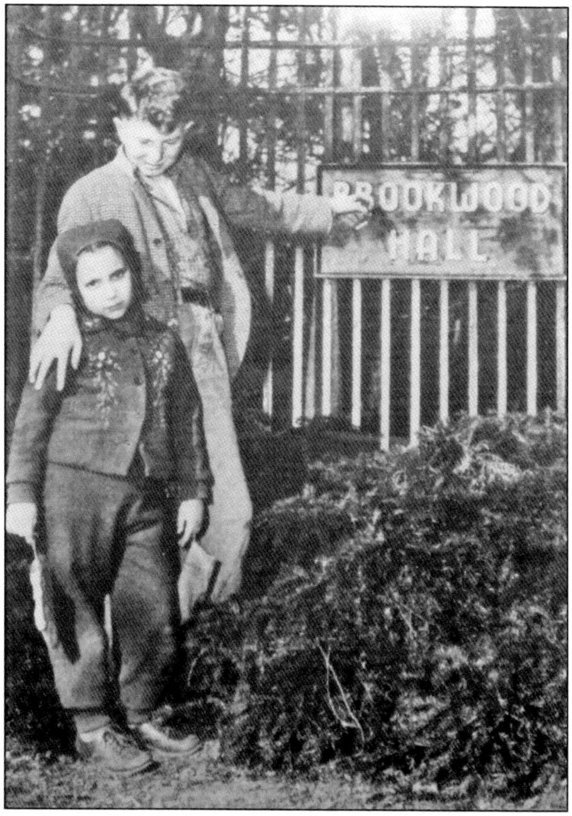

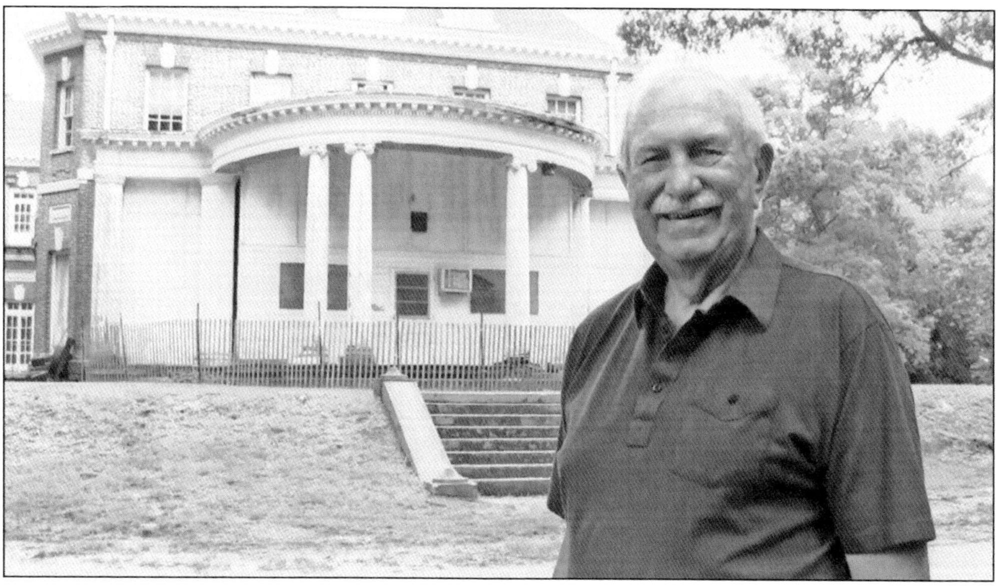

Frank Szemko today says he is happy the mansion still stands but is disappointed that some areas of the mansion, like the front porch, are deteriorating. "When I was here as a kid, this was a showplace, especially the front porch," says Szemko. When he sees the condition it is in, he says it bothers him. "It makes me think what did this building do to deserve that?" (Photograph by Christopher Collora.)

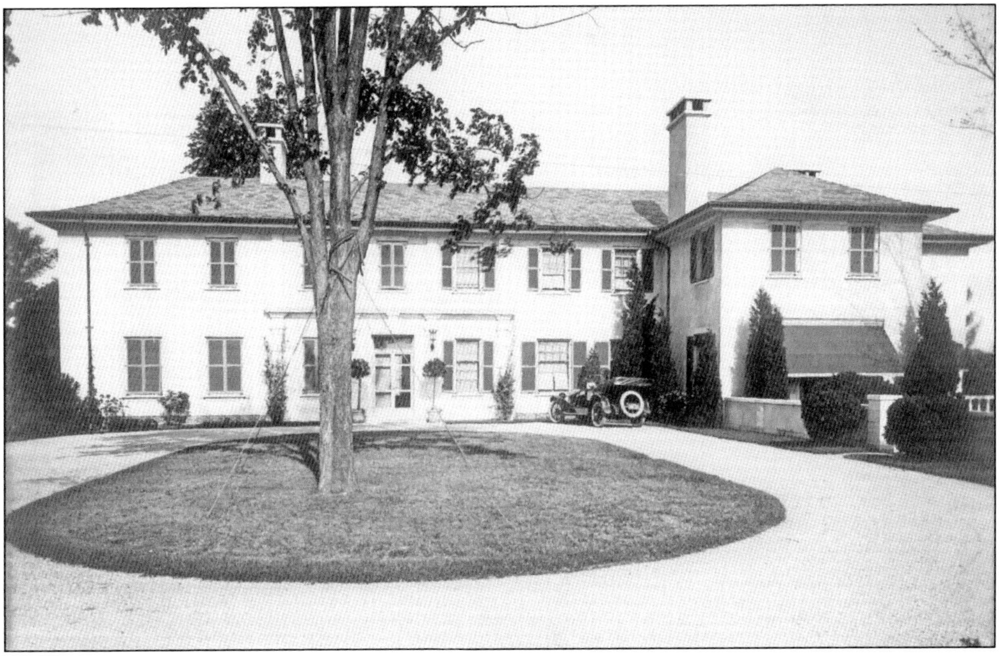

This Mediterranean villa–style mansion, named Rosemary, on Suffolk Lane was built in 1917 by stockbroker and financier Jay Freeborn Carlisle (1868–1937). The estate was designed by Trowbridge and Ackerman. The home also had several construction innovations unique to the time. The house was built to be fireproof and had a waterproof "tub" style basement. The mansion was demolished in 1938. (Courtesy East Islip Historical Society.)

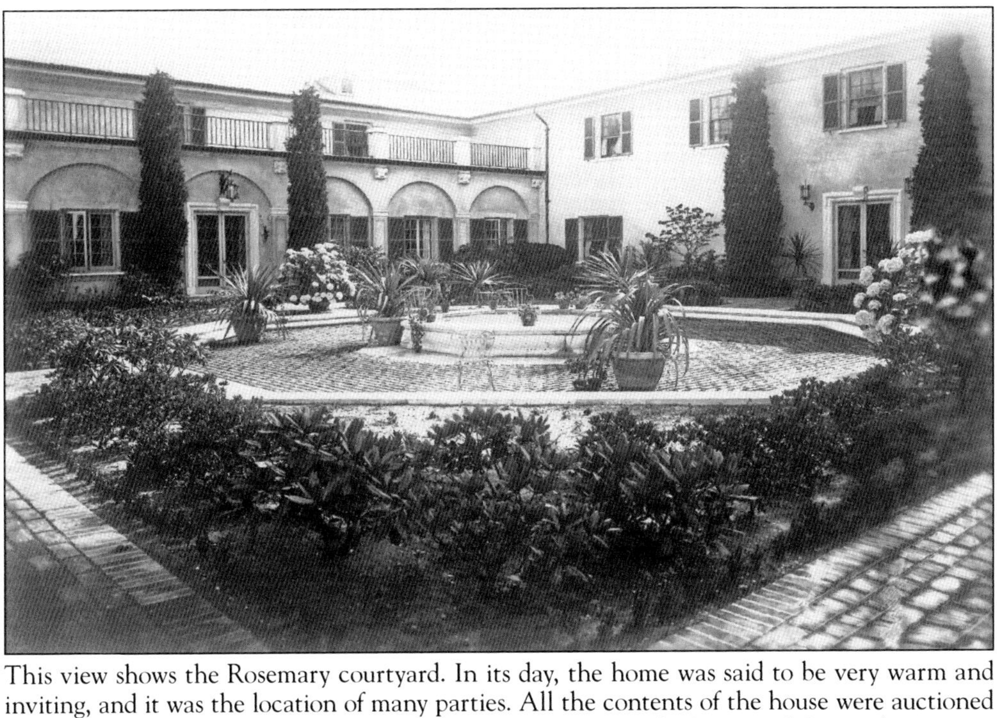

This view shows the Rosemary courtyard. In its day, the home was said to be very warm and inviting, and it was the location of many parties. All the contents of the house were auctioned off by Sotheby's in its first American auction. (Courtesy East Islip Historical Society.)

Pictured here are Jay Freeborn Carlisle and his wife, Mary Pinkerton Carlisle. The couple died within a few months of each other. None of the children wanted the mansion or its contents. (Courtesy East Islip Historical Society.)

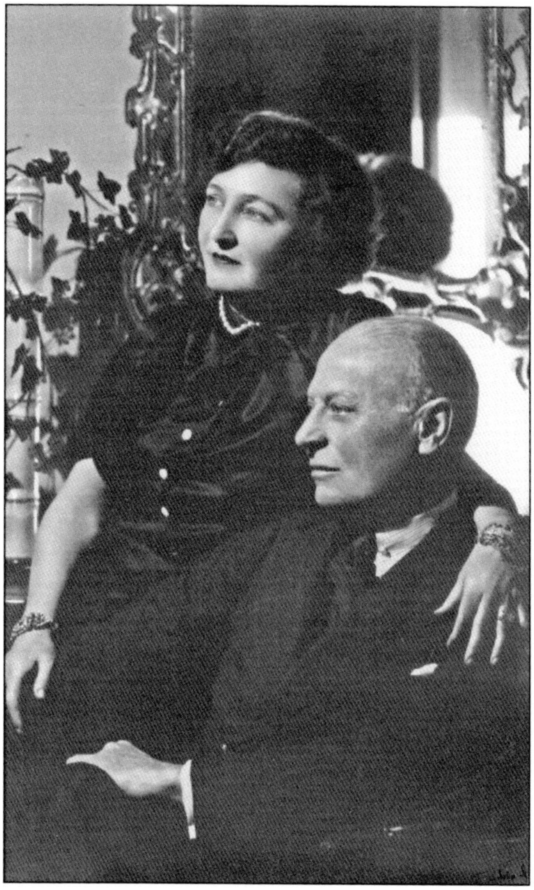

This Shingle-style mansion, named Pine Acres, was built in 1911 by theater owner and entertainer Percy Williams. After his wife's death, the house was used as a rest home for actors at Williams's bequest. The actors were to be treated in the lifestyle they had become accustomed to. The house was demolished in 1975. (Courtesy East Islip Historical Society.)

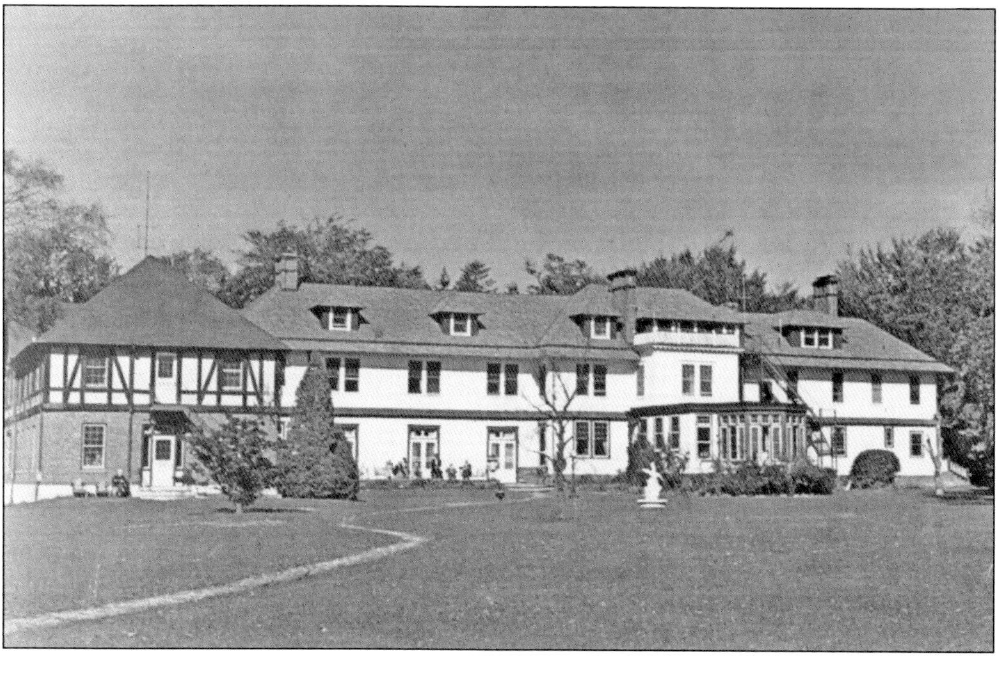

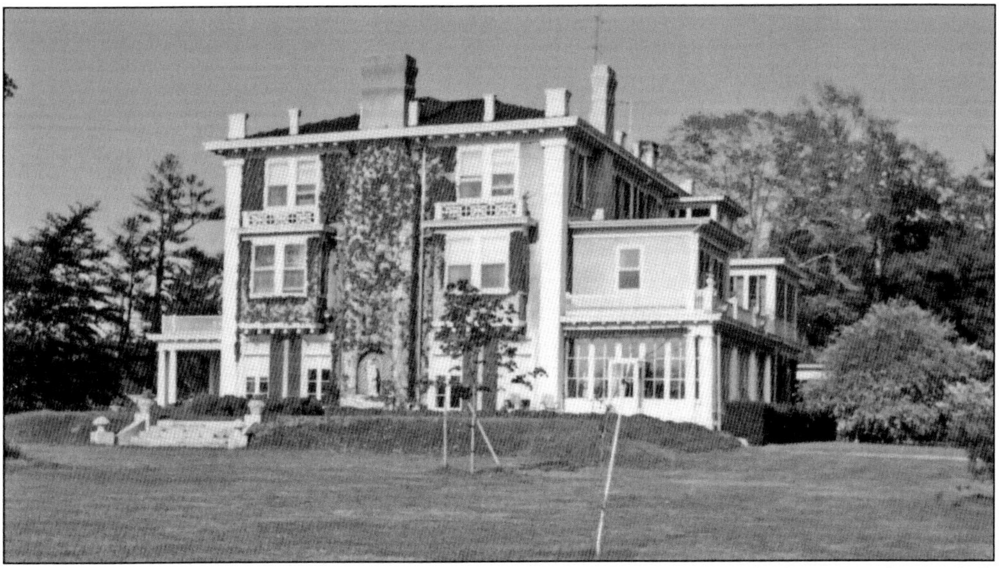

This Neo-Federal-style mansion, named Woodland, on Suffolk Lane was built in 1909 by Bradish Johnson Jr. (1853–1918). The original home on the site, also named Woodland, burned down in 1905. The new home was designed by architect Isaac Henry Green. In 1942, the family sold the estate to the Hewlett School. (Courtesy East Islip Historical Society.)

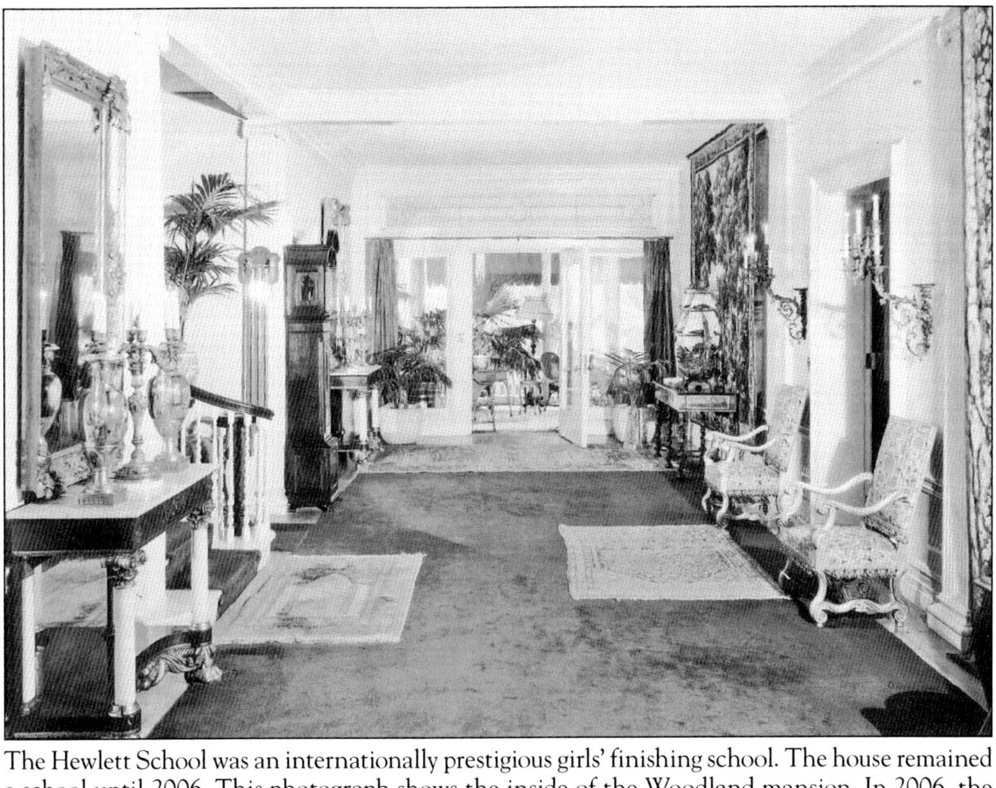

The Hewlett School was an internationally prestigious girls' finishing school. The house remained a school until 2006. This photograph shows the inside of the Woodland mansion. In 2006, the home was sold to a developer. The house still stands today and is for sale awaiting its fate. (Courtesy East Islip Historical Society.)

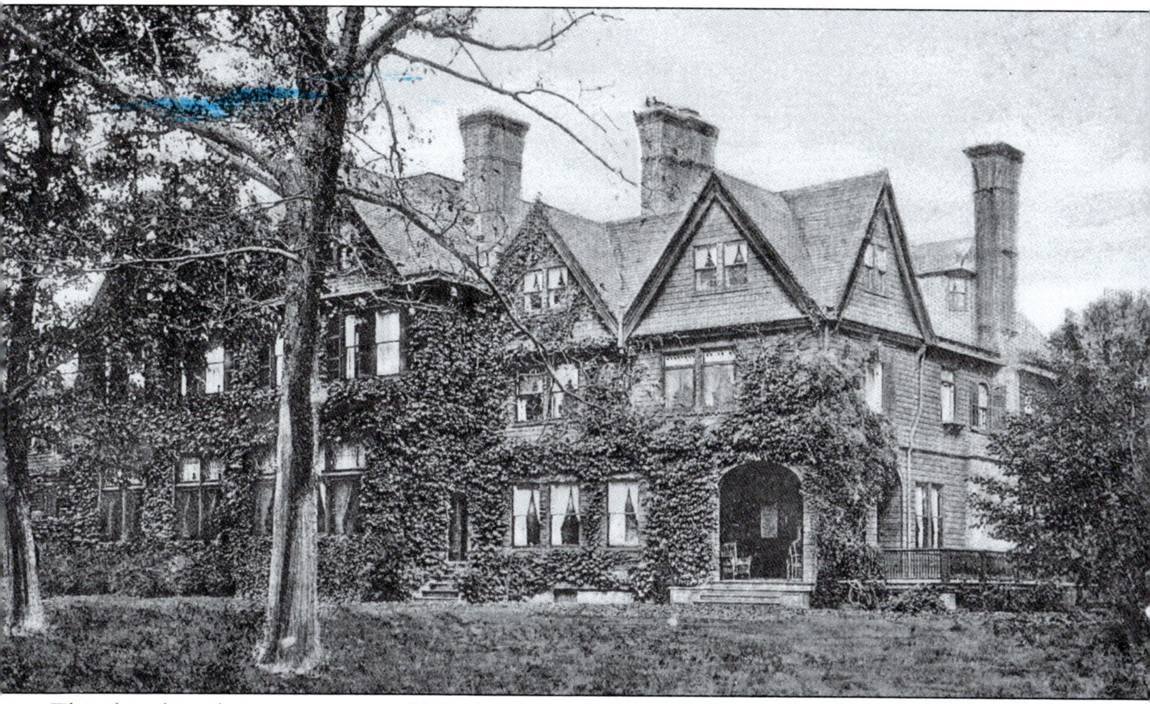

This shingle-style mansion, named Meadow Farm, was built around 1880 by stockbroker Harry Hollins (1854–1939). Hollins was the stockbroker for William K. Vanderbilt Sr. In 1917, Hollins sold the home to inventor Charles Lawrance, who lived there until 1940. The house has been redesigned several times over the years and can no longer be said to be the original home. Lawrance, the longest owner of Meadow Farm, designed and invented the Wright whirlwind engine used on airplanes, including ones flown by Charles Lindbergh and Amelia Earhart. (Courtesy East Islip Historical Society.)

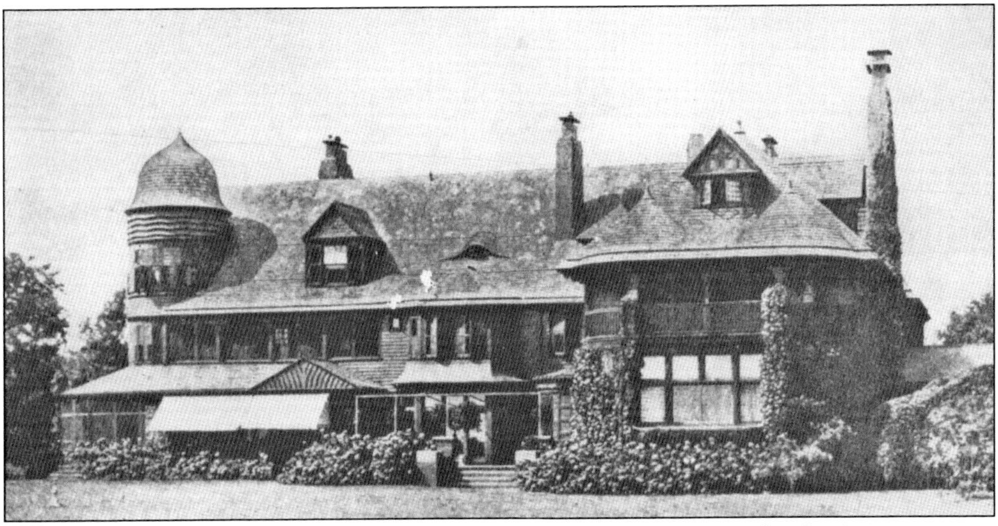

Timber Point was built in 1882 by William Laurence Breese (1852–1888). The 300-acre estate offered views of Great River and the Great South Bay. Later, the house and land was leased to the South Side Sportsman's Club for hunting. In 1905, Julian Tappan Davies purchased the mansion. He died in 1920, and his family sold the mansion to the Great River Club in 1923. (Courtesy Suffolk County Parks Department.)

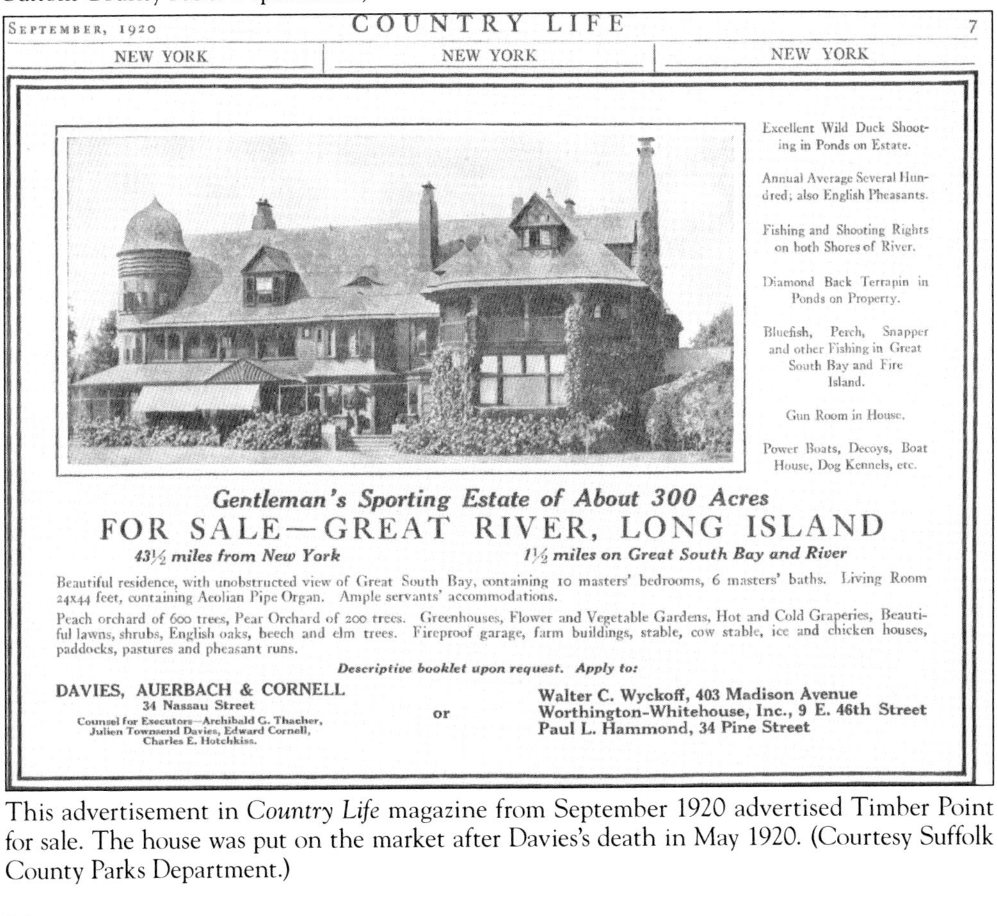

SEPTEMBER, 1920 COUNTRY LIFE 7

NEW YORK | NEW YORK | NEW YORK

Excellent Wild Duck Shooting in Ponds on Estate.

Annual Average Several Hundred; also English Pheasants.

Fishing and Shooting Rights on both Shores of River.

Diamond Back Terrapin in Ponds on Property.

Bluefish, Perch, Snapper and other Fishing in Great South Bay and Fire Island.

Gun Room in House.

Power Boats, Decoys, Boat House, Dog Kennels, etc.

Gentleman's Sporting Estate of About 300 Acres

FOR SALE—GREAT RIVER, LONG ISLAND

43½ miles from New York ***1½ miles on Great South Bay and River***

Beautiful residence, with unobstructed view of Great South Bay, containing 10 masters' bedrooms, 6 masters' baths. Living Room 24x44 feet, containing Aeolian Pipe Organ. Ample servants' accommodations.

Peach orchard of 600 trees, Pear Orchard of 200 trees. Greenhouses, Flower and Vegetable Gardens, Hot and Cold Graperies, Beautiful lawns, shrubs, English oaks, beech and elm trees. Fireproof garage, farm buildings, stable, cow stable, ice and chicken houses, paddocks, pastures and pheasant runs.

Descriptive booklet upon request. Apply to:

DAVIES, AUERBACH & CORNELL
34 Nassau Street
Counsel for Executors—Archibald G. Thacher, Julien Townsend Davies, Edward Cornell, Charles E. Hotchkiss.

or

Walter C. Wyckoff, 403 Madison Avenue
Worthington-Whitehouse, Inc., 9 E. 46th Street
Paul L. Hammond, 34 Pine Street

This advertisement in *Country Life* magazine from September 1920 advertised Timber Point for sale. The house was put on the market after Davies's death in May 1920. (Courtesy Suffolk County Parks Department.)

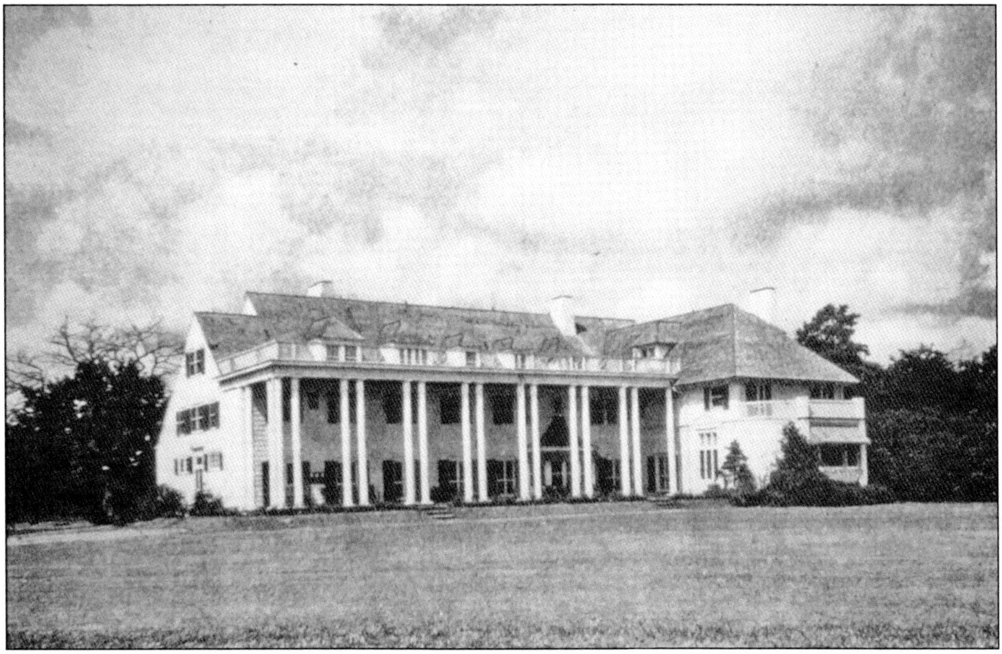

The Great River Club changed its name to Timber Point Country Club in 1925, and the mansion was altered. It was owned by the Republican Party of Suffolk County before being purchased by Suffolk County in 1970. Timber Point stands today as the clubhouse for Timber Point Country Club and Golf Course. (Courtesy East Islip Historical Society.)

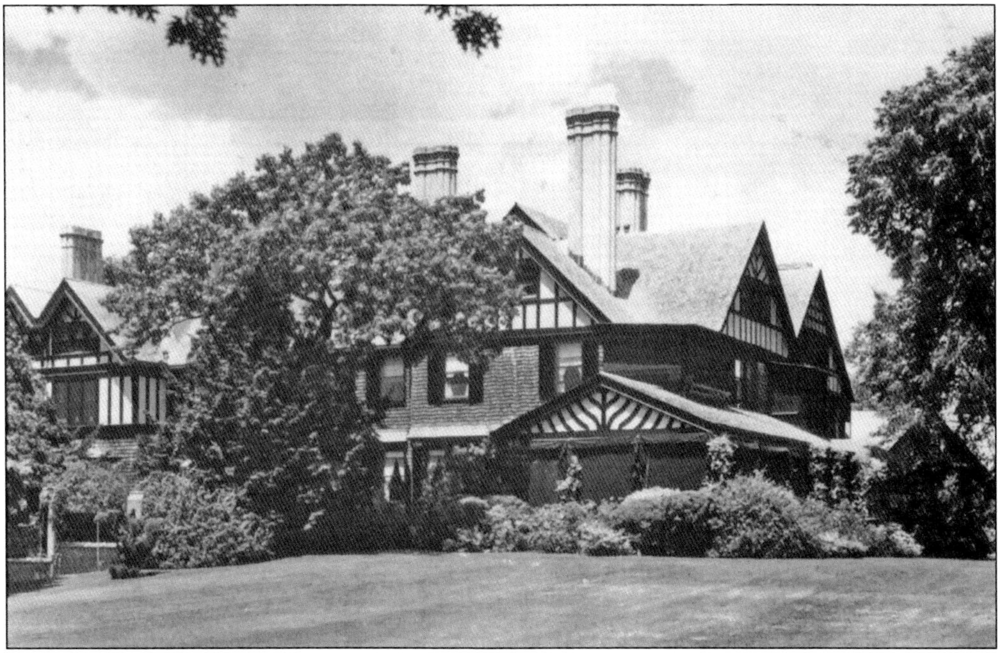

This Neo-Tudor-style mansion, named Westbrook, was built in 1886 by William Bayard Cutting (1850–1912). The home sits on the 931-acre former Robert Maitland-George Lorillard estate. In 1936, the mansion and 200 acres were donated to New York State. Today, the grounds and mansion are open to the public as Bayard Cutting Arboretum. (Courtesy East Islip Historical Society.)

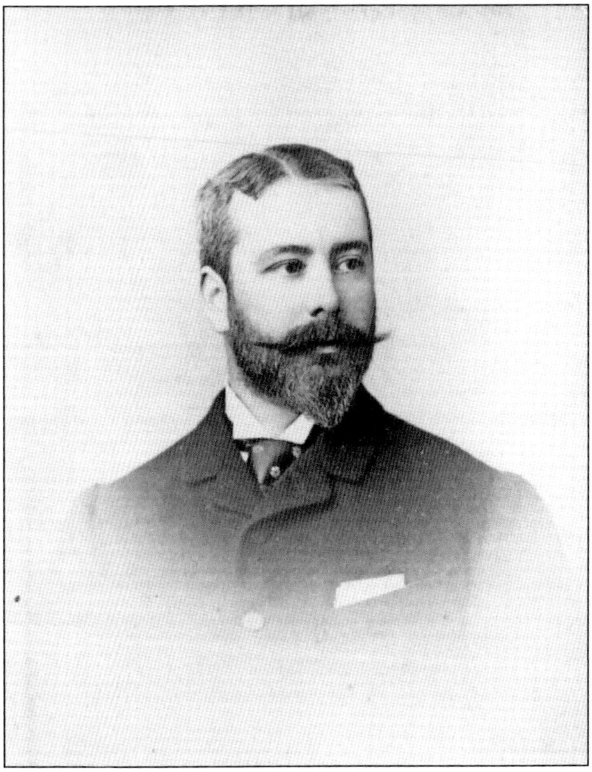

William Bayard Cutting (1850–1912) was an attorney and businessman. He was director of several railroads and founded the Oxnard Sugar Beet Company in 1888. He also took on several charity responsibilities. Cutting was a member of the South Side Sportsman's Club, a lover of nature, and a gardener. A rich variety of plants from around the world are found in the arboretum. (Courtesy Suffolk County Parks Department.)

This is an aerial shot of the area that was Westbrook farm. It gives an idea of the scope of land it occupied as a private estate and today as a public arboretum. (Courtesy East Islip Historic Society.)

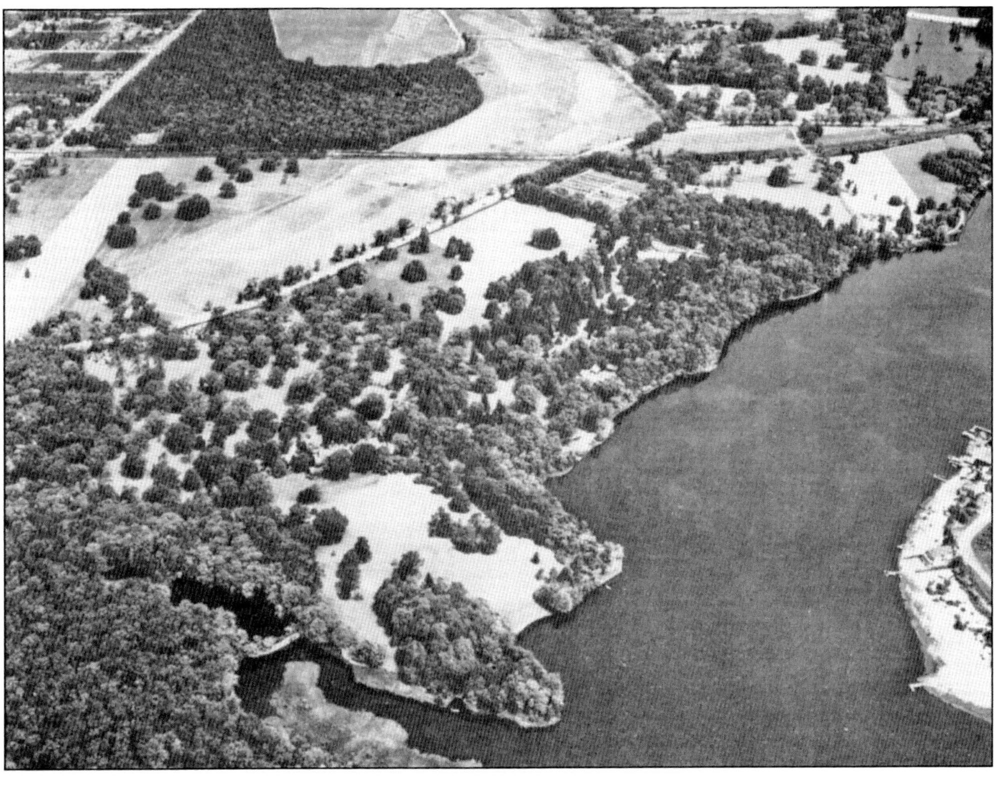

Seven

OAKDALE AND SAYVILLE

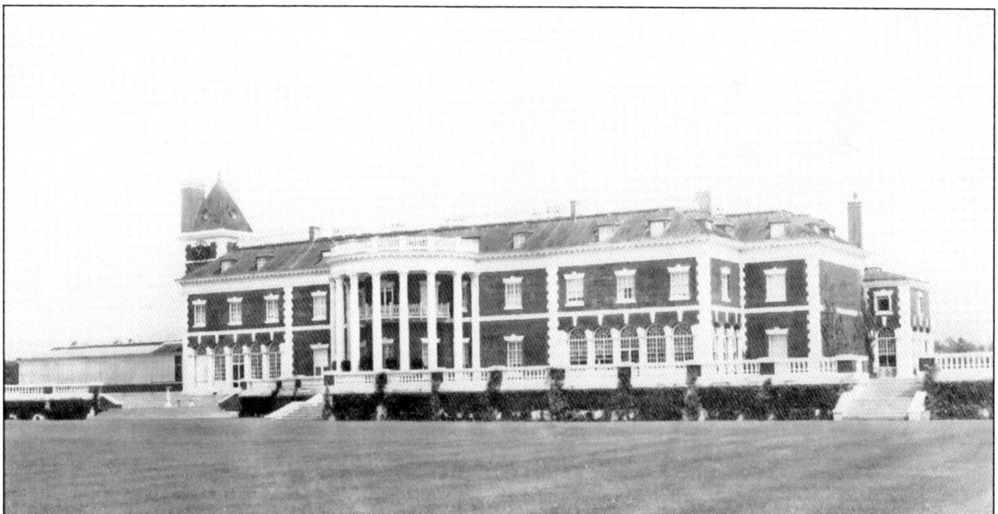

This Neo-Federal mansion, named Indian Neck Hall, was completed in 1900 and was built by Frederick Gilbert Bourne (1851–1919). The mansion was designed by architect Ernest Flagg. It sat on a 2,000-acre estate and was said to be the largest mansion on the South Shore of Long Island at the time. (Courtesy East Islip Historical Society.)

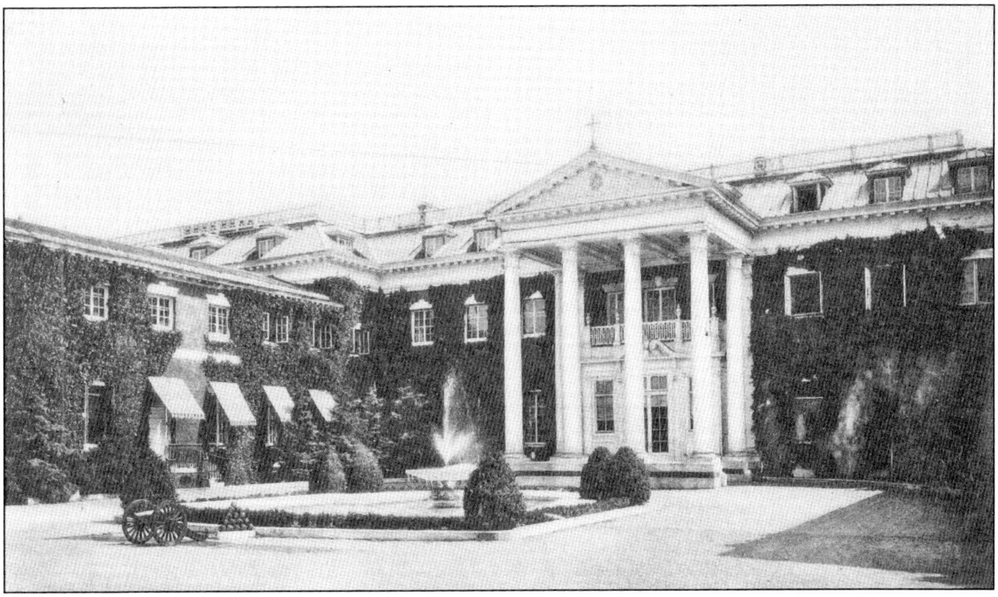

In 1925, the family sold the mansion to a developer. In 1926, Clason Point Military Academy purchased it and established LaSalle Military Academy. After that, it was sold to St. John's University in 2001. The mansion still stands today as part of the university. (Courtesy Suffolk County Historical Society.)

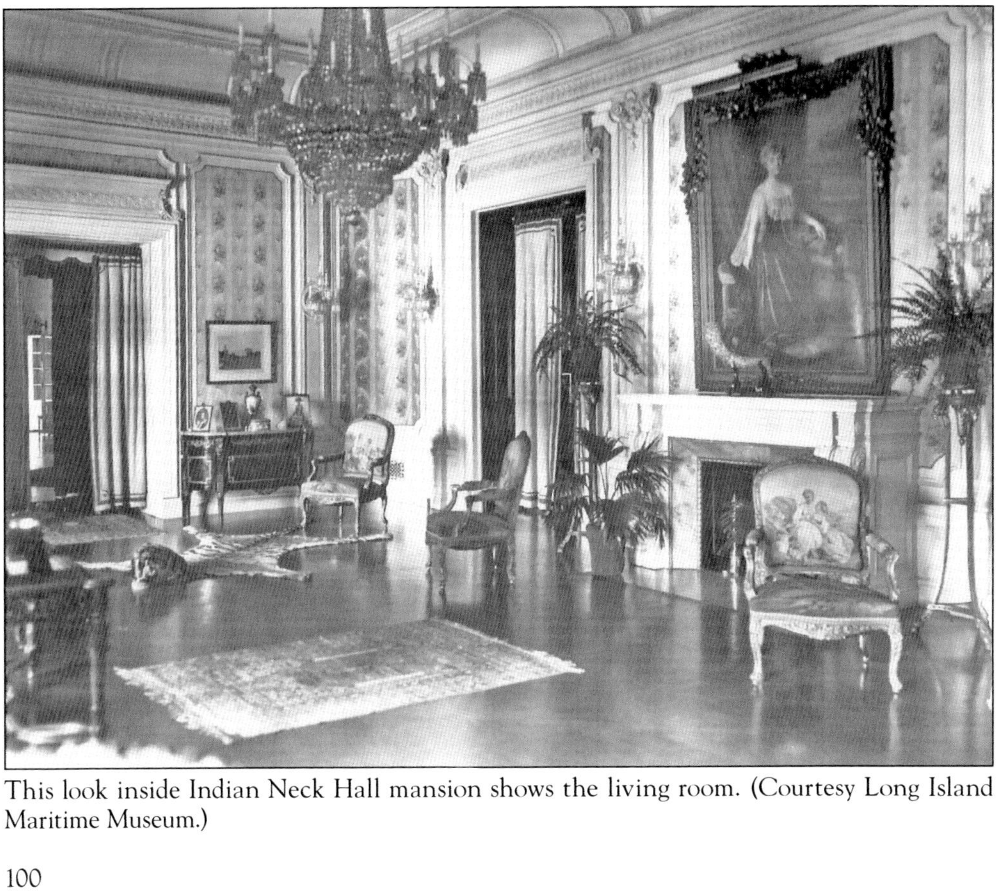

This look inside Indian Neck Hall mansion shows the living room. (Courtesy Long Island Maritime Museum.)

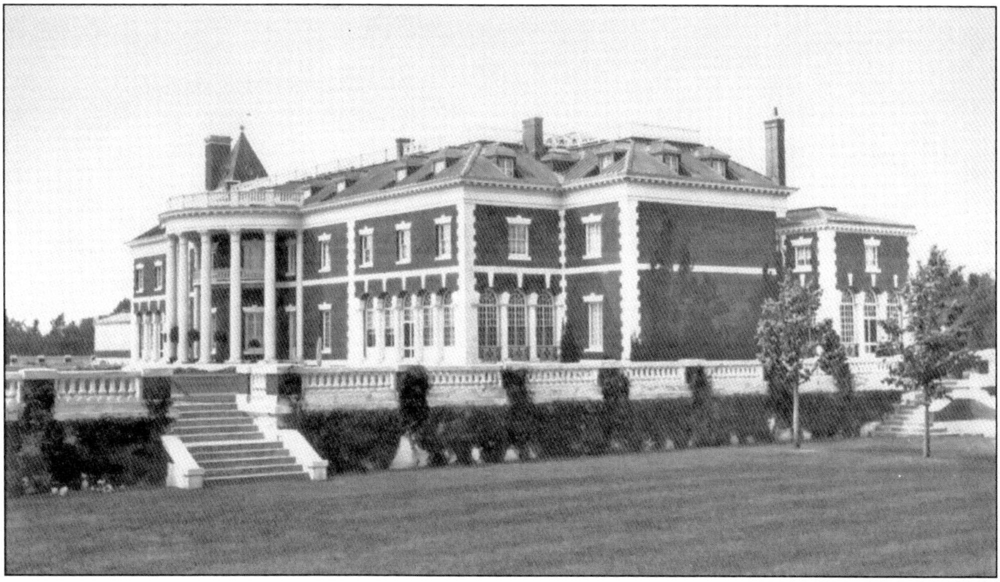

The Indian Neck Hall mansion, seen in this side view, was built and owned by the Bourne family. (Courtesy Long Island Maritime Museum.)

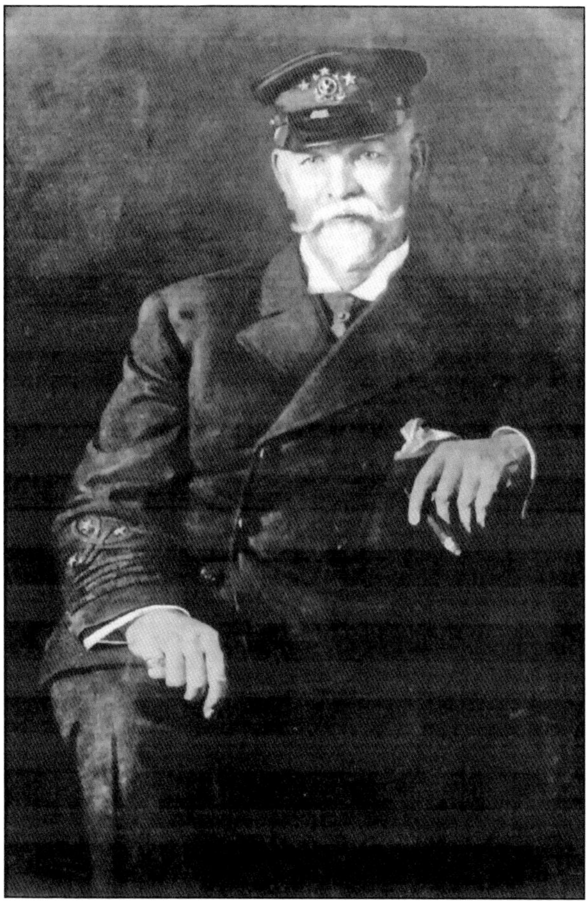

Frederick Gilbert Bourne (1851–1919) was the president of Singer Sewing Machine Company and director of several other companies, including the Long Island Rail Road and the Bank of Manhattan. (Courtesy Long Island Maritime Museum.)

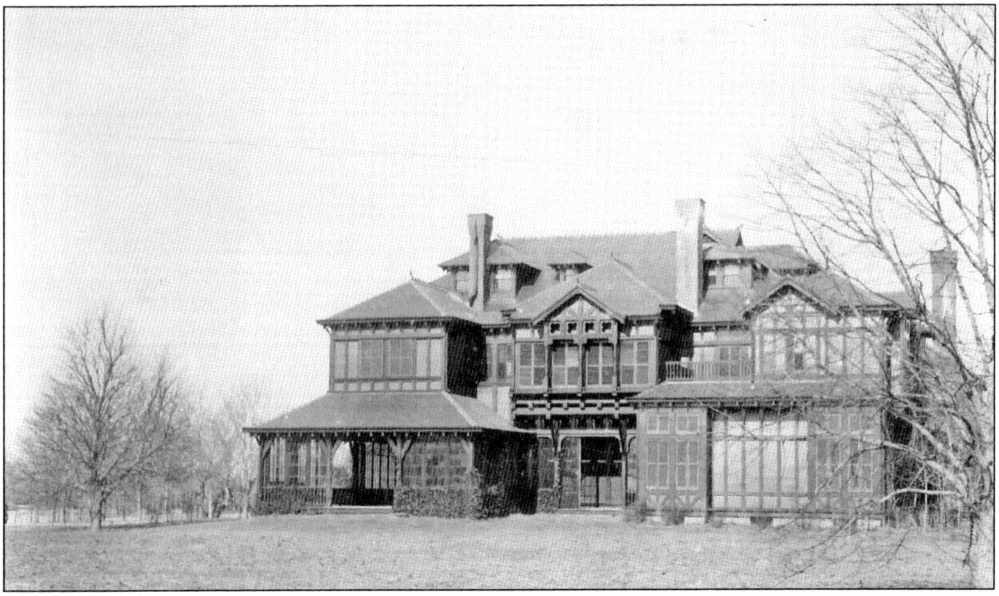

The 110-room mansion Idlehour was built in 1878 by William Kissam Vanderbilt Sr. It was designed by architect Richard Morris Hunt. Vanderbilt was friends with Schuyler Parsons Sr., and supposedly they both liked the name Idlehour for their estates, so they tossed a coin to decide who would get to use the name. The original Idlehour burned down in 1899. (Courtesy Dowling College Library Archives and Special Collections.)

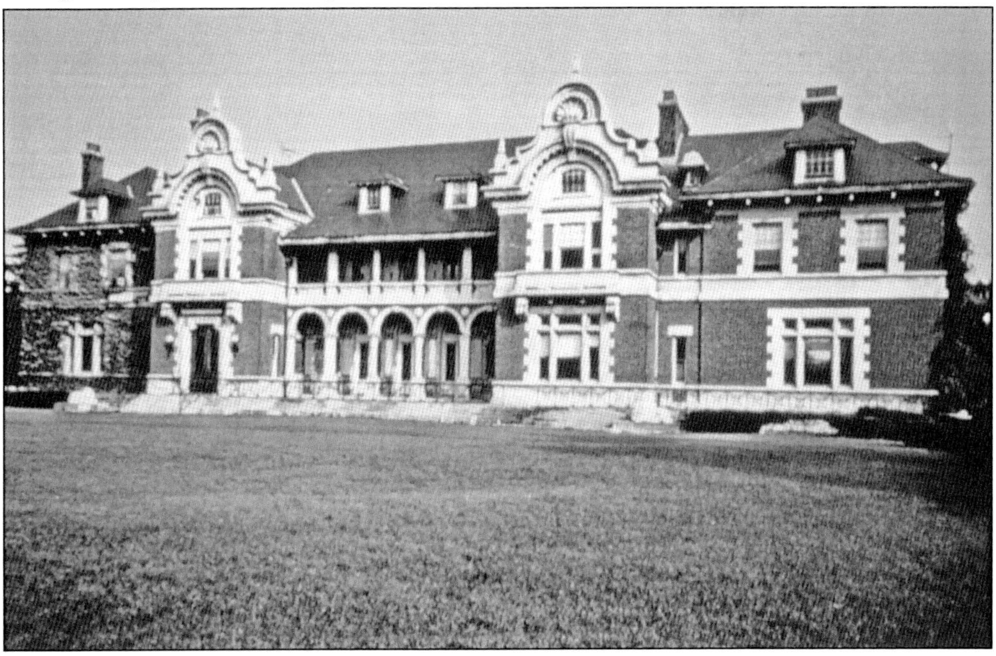

This Beaux-Arts–style mansion, named Idlehour, was built in 1900 to replace Vanderbilt's original Idlehour mansion, which burned down. From the 1920s through the 1960s, it had several different owners. Adelphi Suffolk moved into the Idle Hour mansion in January 1963. The school changed its name to Dowling in 1968. It is still used by Dowling College today. (Courtesy East Islip Historical Society.)

William Kissam Vanderbilt Sr. (1849–1920), here with his wife, Alva, was a member of the famous Vanderbilt family, which made its fortune in railroads. The Vanderbilts built and owned Grand Central Terminal in New York City. He was also the father of William Kissam Vanderbilt II, who built Vanderbilt Motor Parkway and Eagle's Nest in Centerport. (Courtesy Dowling College Library Archives and Special Collections.)

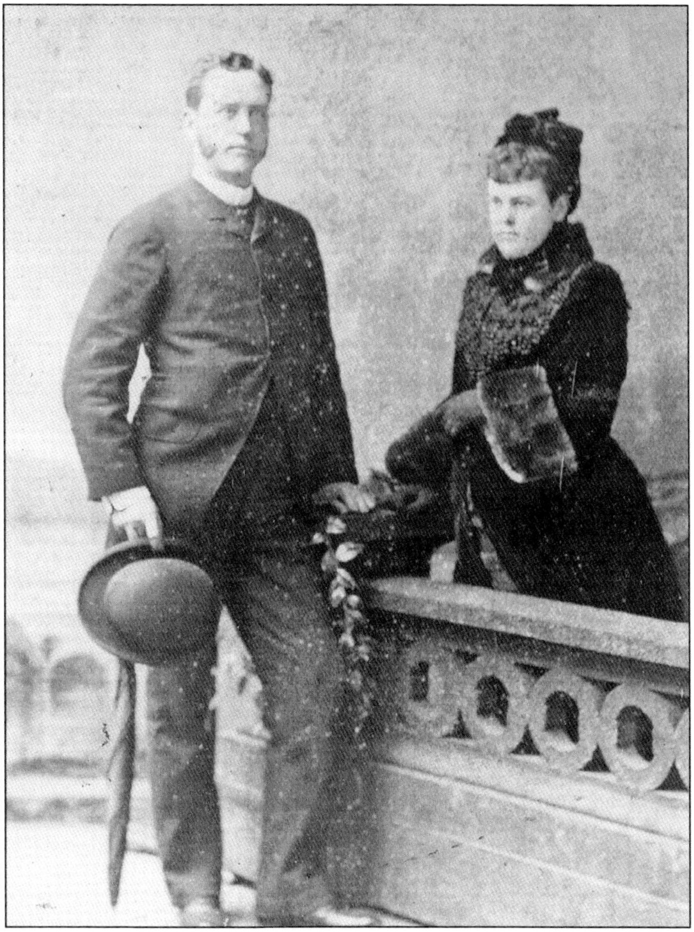

Idlehour still stands today as the Dowling College campus. (Courtesy East Islip Historical Society.)

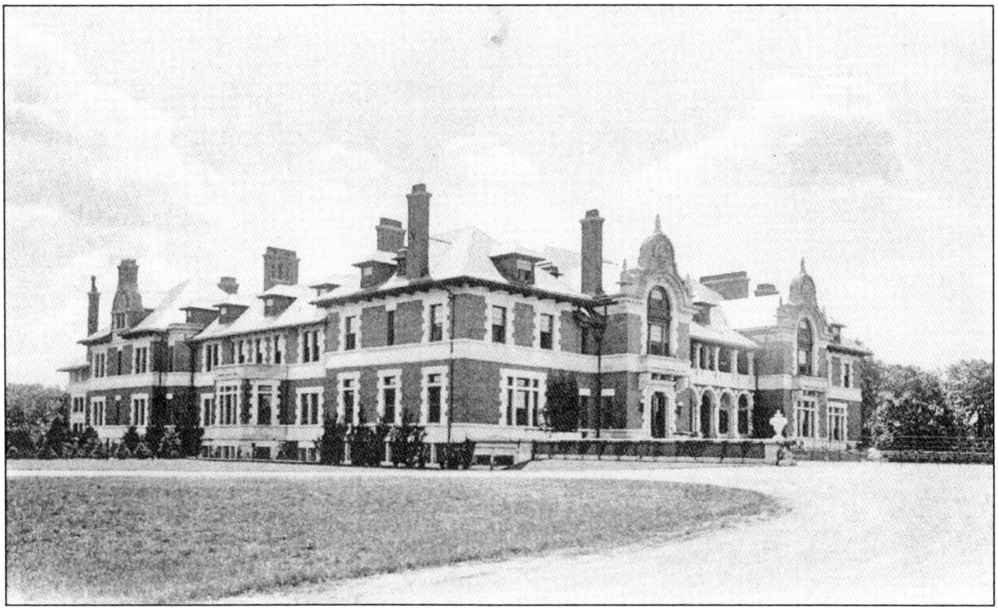

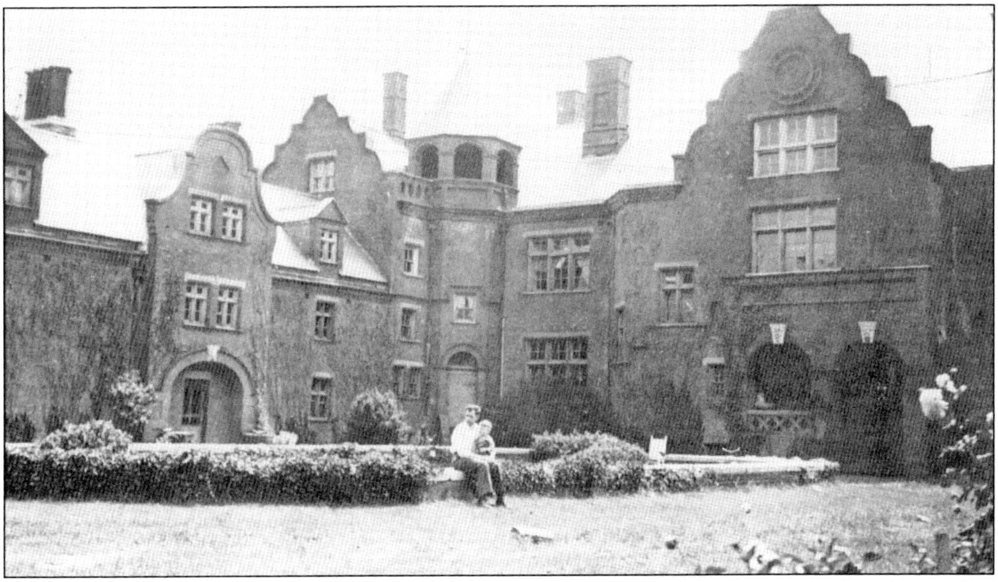

This French chateau–style mansion, named Peperidge Hall, was built around 1890 by Christopher Rhinelander Robert (1830–1898). The entire interior was from a chateau in Normandy. Roberts had it brought to Long Island and reassembled. The mansion was sold to a developer in 1896. The mansion was demolished in 1941. (Courtesy East Islip Historical Society.)

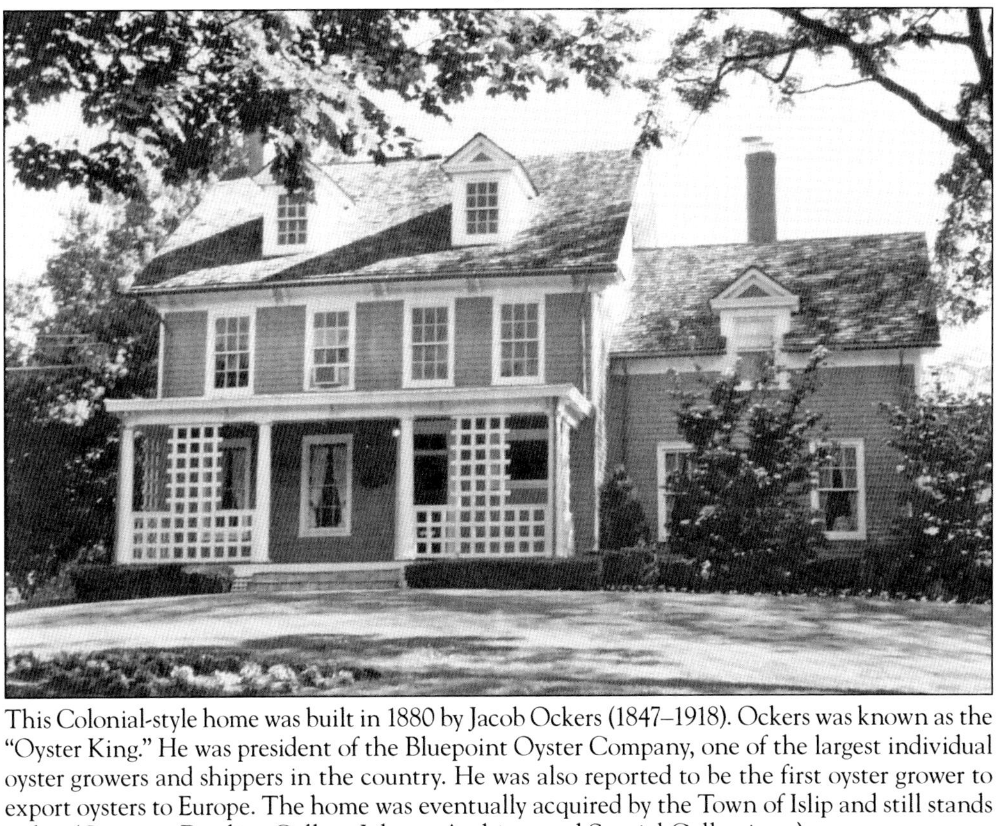

This Colonial-style home was built in 1880 by Jacob Ockers (1847–1918). Ockers was known as the "Oyster King." He was president of the Bluepoint Oyster Company, one of the largest individual oyster growers and shippers in the country. He was also reported to be the first oyster grower to export oysters to Europe. The home was eventually acquired by the Town of Islip and still stands today. (Courtesy Dowling College Library Archives and Special Collections.)

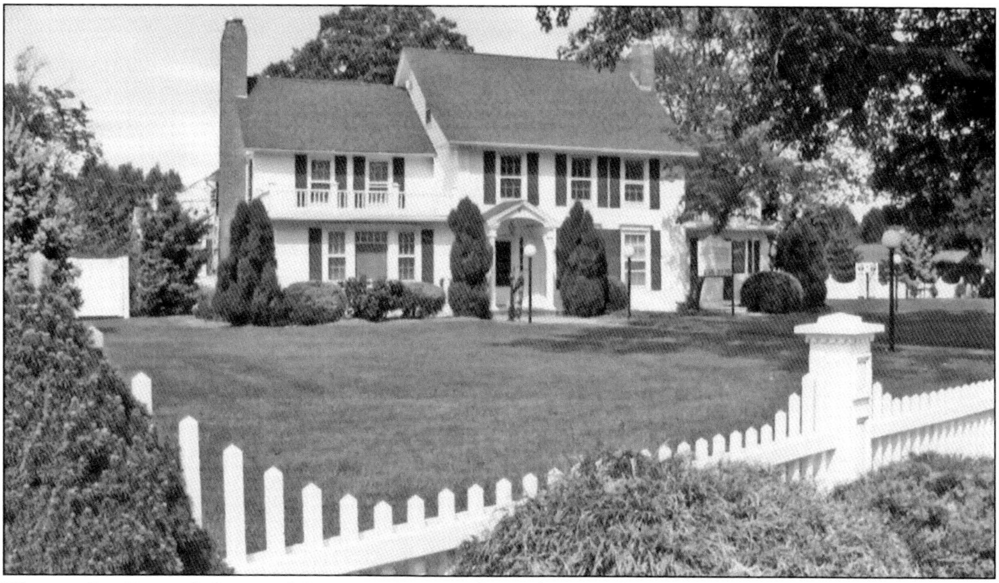

This is the Samuel Greene Home on Montauk Highway. The house is famous for being George Washington's third South Shore stop on his 1790 tour of Long Island. It is noted in his diary that he stopped here to rest and refresh his horses. The home still stands as a professional office building. (Photograph by Christopher Collora.)

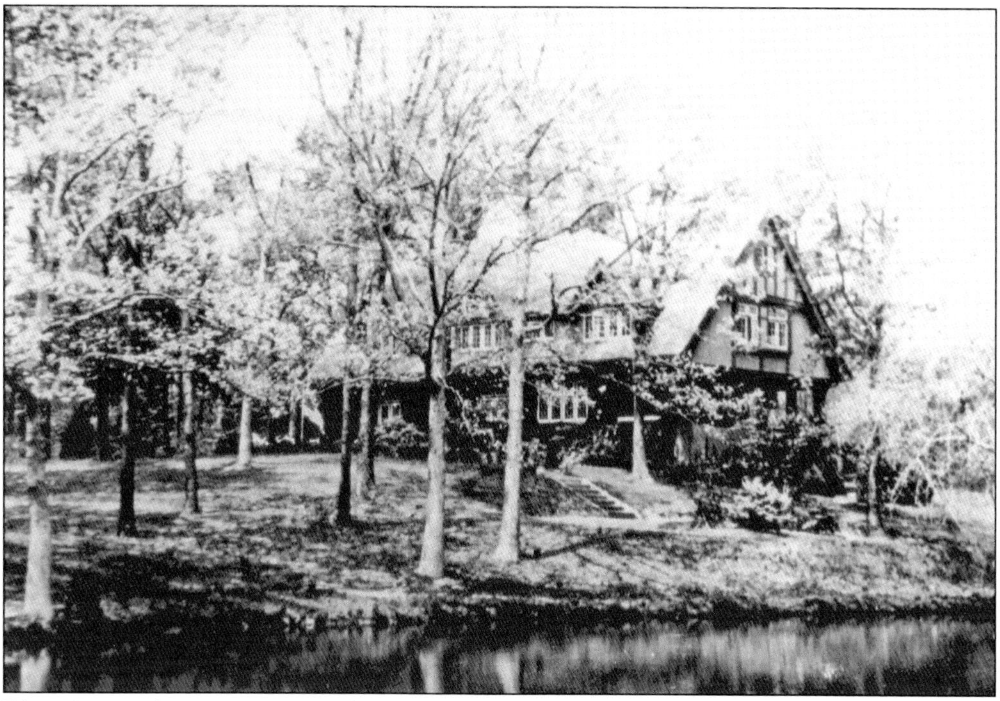

This Tutor-style mansion, named Brookside, was completed in 1897. It was home to architect Isaac Henry Greene (1859–1937), who designed his own home. The main house burned down in 1970. Part of the estate was purchased by Suffolk County, and it is now a county water park. The gatehouse still stands and is home to the Great South Bay Audubon Society. (Courtesy Suffolk County Parks Department.)

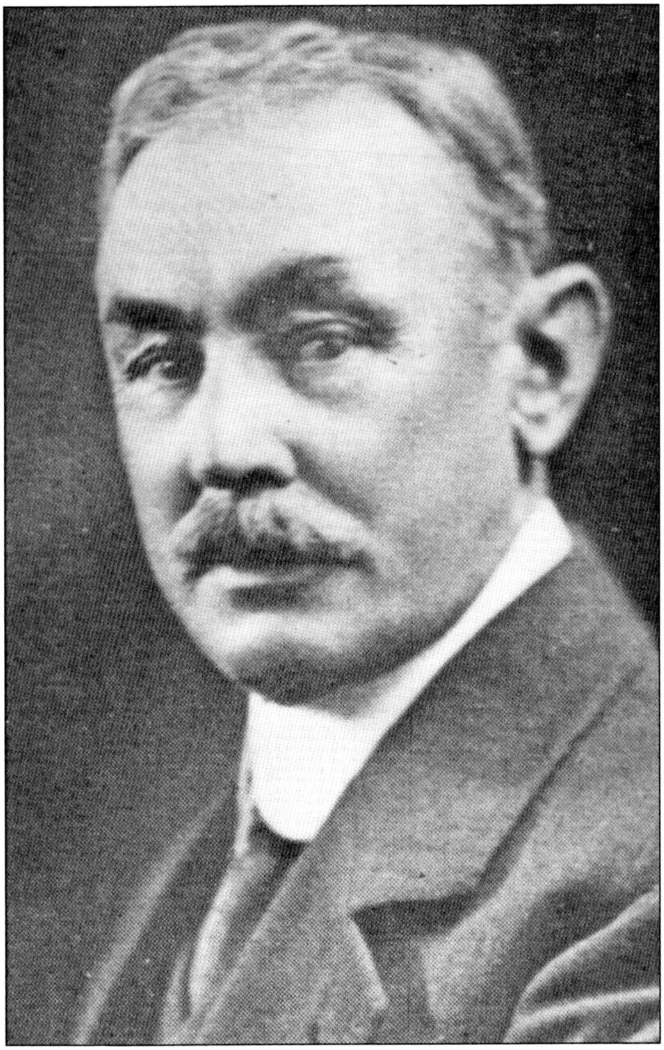

Architect Isaac Henry Green (1859–1937) designed over 200 structures on Long Island. He designed everything from houses to churches, schools, industrial buildings, and windmills. He also worked on many of the Bourne and Vanderbilt estate buildings on Long Island as well as many other large mansions and homes in the area. (Courtesy Constance Currie, Sayville historian, Sayville Historical Society.)

Meadow Croft was built in 1891 for lawyer John Ellis Roosevelt, cousin of Pres. Theodore Roosevelt. The Colonial Revival residence was expanded from an older existing Woodward farmhouse on the property. The home was designed by architect Isaac Henry Green. (Courtesy Bayport Heritage Association.)

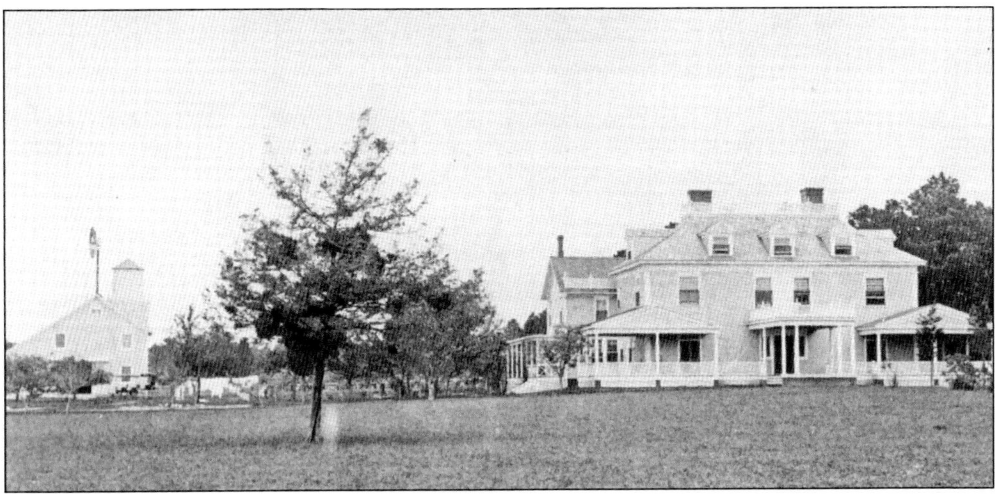

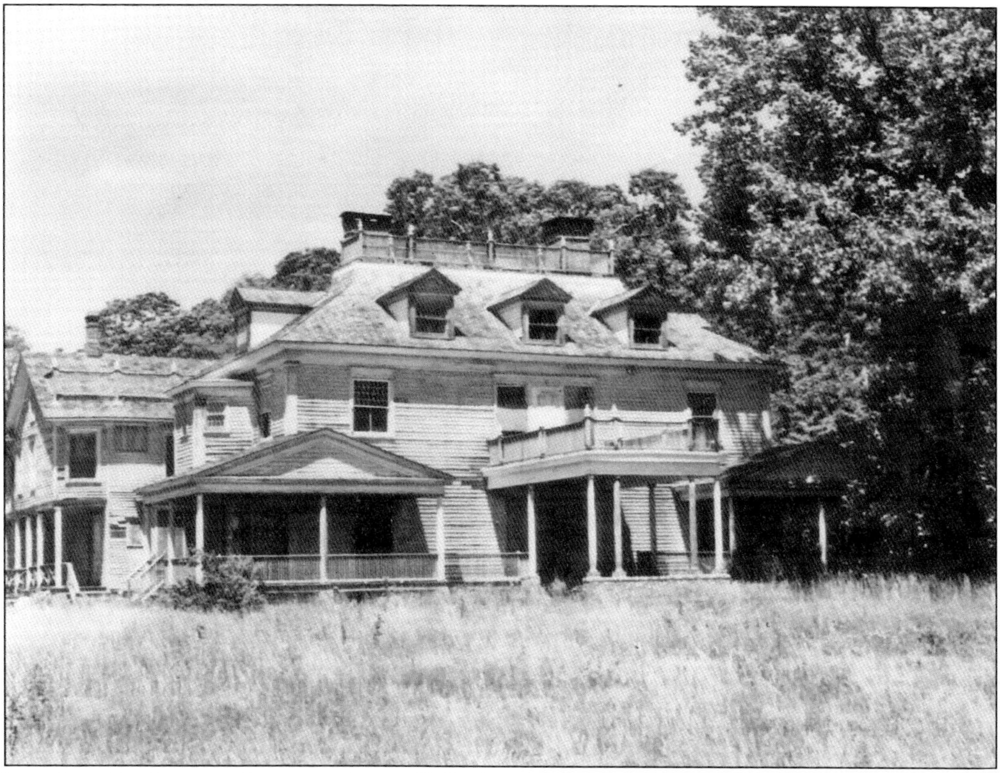

Meadow Croft was taken over by Suffolk County by eminent domain in 1975. The house underwent a much-needed 12-year restoration that started in 1983. In 1995, it opened to the public as a house museum. Today, it is part of the Suffolk County Sans Souci Lake Nature Preserve and is a house museum operated by the Bayport Heritage Historical Society and the Suffolk County Parks Department. (Courtesy Bayport Heritage Association.)

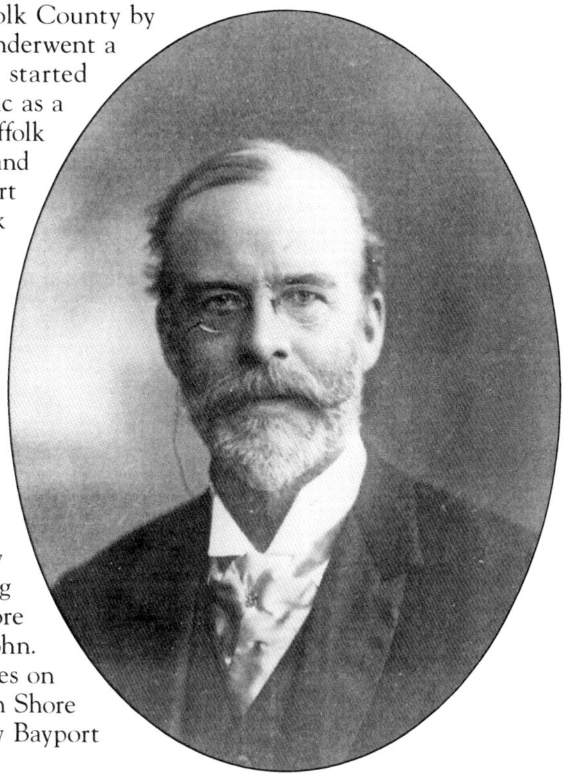

John Ellis Roosevelt (1853–1939), pictured here, was a cousin of Pres. Theodore Roosevelt, who would often visit Meadow Croft. Legend has it that while vacationing at Sagamore Hill in 1903, Pres. Theodore Roosevelt and his sons decided to visit John. They set off at 4:00 a.m., riding 35 miles on horseback from Oyster Bay on the North Shore to Meadow Croft in Sayville. (Courtesy Bayport Heritage Association.)

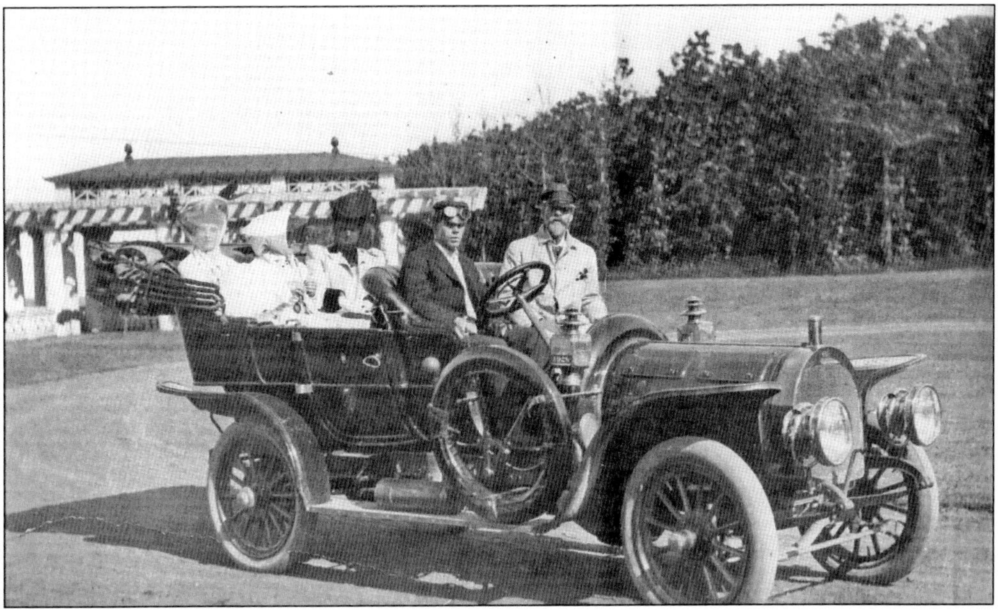

The Roosevelt family (from left to right), Jean and Gladys Roosevelt, Nannie Mitchell Vance Roosevelt, and John E. Roosevelt, and their driver are out for a spin in their car. (Courtesy Bayport Heritage Association.)

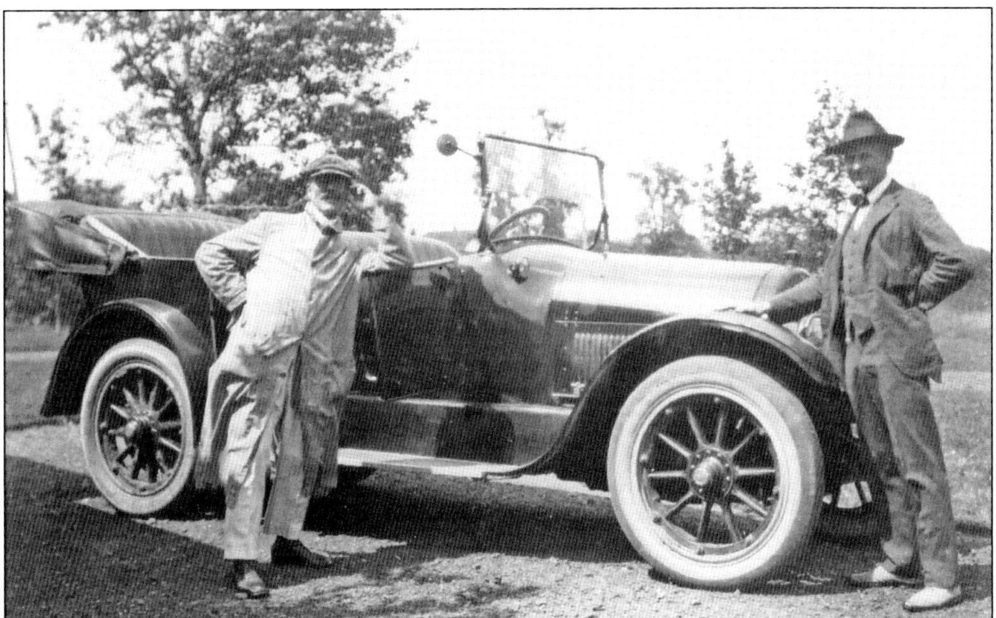

John Roosevelt was apparently an avid car collector. Above, he leans on one of his cars. (Courtesy Suffolk County Parks Department.)

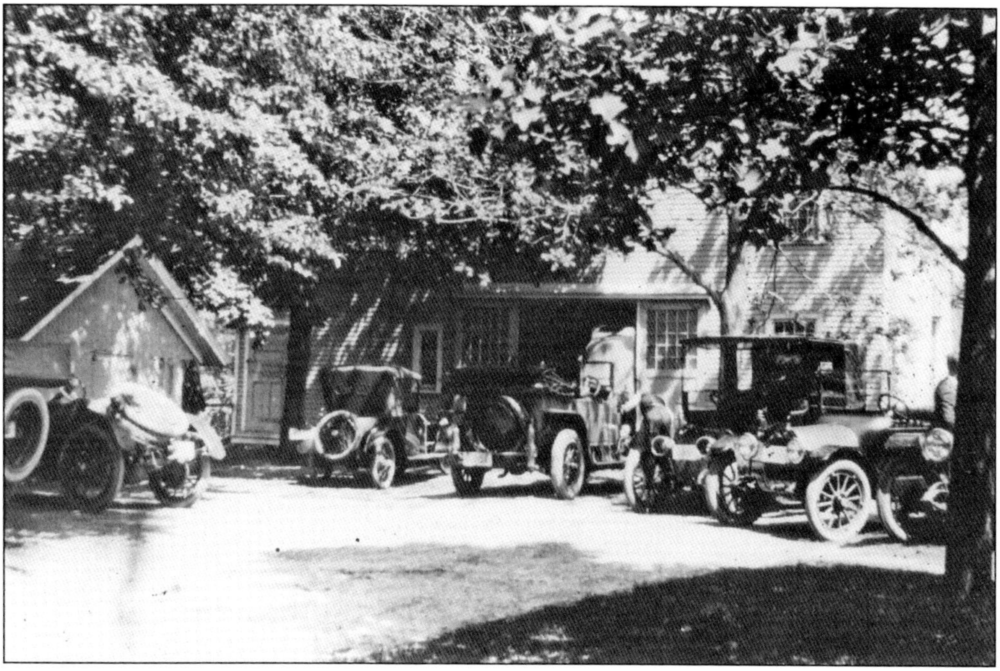

This is Roosevelt's car collection at Meadow Croft. (Both, courtesy Suffolk County Parks Department.)

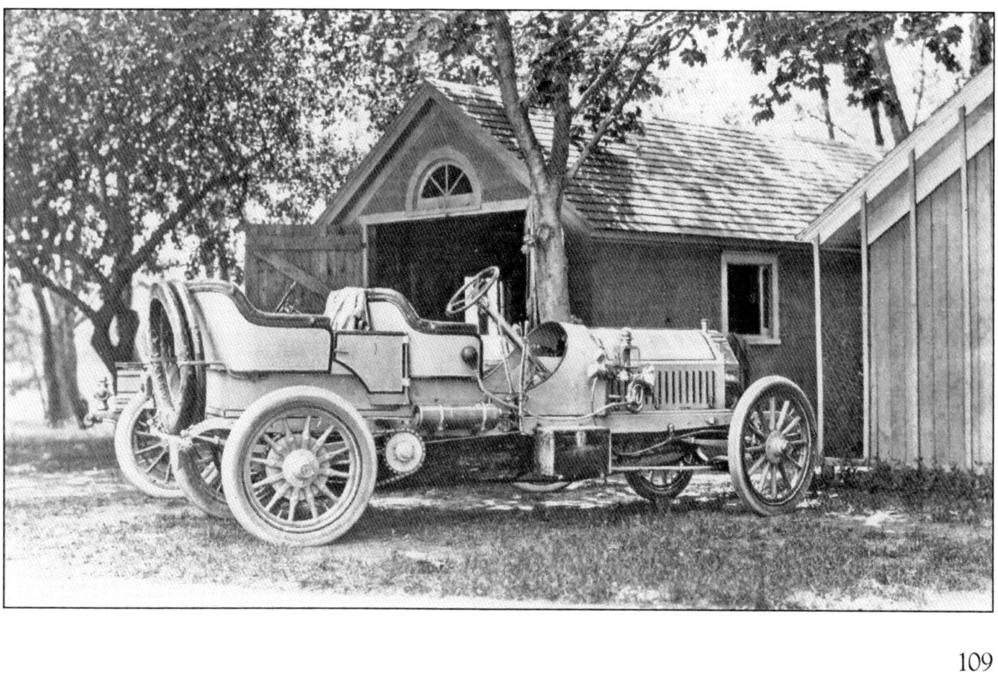

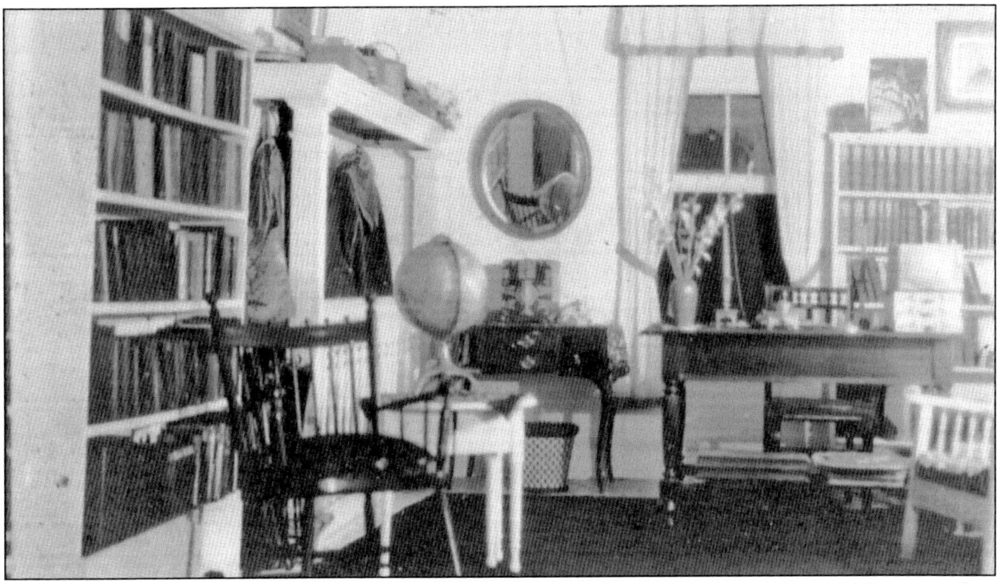

Meadow Croft sits on a picturesque 75-acre landscape. It has 26 rooms and is 8,000 square feet altogether. The original farmhouse was constructed in 1850, and the rest of the modern house was built attached to it. Today, it is furnished as it was when the Roosevelts lived there, and most of the rooms were restored according to interior photographs of the house from that time. (Courtesy Bayport Heritage Association.)

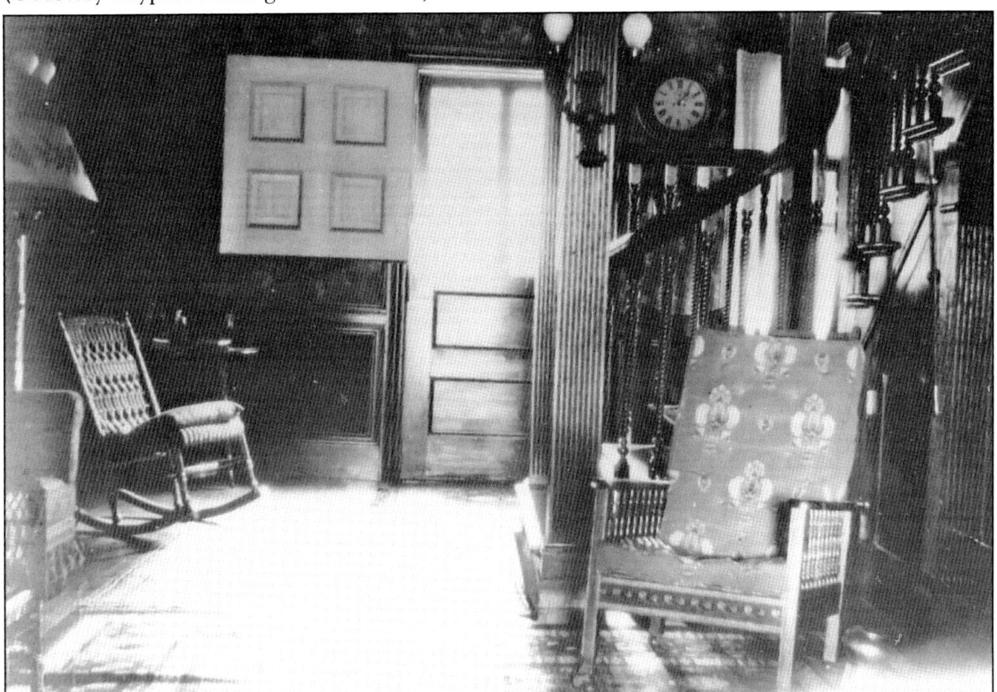

The home was restored based on these interior photographs. This is a photograph of the front entrance hall, used to restore the current entrance hall as it looked in the early 1900s. (Courtesy Suffolk County Parks Department.)

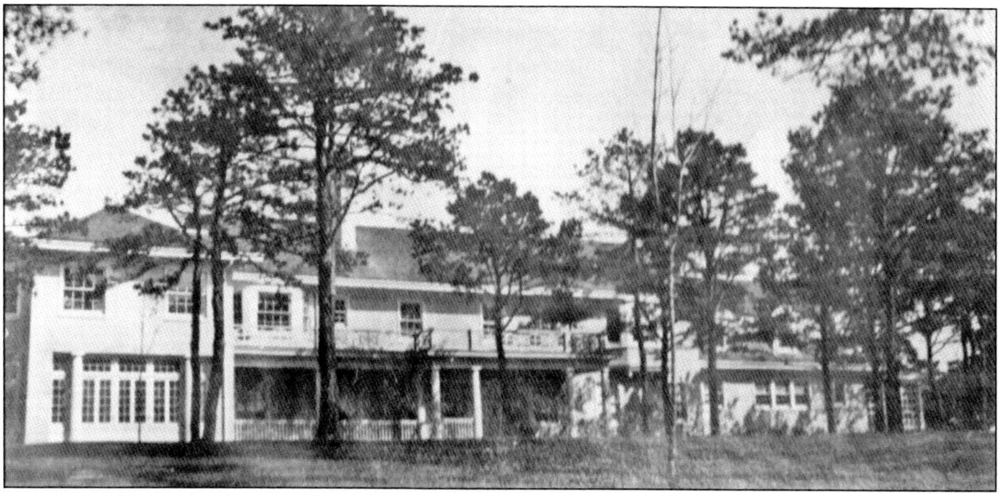

Meadow Edge was built in 1909 in a Colonial style and was designed by architect Isaac Henry Green for Anson and Florence Bourne Hard. The 250-acre estate was originally part of the eastern end of Indian Neck Hall and was given to the couple as a wedding gift from Florence's father, Frederick Bourne. In 1966, the estate was sold to Suffolk County. The main residence and grounds are now home to the Suffolk County Parks Department. (Courtesy Long Island Maritime Museum.)

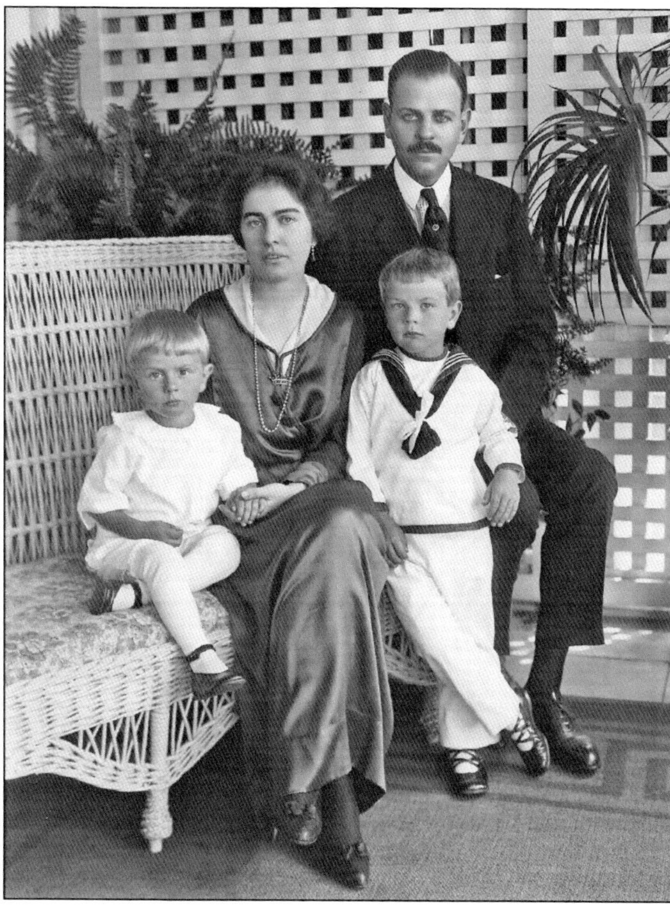

Anson Hard (1886–1935), pictured here with his family, was a stockbroker and financier. In 1908, he married Florence Bourne (1886–1969), daughter of Frederick and Emma Bourne from Oakdale. (Courtesy Long Island Maritime Museum.)

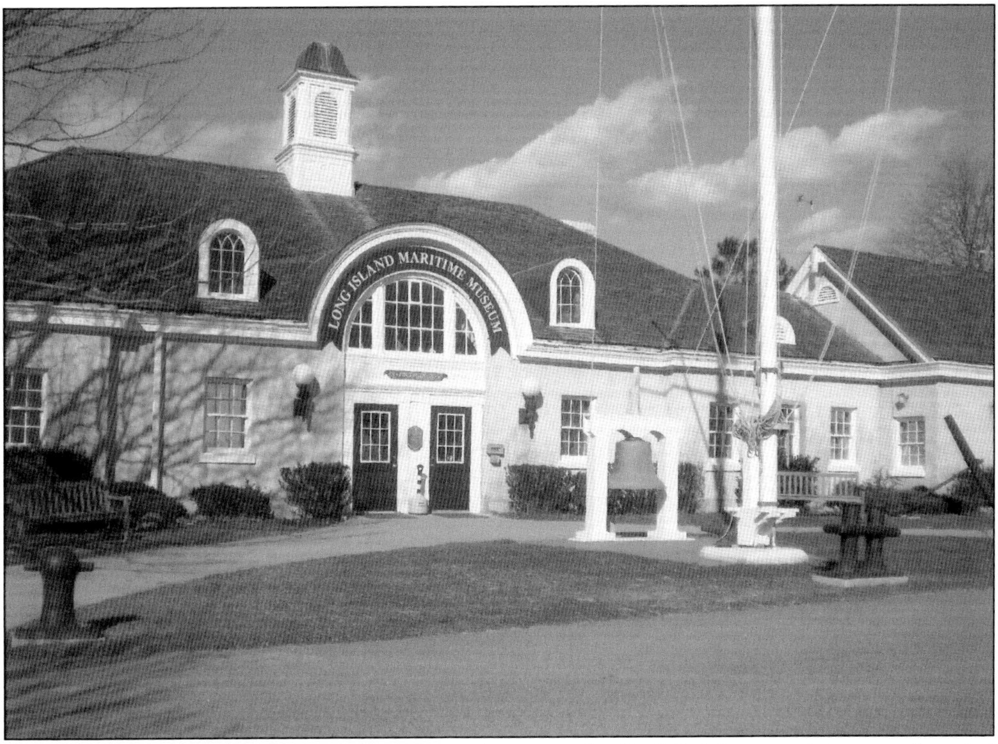

The Meadow Edge garage eventually became home to the Suffolk Maritime Museum, founded in 1966. Today, the museum is the Long Island Maritime Museum and is open to the public. (Photograph by Christopher Collora.)

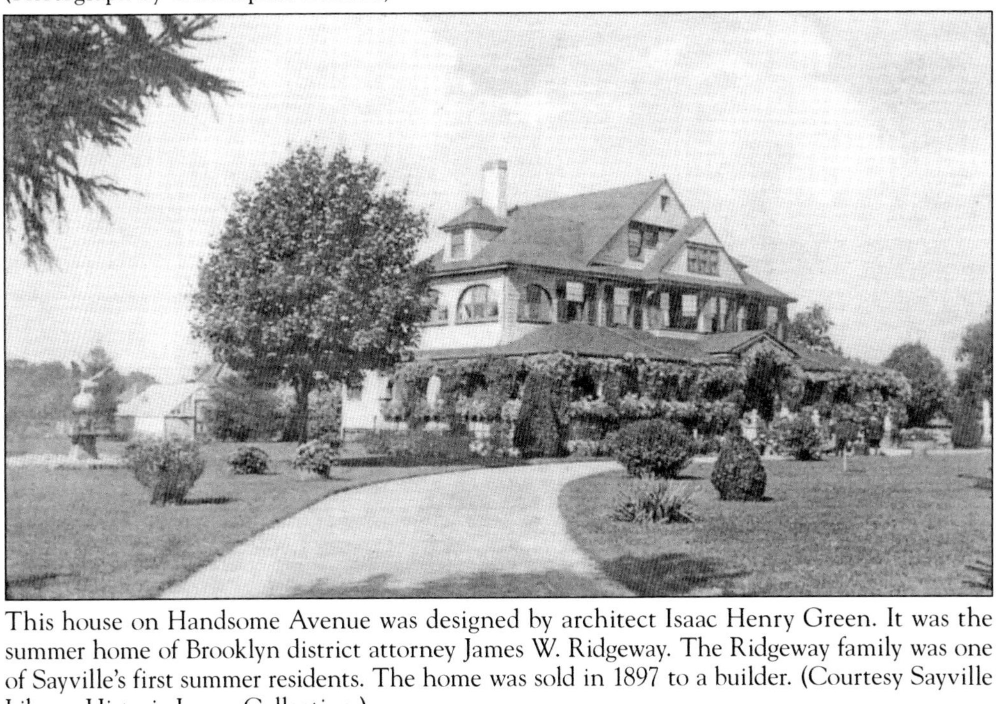

This house on Handsome Avenue was designed by architect Isaac Henry Green. It was the summer home of Brooklyn district attorney James W. Ridgeway. The Ridgeway family was one of Sayville's first summer residents. The home was sold in 1897 to a builder. (Courtesy Sayville Library Historic Image Collection.)

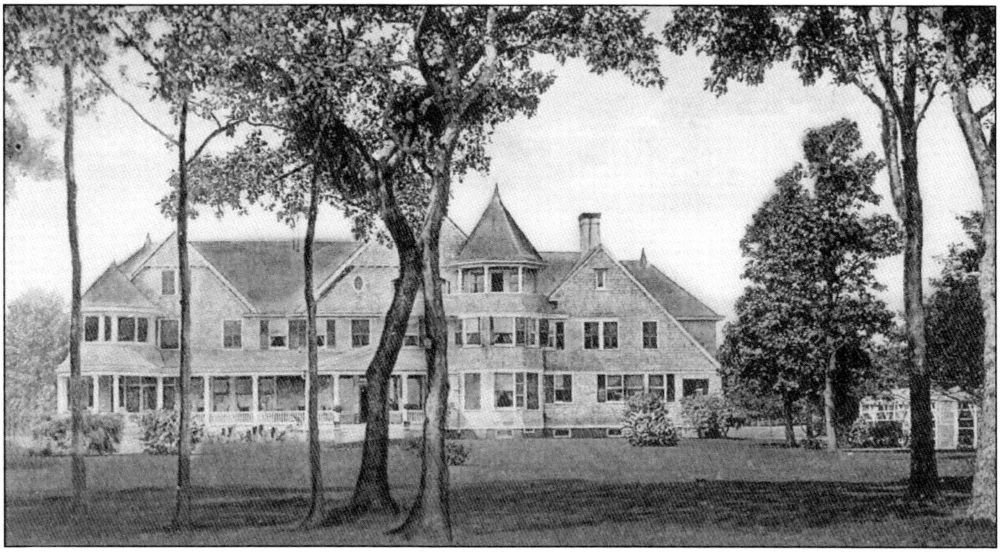

This shingle-style estate, named Beechwold, on Handsome Avenue was built in 1875 by publisher and businessman Edward Russell Wilbur (1849–1905). The home was designed by architect Isaac Henry Greene. In 1902, it was sold to Grand Union Tea Company president Frank Smith Jones (1847–1927) as his summer residence. The house was destroyed by fire in 1957. (Courtesy Sayville Library Historic Image Collection.)

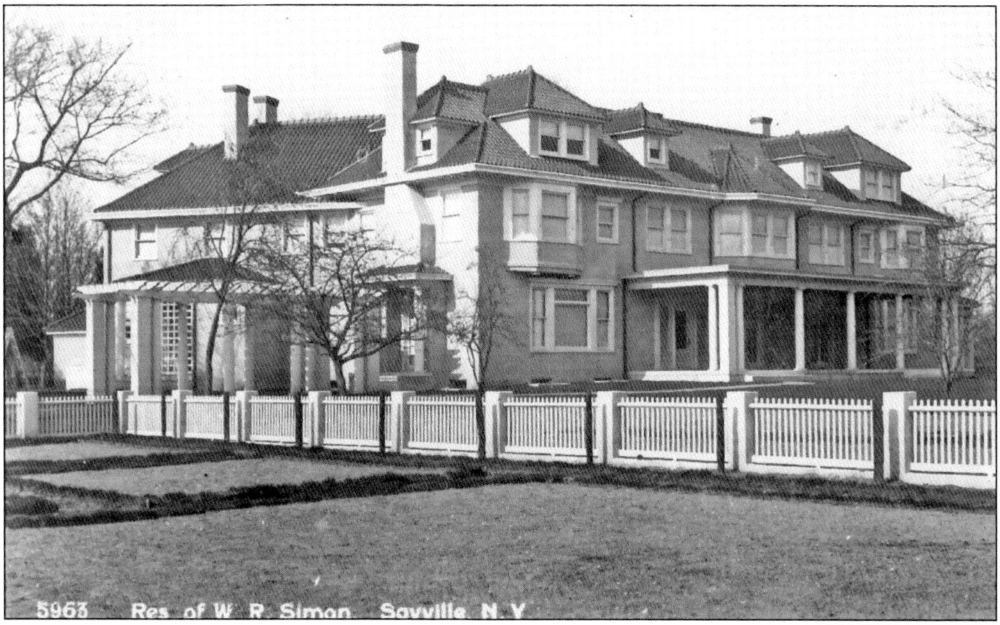

This Colonial Revival–style house, named Wyndemoor, on Benson Avenue was built in 1909 by stockbroker William Robinson Simonds (1878–1933). The house was designed by architect Isaac Henry Green. In 1930, the house was divided and moved to Benson Avenue. It still stands as a private residence. (Courtesy Sayville Library Historic Image Collection.)

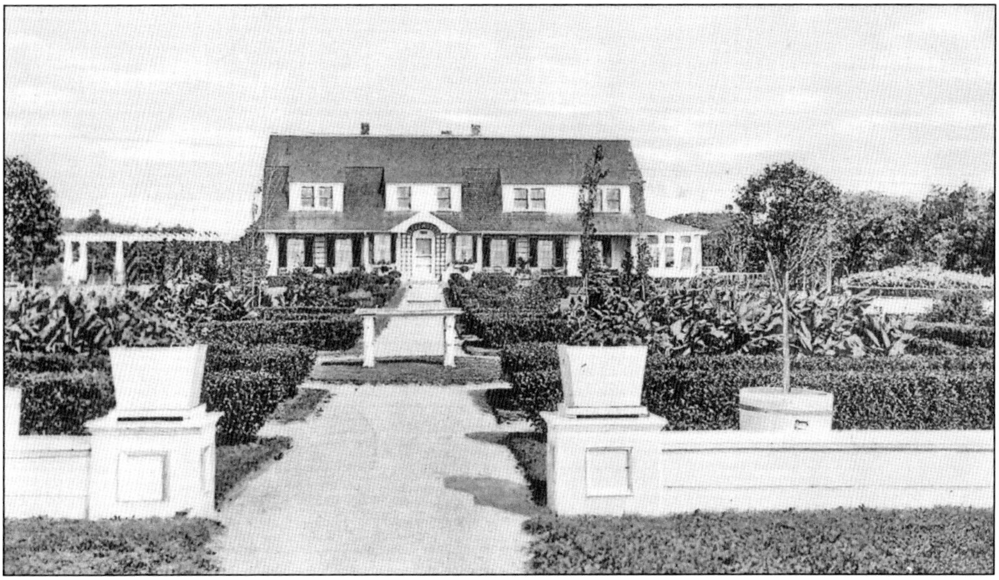

This shingle-style house on Greene Avenue called Joy Farm, built around 1892, was the summer residence of Frank Earl Haywood (1867–1923). (Courtesy Sayville Library Historic Image Collection.)

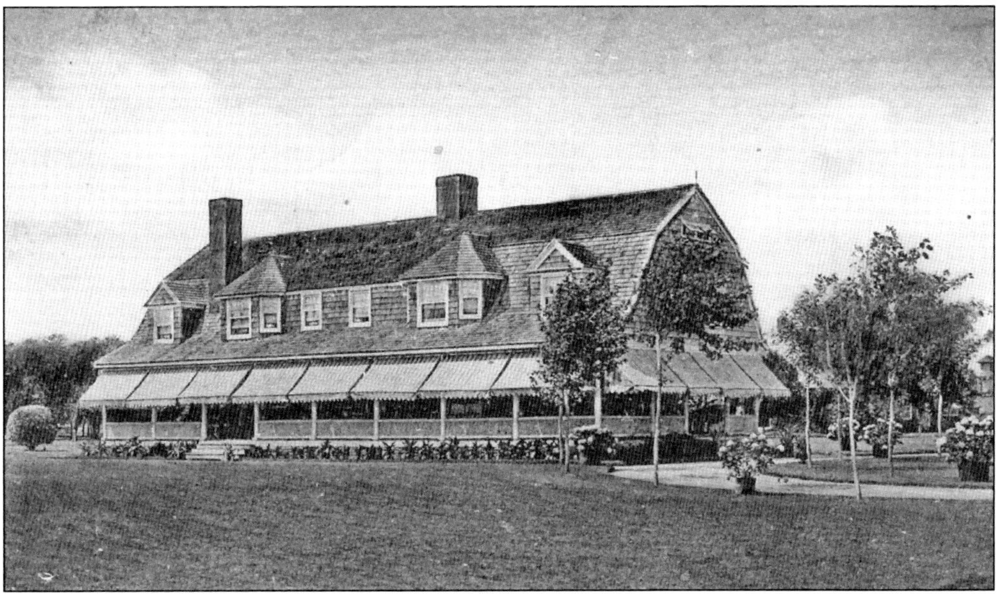

This shingle-style house called The Anchorage on Greene Avenue was built in 1892 by William Tyson Haywood (1857–1921). The house was designed by architect Isaac Henry Greene. In 1920, it was sold to a developer who divided it and sold it as two separate residences. (Courtesy Sayville Library Historic Image Collection.)

Eight

BAYPORT AND PATCHOGUE

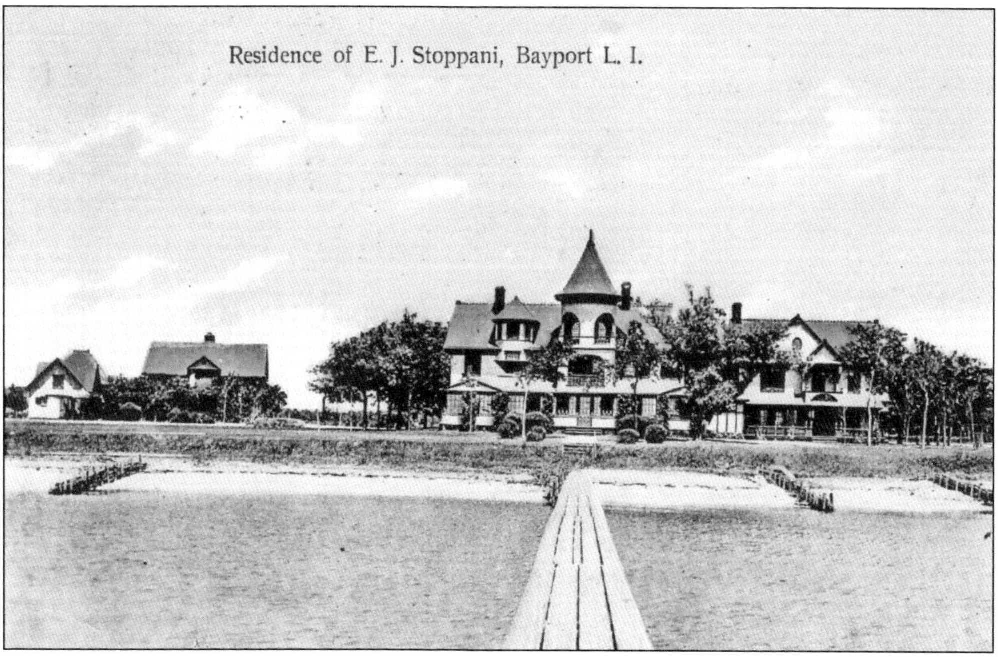

This impressive mansion, named Arcadia, was built in 1888 by Charles F. Stoppani (1832–1892). The mansion sat on 50 acres overlooking the Great South Bay and was designed by architect Isaac Henry Greene. It was later inherited by Stoppani's daughter. The house no longer stands. (Courtesy Bayport Heritage Association.)

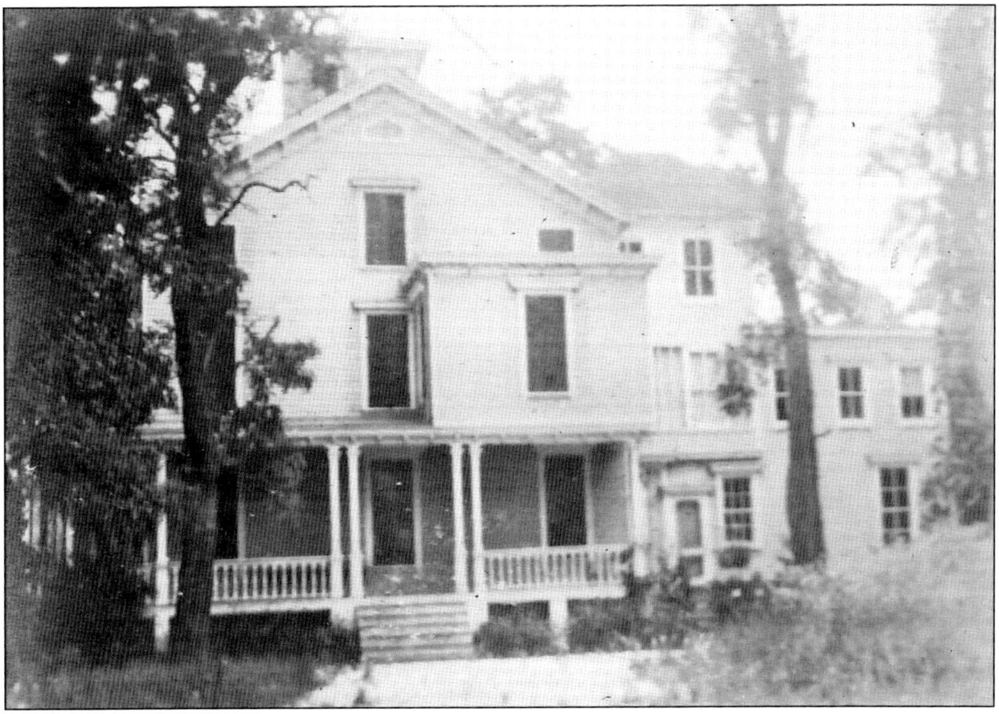

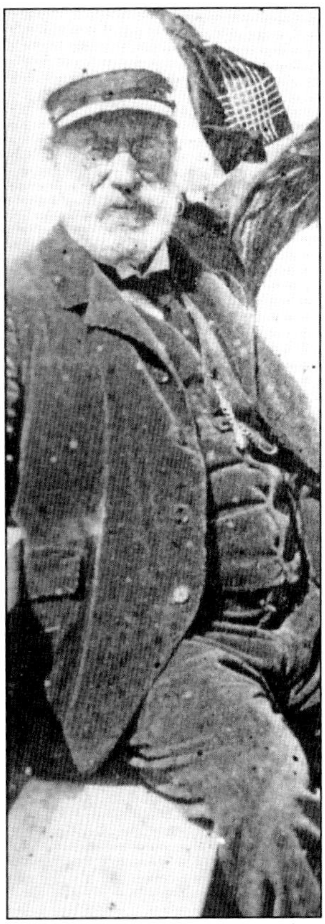

This eclectic/Italianate mansion, named Lotus Lake, was built on a 200-acre estate around 1873 by Robert Barnwell Roosevelt Sr. (1829–1906). The mansion was destroyed by fire in 1958. (Courtesy Bayport Heritage Association.)

Robert B. Roosevelt Sr. (1829–1906), seen here, was the uncle of Pres. Theodore Roosevelt and the father of John Ellis Roosevelt of Sayville. Roosevelt served as US ambassador and US congressman, and he was also well known as a writer, publisher, and environmental preservationist who may have influenced some of Theodore Roosevelt's environmental policies. (Courtesy Bayport Heritage Association.)

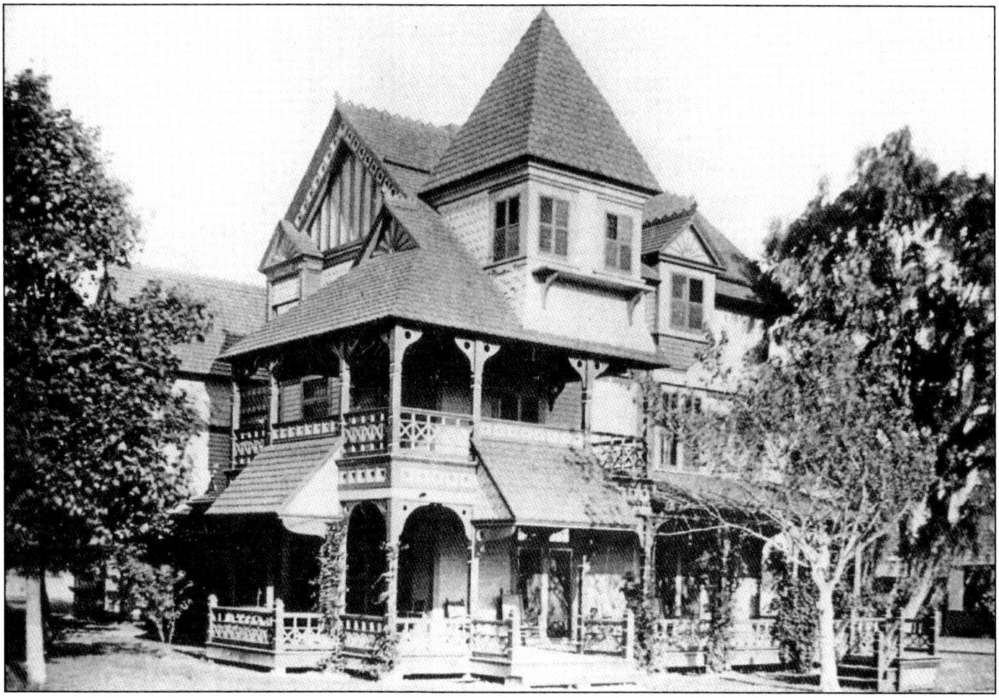

This shingle-style mansion, called Edgemere, was built around 1883 by Charles Robert Purdy. The house was cut in half by Robert H. Koehler, who eventually purchased it from the family. It still stands as two residences on Connetquot Road. (Courtesy Bayport Heritage Association.)

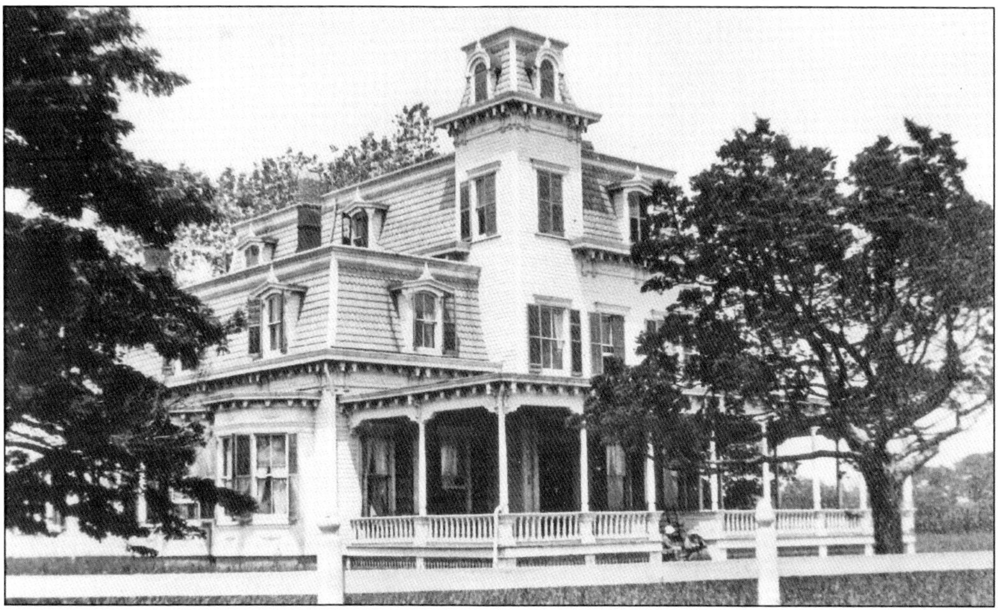

This Second Empire–style mansion, called the White House, on Fairview Avenue was built in 1881 by real estate developer Edward Edwards (1831–1897). It was purchased by several owners through 1925, including W.K. Post and James H. Snedecor, before it became a schoolhouse briefly for two years until 1926. The home was destroyed by fire around the 1940s. (Courtesy Bayport Heritage Association.)

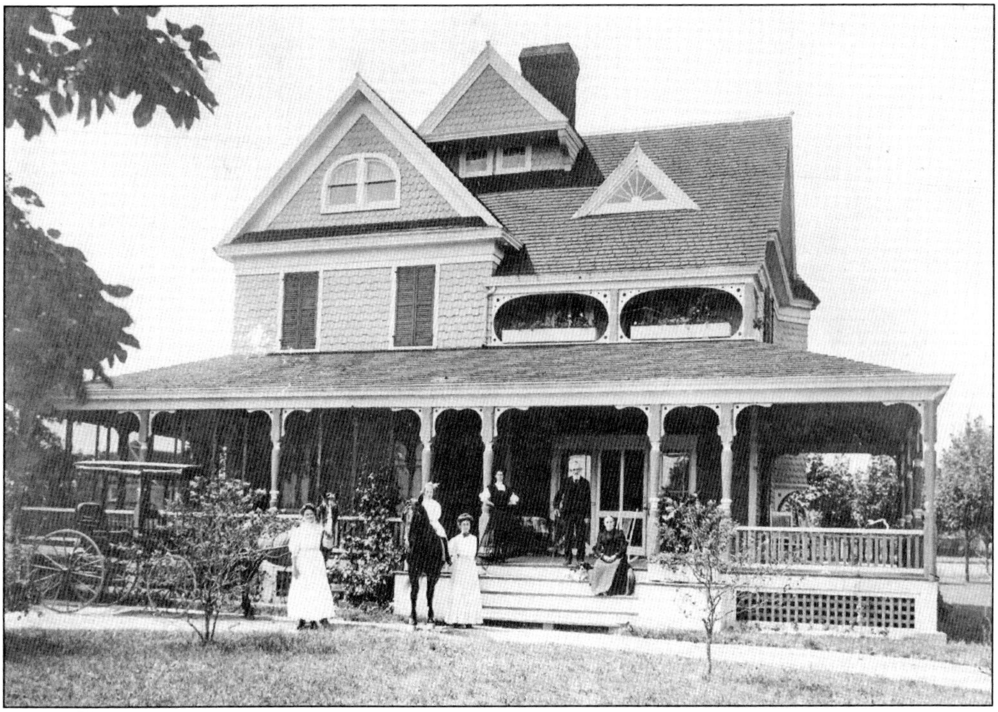

This impressive house, named The Namkee, was built in 1891 for Capt. Edward Gillette. Here, the family is pictured outside on the porch. (Courtesy Bayport Heritage Association.)

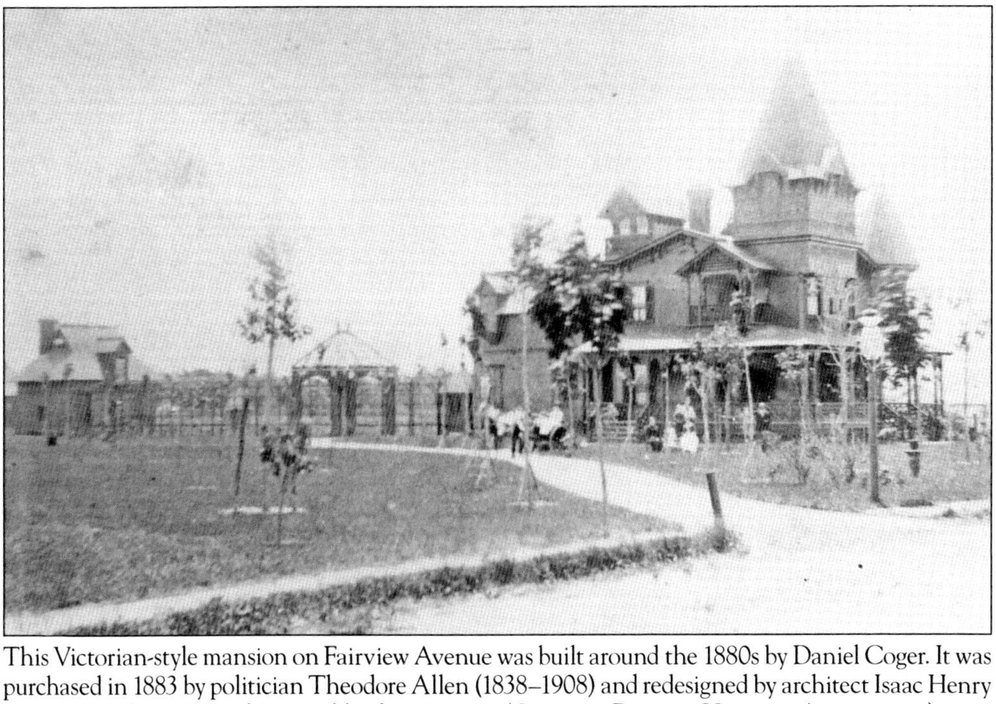

This Victorian-style mansion on Fairview Avenue was built around the 1880s by Daniel Coger. It was purchased in 1883 by politician Theodore Allen (1838–1908) and redesigned by architect Isaac Henry Green. The house was destroyed by fire in 1911. (Courtesy Bayport Heritage Association.)

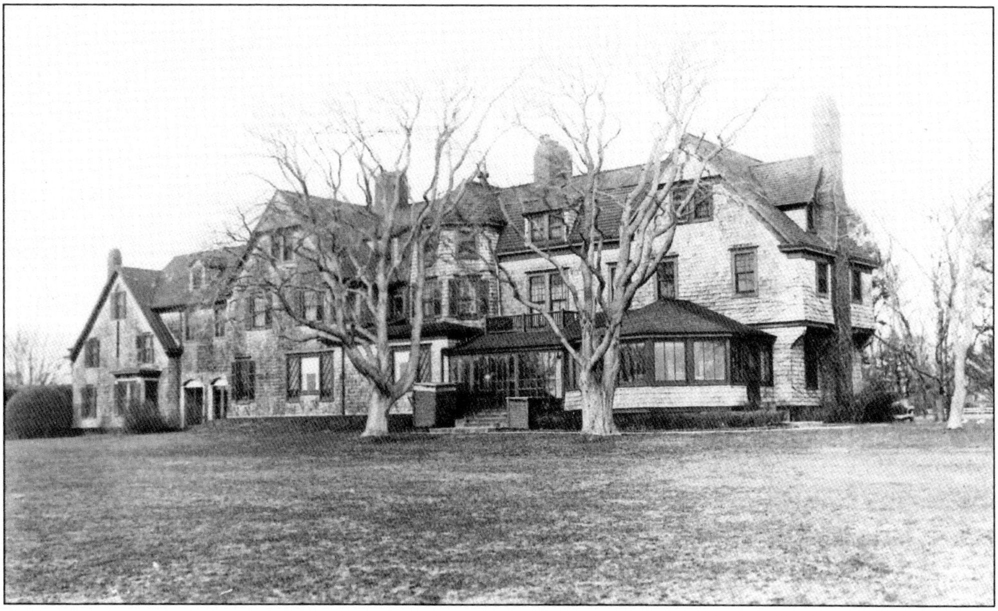

This shingle-style mansion, named Strandhome, on Ocean Avenue was built in 1887 by William R. Foster Jr. It was designed by architect Isaac Henry Greene. In 1890, it was purchased by attorney Charles Alfred Post (1844–1921). Strandhome was inherited by his son Waldron Post. The family sold it off in 1953. The 22-acre estate was subdivided and the home demolished. (Courtesy Bayport Heritage Association.)

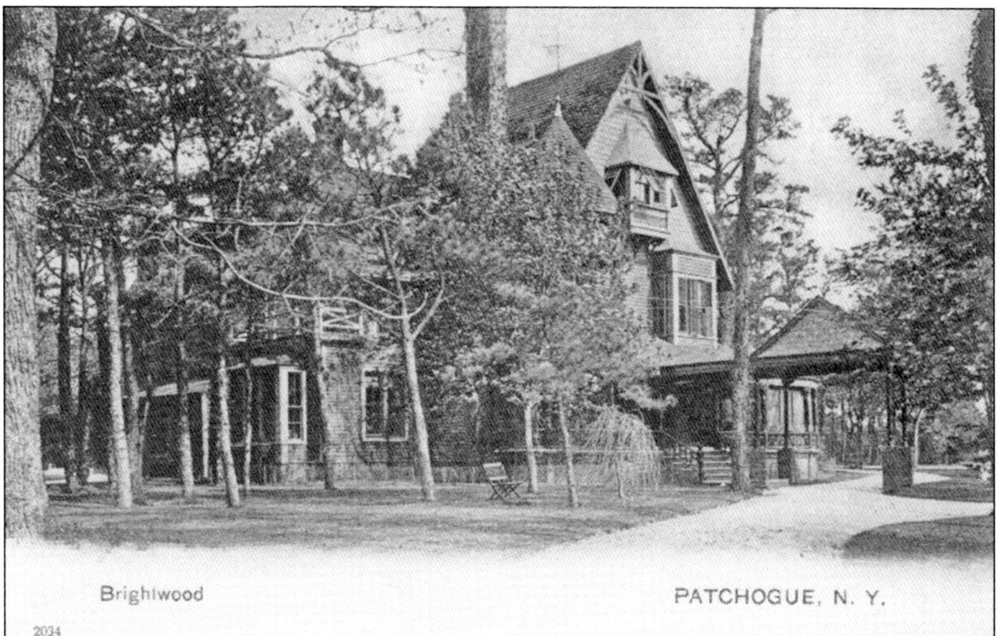

This shingle-style estate, named Brightwood, was the home of K.L. Gilbert. The mansion was demolished and is now the site of the Sandspit park and ferry terminal. (Courtesy Patchogue Historical Society, Steve Lucas.)

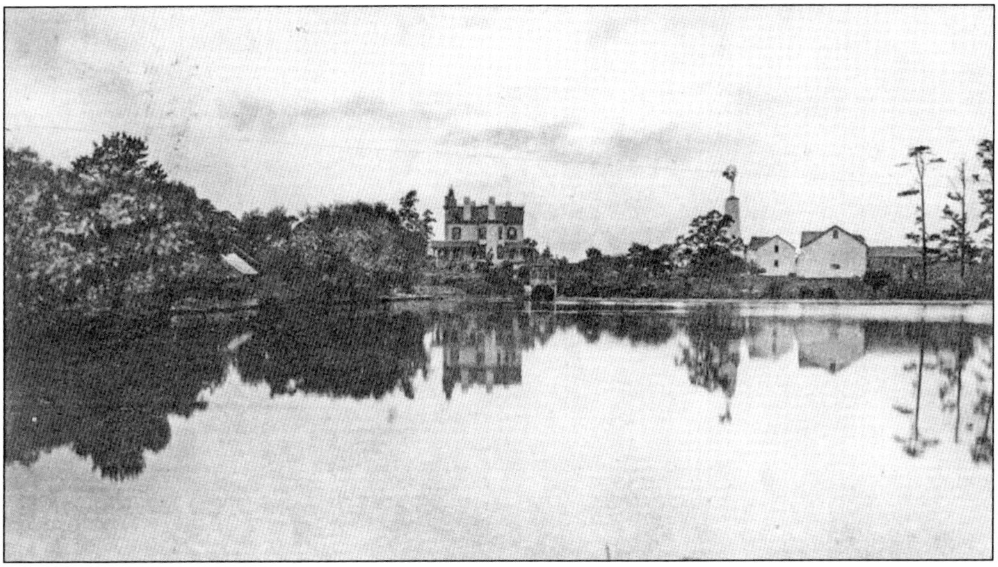

This was the home of Adm. George Watson Sumner (1841–1924). During the Civil War, Sumner fought against Confederate forts on the Mississippi River. After the war, he commanded the USS *Monocacy* and carried out diplomatic missions in Asia. He met King Chulalongkorn of Siam and was presented with a bear as a gift, which he later donated to the New York City Zoo. (Courtesy Patchogue Historical Society, Steve Lucas.)

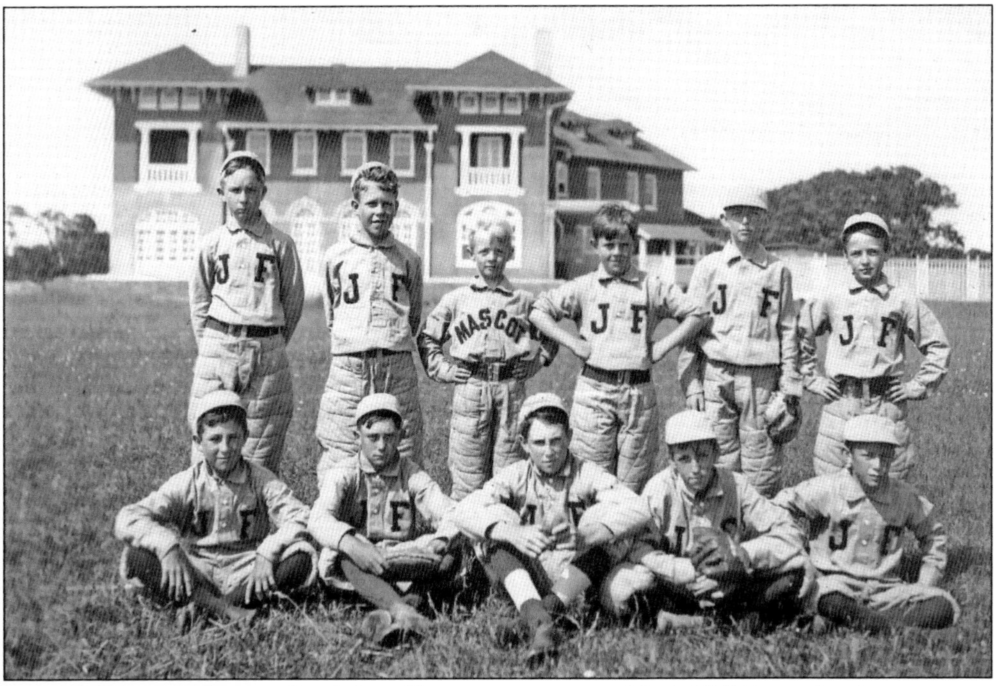

Pictured here is the home of Ruth Litt. Her estate was named Jack Will Farm after her two sons. In the foreground is the local baseball team she funded and organized for boys around 1908. Litt also organized a summer camp for boys and founded the Patchogue Christian Science Church. The home no longer stands. The area is now Patchogue Shores. (Courtesy Barbara M. Russell, Town of Brookhaven historian.)

Nine

Bellport-Brookhaven and Mastic

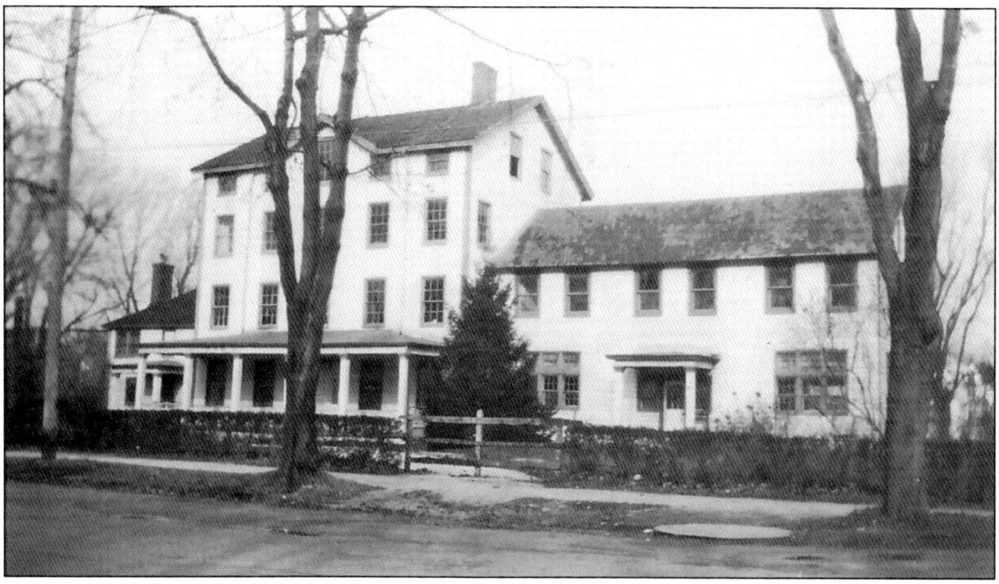

This home was built around the 1830s by Bellport Village founders and brothers Thomas and John Bell as a private home for their families. The home was later enlarged and used as an inn to accommodate increasing tourism to the area. Around 1900, the home became known as the Mallard Inn. It was sold in 1911 and was renamed the Bell Inn. It was demolished around the 1930s. The Bell brothers had envisioned creating a commercial seaport in the area, but the inlet allowing access to the Atlantic Ocean closed up. Tourism became the main industry instead. Before being named Bellport, the village was called Occumbomuck. The Bell family originally named the village Bellville, but it was later changed to Bell Port and became one word, "Bellport," in 1861. (Courtesy Bellport-Brookhaven Historical Society.)

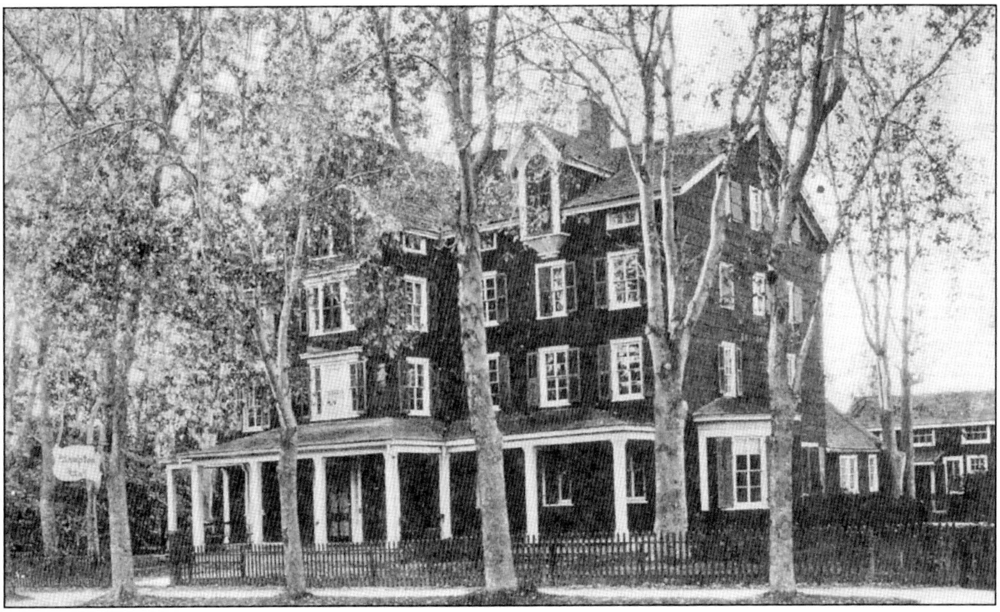

This house on South Country Road was known as the Titus House. It was built in the early 1800s by Hampton Howell as his private home. In 1840, it was sold to Henry Weeks, who eventually converted it into a four-story boardinghouse. The name changed to Hampton Hall. It was demolished in 1937. (Courtesy Bellport-Brookhaven Historical Society.)

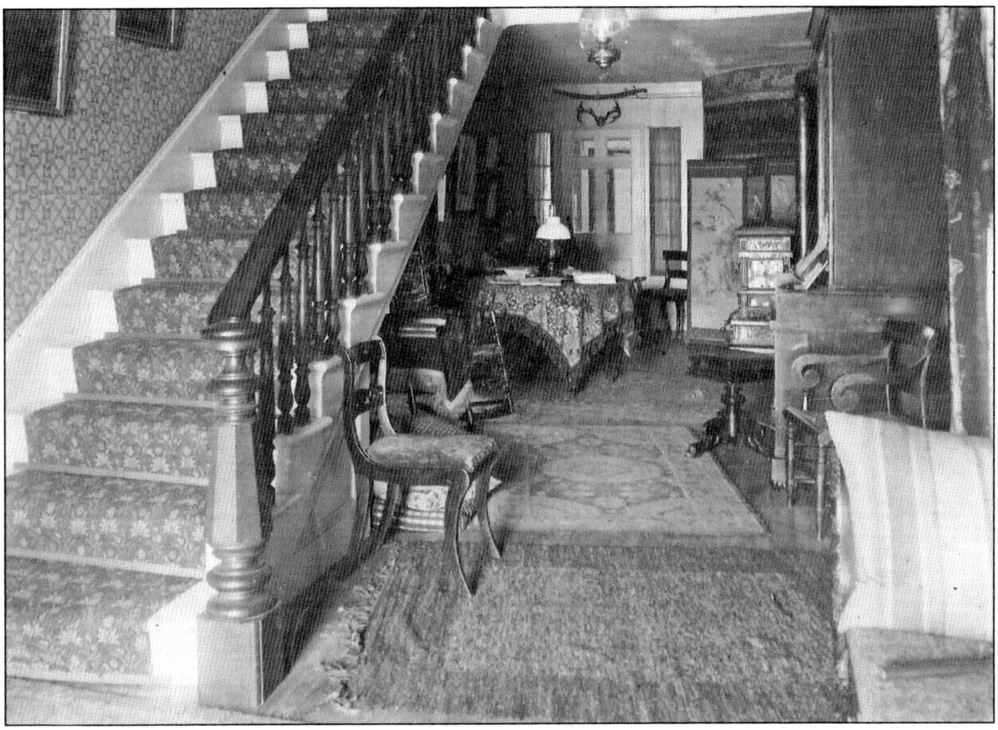

This is an internal look at Hampton Hall from around 1900. The photograph above is of the front entranceway. It could accommodate 50 guests. (Courtesy Bellport-Brookhaven Historical Society.)

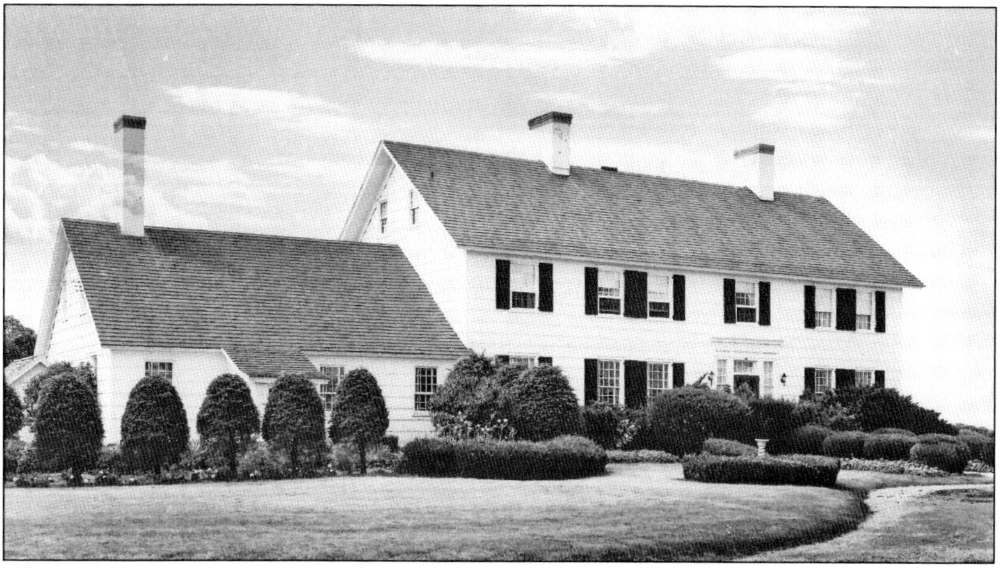

The Manor of St. George was built around the 1690s as the home of Col. William Tangier Smith (c. 1650s–1705) and was the Tangier Smith family house through 1954. The home has about 20 rooms. One of the estate's major historical significances is that it was the site of a Revolutionary War battle. The last member of the Smith family to live in the manor was Eugenia Annie Tangier Smith, who died in 1954. Today, the manor is open to the public as a park and house museum. (Courtesy Suffolk County Historical Society.)

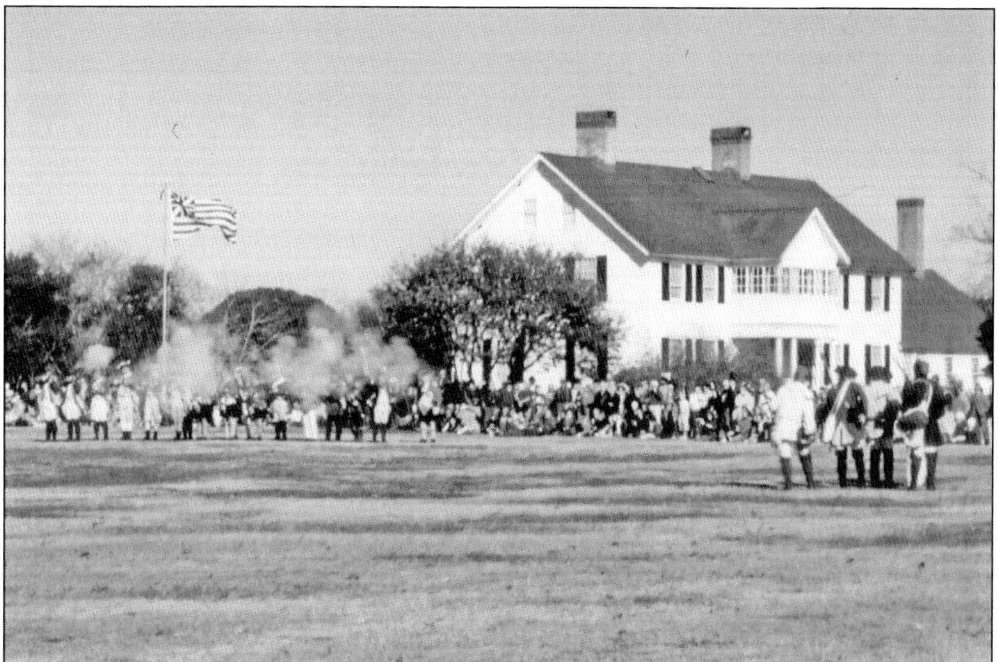

This is a reenactment of the battle. During the Revolutionary War, the British occupied the manor and built a fort nearby. On November 23, 1780, Patriot forces under Col. Benjamin Tallmadge conducted a surprise 4:00 a.m. attack, recaptured the manor, and destroyed the fort. (Courtesy Beverly C. Tyler, *History Close at Hand* website.)

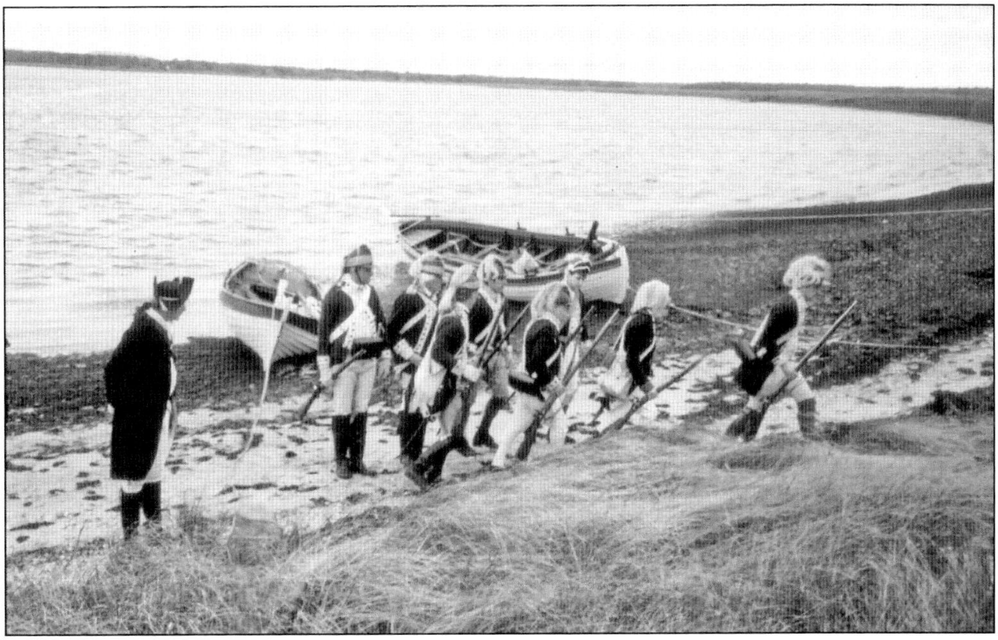

This is a reenactment of the Patriot solders arriving on the beach at Mount Sinai. The solders sailed across the Long Island Sound from Connecticut with 80 men in eight whaleboats. (Courtesy Beverly C. Tyler, *History Close at Hand* website.)

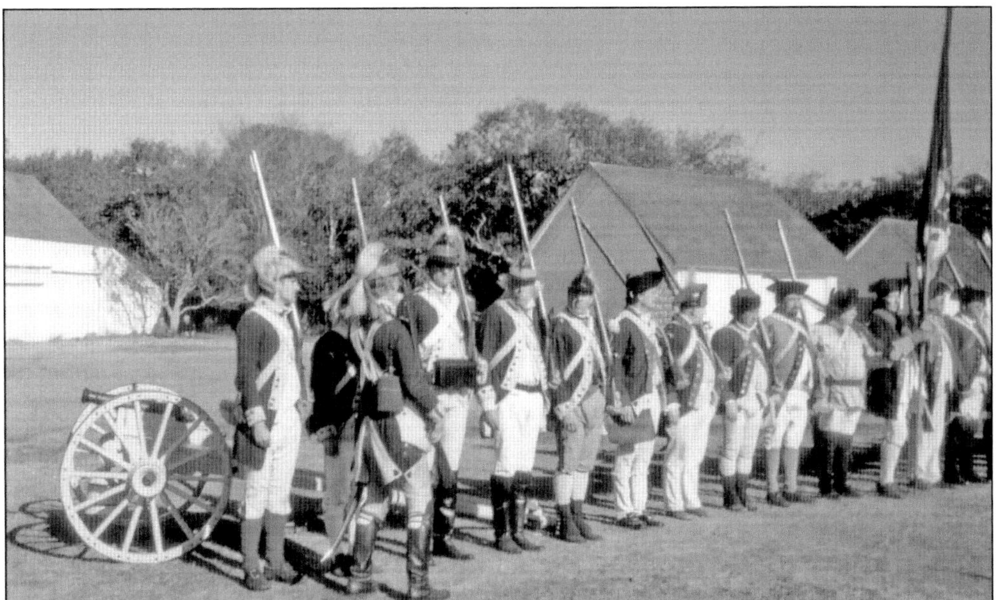

Here, the Patriot forces line up to prepare for the battle. Remarkably, the battle lasted 10 minutes and the Patriots did not lose any men. They killed seven British soldiers, captured the rest as prisoners, then burned the fort. (Courtesy Beverly C. Tyler, *History Close at Hand* website.)

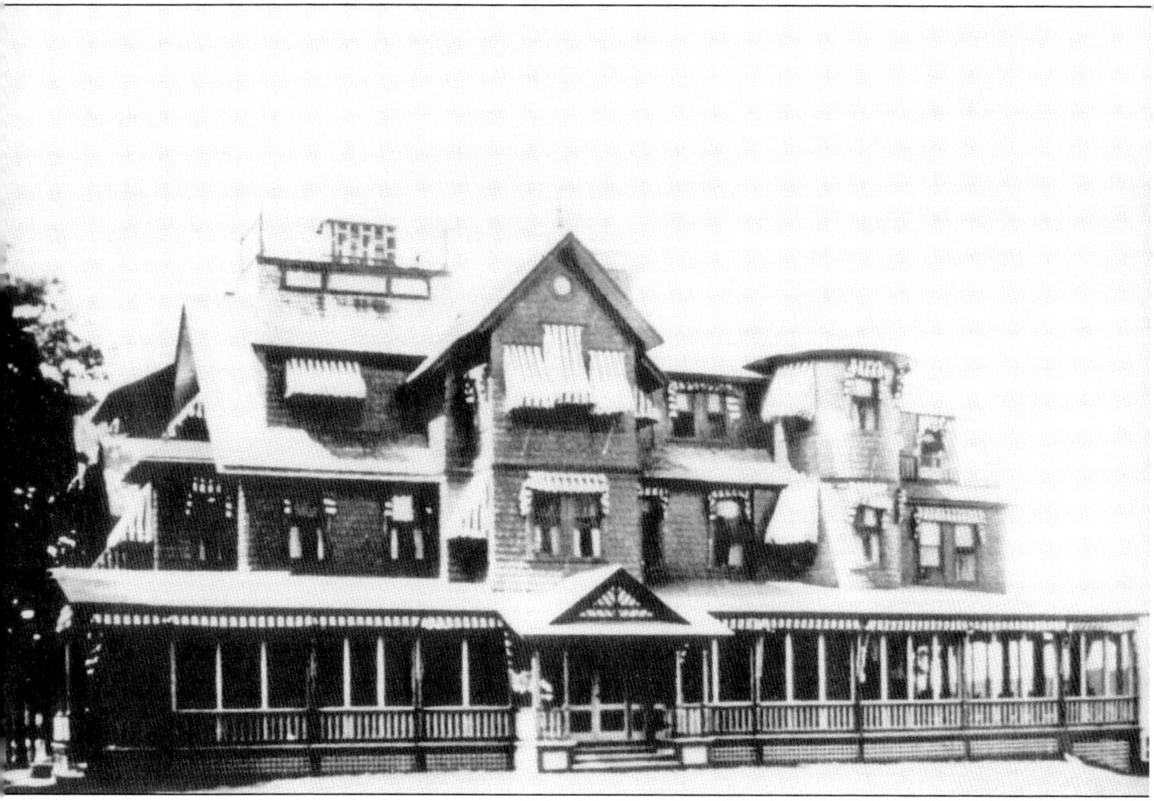

This 25-room mansion, named Moss Lots, was built around 1883 by William Buck Dana, who married Catherine Floyd. The house was later inherited by his son William Shepherd Dana (1892–1939) and his wife, Ella Marian Dana. Moss Lots was located on the Forge River. This is a view of the south side of the estate. The home burned down in 1969. (Courtesy Ken Spooner, *The Knapps Lived Here* website.)

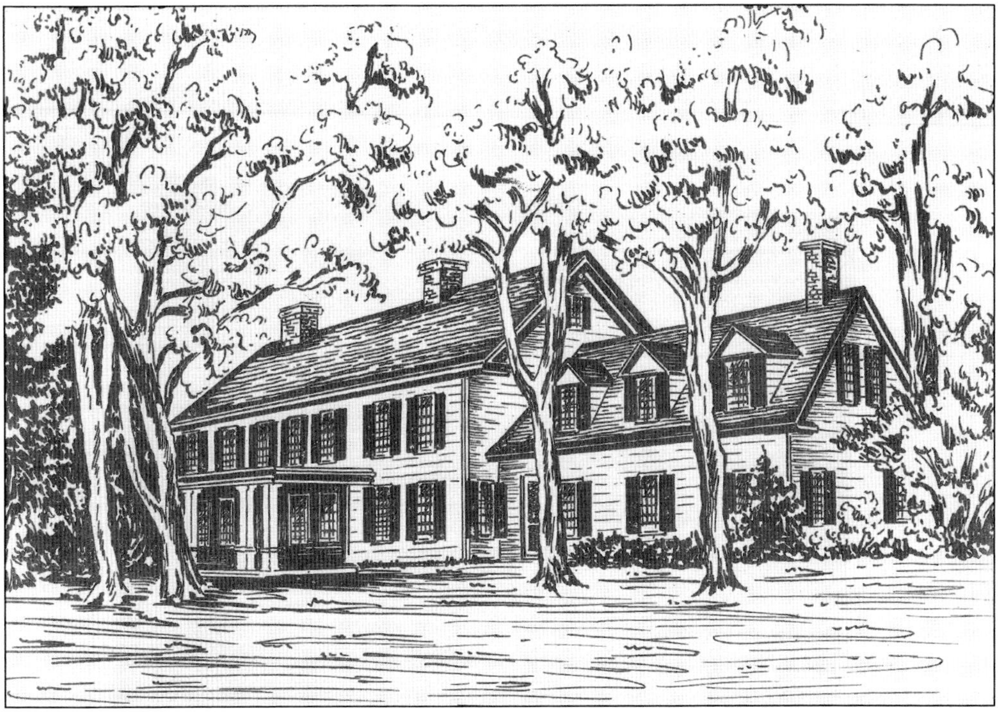

This 4,400-acre estate, named Old Mastic House, was first purchased in 1718 by Richard Floyd II (1665–1738). The house was built around 1724 and would become the estate of Gen. William Floyd (1734–1821). The home slowly grew through additions to 25 rooms with 12 outbuildings. In 1976, the Floyd family donated the home and its contents to the National Park Service. (Courtesy George Weeks Library, West Islip.)

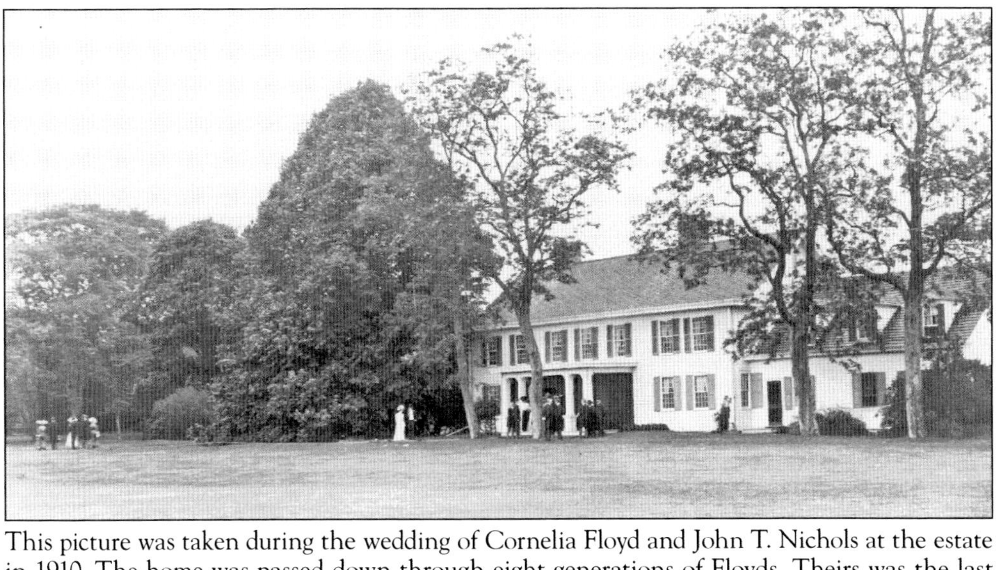

This picture was taken during the wedding of Cornelia Floyd and John T. Nichols at the estate in 1910. The home was passed down through eight generations of Floyds. Theirs was the last marriage in the house and their children were the last Floyd children to grow up in the house. (Courtesy William Floyd Estate Archives, Fire Island National Seashore [FINS].)

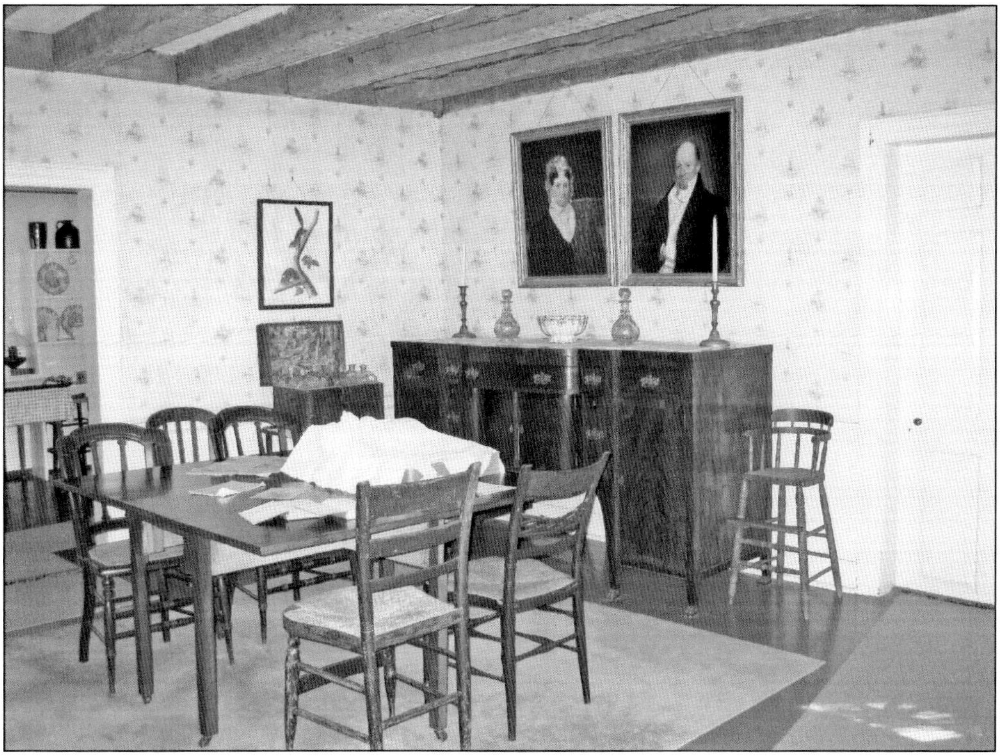

Today, the William Floyd estate is open to the public as a park and house museum. It is managed and maintained by the Fire Island National Seashore. Visitors can take a tour and see how the house used to look when the Floyd family lived there. (Courtesy William Floyd Estate Archives, FINS.)

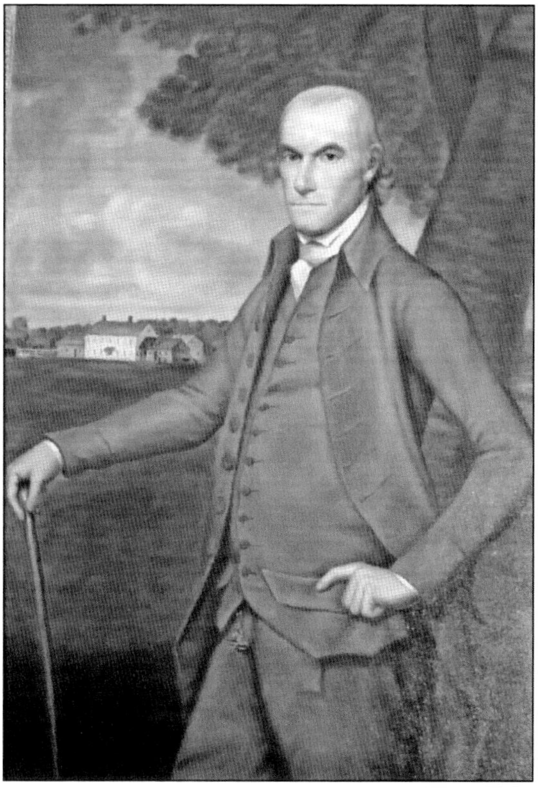

Gen. William Floyd (1734–1821) was one of the signers of the Declaration of Independence. He represented New York at the Continental Congress in 1774 and in 1775. After the Revolution, he returned to Mastic to rebuild his estate. Soon after, he returned to politics, serving in the state senate and as a representative in the first US Congress. (Courtesy William Floyd Estate Archives, FINS.)

Consistent with our mission to preserve history on a local level, this book was printed in South Carolina on American-made paper and manufactured entirely in the United States. Products carrying the accredited Forest Stewardship Council (FSC) label are printed on 100 percent FSC-certified paper.

MADE IN THE USA